Warrior Woman

Also by Peter Aleshire

▼

The Fox and the Whirlwind

Reaping the Whirlwind

Cochise: The Last War Won

Warrior Woman

The Story of Lozen, Apache Warrior and Shaman

PETER ALESHIRE

ST. MARTIN'S PRESS
NEW YORK

www.stmartins.com

Design by Kathryn Parise

LIBRARY OF CONGRESS CATALOGING-IN-PUBLICATION DATA

Aleshire, Peter.
Warrior woman : the story of Lozen, Apache warrior and shaman / by
Peter Aleshire—1st ed.
p. cm.
Includes bibliographical references.
ISBN 0-312-24408-8 (hardcover : alk. paper)
1. Lozen. 2. Chiricahua women—Biography. 3. Women shamans—
Southwest, New—Biography. 4. Chiricahua Indians—Social conditions.
5. Apache Indians—Wars, 1883–1886. I. Title.

E99.C68 L693 2001
978.9'004972—dc21
[B]
00-046030

First Edition: April 2001

10 9 8 7 6 5 4 3 2 1

CONTENTS

▼▼

Warrior Woman

INTRODUCTION

▼▼▼

Upon this earth
On which we live
Ussen has Power.
This Power is mine
For locating the enemy.
I search for that enemy
Which only Ussen the Great
Can show to me.[1]
— LOZEN'S CHANT

The stories of Geronimo, Crazy Horse, and Custer pale beside the tale of another warrior—one who fought relentlessly, successfully, and against all odds almost continuously for forty years. This warrior fought longer than Geronimo or Crazy Horse and more effectively than Custer. History suggests this warrior wielded supernatural powers, evaded successfully a full one-quarter of the United States Army, and displayed an epic personal courage and heroism.

But you've probably never heard of her.

Lozen, the war shaman of the Apache, represents one of the most successful, respected, and influential woman warriors in history. Yet historians have almost entirely overlooked her remarkable life story.

Every other major figure in the struggle between the Apache and the Americans fought for only a portion of the final, thirty-year confrontation, but Lozen fought throughout. Lozen[2] began fighting Mexican soldiers and scalp hunters, eternal enemies of her band, when she came of age in the 1840s. After the Americans arrived in 1848 to lay claim to her homeland, she battled them as well. She fought at the Battle of Apache Pass, in her brother Victorio's struggle for his homeland, in the massacre at Cibecue, and throughout the Geronimo campaigns.

She played a crucial role in each phase of the struggle, in part because the Apache believed she had the supernatural ability to sense the proximity of the enemy, had power over horses, and could heal wounds. "When Victorio wished to know the location of the enemy," said James Kaywaykla, who was an apprentice warrior in Victorio's band, "Lozen stood with outstretched arms, palms up, and prayed to Ussen. As she turned slowly, following the sun, her hands tingled and the palms changed color when they pointed toward the foe. The intensity of the sensation indicated the approximate distance of the enemy. The closer the adversary, the more vivid the feeling. Time after time I have seen her stand thus to ascertain the direction and proximity of the pursuers. I have always believed, along with many other Apaches, that had Lozen been with us at Tres Castillos her brother would never have ridden into the trap of the Mexican cavalry."[3]

The enigmatic figure of Lozen provides a link to an ancient world with surprising relevance to modern readers. For one thing, her ability to excel in a brutally male-dominated setting provides a way to examine a whole set of alternatives for women. Apache women played a crucial role in the life of their bands. They were at the center of the matriarchal relationships linking the scattered, autonomous bands, since when a man married, he moved to his wife's band, offering deference and support to her parents.

The Apache culture emphasized female chastity and monogamy and gave men the right to cut off their wives' noses if they proved unfaithful. However, women retained considerable power and independence within the family. They remained free to divorce at will an unreliable, unfaithful, or brutal husband. In return for this relatively high status and independence, the women performed most of the hard work of gathering and preparing food.

But in the Apache's war-dominated culture, status flowed from success in the constant raids against neighboring people. As descendants of the restless Athapascan people who had fanned out across North America from their starting point in Alaska, the Apache readily adapted to the conditions they encountered. When they reached the Southwest, they came up against settled Pueblo peoples, with their irrigated fields, walled towns, and stored food. The more warlike Apache turned to raiding to augment their own hunting and gathering. This pattern of not very violent, small-scale raiding changed dramatically when the Spanish arrived and introduced livestock, which transformed everything for the Apache. The ever-adaptable Apache immediately saw the possibilities of horses. Horses enabled the warriors to cover one thousand miles on a single raid and also provided something both portable and well worth taking.

The Apache's collision with the Europeans also injected a dramatic new level of violence into the Apache raiding culture. The Apache recognized two distinct types of raids: one to obtain goods, the other to extract revenge for a death. Stealthy raids to obtain goods rarely resulted in deaths on either side, but the death of a single Apache warrior would trigger an obligatory revenge raid intended to terrorize the enemy and so discourage any other group from killing a warrior. But the Apache's eye-for-an-eye accounting could not cope with the bewildering influx of European settlers; instead it triggered an escalating series of incidents, culminating in massacres, mutilations, and all-out war. This descent into nearly full-time warfare dislocated Apache culture and gradually diminished the role of women in Apache culture as male-dominated raiding, which was increasingly critical to survival and influence, came to dominate the Apache economy.

Raiding and warfare traditionally had been the province of the men. Women often accompanied war parties, but their numbers usually were limited to the wives of warriors who played a largely noncombatant role. Apache girls were generally subjected to the same arduous, physical training as young boys, but few took the training as warriors. Women did play a crucial role in the initiation of warfare, as most war parties were mounted in response to calls for revenge by the female relatives of warriors who had been killed. War parties sometimes brought back prisoners from the offending group who were then killed by the women relatives of the murdered person.

Lozen was one of the great exceptions to this division of roles in warfare. She never married. She sat in the war councils as an equal with the men. She helped Victorio formulate the strategy that made his band the scourge of the West. She wielded spiritual Power that was acknowledged and respected by the entire band. She excelled in stealing horses, one of the most honored skills among the Apache. And she provided the kind of leadership, moral example, and inspiration to her band usually offered only by great chiefs or shamans.

Her life brimmed with drama, tragedy, courage, violence, loss, and triumph. She rode like a phantom, unseen, through most of the great struggles between the Apache and the United States Army, the battles from which the most enduring myths and images of the West have sprung. Her life also provides an opportunity to examine supernatural or spiritual Power among the Apache, concepts that illuminate the complex view of a people who regarded the world with a sense of reverence, for they felt inseparably part of a larger whole. Their world was splintered into the seen and the unseen; they drew no sharp lines between spirit and flesh, suffered no contradictions between physical and mental realities, and greeted the world with a courageous fatalism that fascinates the modern reader, who lives estranged from nature.

However, telling Lozen's story presents some problems that make it impossible to do justice to her life by relying on a conventional historical narrative. The biggest problem lies in the nature of the few surviving firsthand Apache accounts of Lozen's life or the events in which she participated. The Apache left few firsthand versions of their side in this unequal struggle. None of the principal warriors could write, and so we are mostly limited to Apache oral traditions or the conversations their enemies wrote down. In addition, the Apache prisoners of war deliberately protected Lozen by hiding her importance from their captors, convinced the treacherous whites might execute the leaders at any time. Historian Eve Ball gathered the most telling accounts among the Chihenne and Chiricahua Apache, working years later with some informants who were mostly children when these events unfolded. Anthropologist Grenville Goodwin also gathered some fascinating firsthand accounts by people from Western Apache tribes who sometimes intermarried with the Warm Springs, or Chihenne, clans, but none of them spoke of Lozen. Geronimo left his own account, but he also does not mention Lozen, perhaps out of an effort to protect her. In fact, only a few surviving primary sources mention Lozen's childhood and her time with the Warm Springs Apache. We do know enough, however, to connect her to the most important events of this long, fascinating conflict: She was present at Victorio's brilliant ambushes of Mexican soldiers, Nana's raid through the Southwest, the execution of the Prophet during the battle at Cibecue, Geronimo's slashing raids, and Geronimo's final negotiations. Therefore, her life is a thread connecting many crucial conflicts, even if we often lack details of her actions in these incidents.

Historians of the Apache wars have struggled with these prob-

lems for decades. They have made vivid use of the detailed recollections by wonderful diarists like Captain John Bourke, John
Cremony, and Lieutenant Britton Davis to reconstruct battles,
cultures, and events. In recent years, they have also made use of
the more low-key but absorbing accounts of Apache like Jason
Betzinez, John Rope, James Kaywaykla, and Ace Daklugie.

This account of Lozen's life remains faithful to the facts and
to the spirit of the warrior people she led. I offer a full telling of
the sweeping events in which she was involved and all that is
known now of her life and character. However, the narrative style
of this biography represents a difficult trade-off. We lack the firsthand accounts on which conventional biographies rely when it
comes to reconstructing thoughts and viewpoints. Should we
therefore turn away from the task and continue retelling the story
from the accounts left mostly by her enemies? That seems neither
fair nor "truthful." Therefore, inspired by Maria Sandoz's compelling biography of Crazy Horse, I decided to combine the chro-
nologies of the whites with the scattering of firsthand Apache
accounts and the fascinating depiction of the complex, lyrical,
tenacious culture offered by several anthropologists who have
worked among the Chiricahua and White Mountain Apache.

So here's the trade-off I made in writing this biography: I
stretched the form of the conventional historical biography, but
provided notes when I made one of these necessary choices. I
presented here every bit of information the conventional primary
sources offer on Lozen, her life and her thoughts. In many cases,
I accepted white accounts when it comes to dates, numbers, and
the sequence of events. However, I accepted Apache versions of
events whenever those versions were not contradicted by known
facts—even if they differ from a plausible account by whites.
Rather than debating all of these points in the text, I chose the
most likely version and then provided a discussion of the alternatives in the notes. In addition, I didn't flinch from suggesting

what Lozen might have been thinking as she made key choices, based on her subsequent actions and on the insight into Apache thought and philosophy offered by anthropologists like Grenville Goodwin and Keith Basso. If I were writing a conventional biography with sufficient primary sources and recollections by the subject herself, I would not try to fill in the gaps in such a fashion. However, it seemed impossible to tell Lozen's story without making some careful guesses. You'll find notes when I included speculation about Lozen's thinking.

Moreover, I mingled the myths, ceremonies, and cultural beliefs of different Apache bands and attributed them to Lozen's own Chihenne Apache, largely because the Chiricahua and White Mountain Apache are far better studied. Therefore, although we have no firsthand account of Lozen's Sunrise Ceremony by which she entered into the responsibilities and privileges of adulthood, I used Goodwin's wonderfully detailed account of that ceremony among the Chiricahua Apache, a band closely related to Lozen's own. Each time I took such liberties, I provided a detailed note on sources. Most historians used the overall term "chiricahua" for a cluster of tribal groups that considered themselves distinct but allied—including the Chokonen, Nednhi, Chihenne, Bedonkohes, and Mimbrenos. Other historians restrict use of "Chiricahua" to the Chokonen.

You'll also find no quotation marks in the text, although I've included many direct quotes from both Apache and white sources and italicized the direct quotations. I avoided quotation marks for two reasons. When the whites recorded the words of the Apache, the thoughts were often translated first into Spanish and then into English, which undercuts the literal authority implied by use of a direct quote. When the Apache informants provide stretches of dialogue, they were almost always recalled years after the actual conversation. Again, I believe use of quotation marks in that case would be at least subliminally misleading. I therefore decided to follow Sandoz's lead in *Crazy Horse* and do without direct quotes. Whenever I have lifted dialogue from direct sources, you'll find a note indicating the source at the beginning or end of the passage.

My hope is that these trade-offs provide a narrative that remains true to Lozen's life and the struggle of the Apache against their enemies. Meanwhile, the discussion in the notes will tell the reader when I have departed from convention.

I am indebted to people who have helped me talk all this through and had the patience to read the manuscript and make cogent suggestions. Beth Deveny has been a friend and an inspiration and a careful editor. Kathy Khoury also provided insight and guidance and a sounding board. Their advice was generally better than my book but it's a better book for their advice. I am also grateful to the Department of American Studies at Arizona State University West for the support and latitude to produce such an unconventional history. I am also indebted to my family. Seth, Caleb, and Noah made me feel like writing history was a useful thing for a grown man to undertake. Elissa taught me to respect and admire women and so, perhaps, prequalified me to write a woman's biography.

I should also note that an Apache woman who'd never heard of Lozen helped convince me to write this book. I met her at a health spa near Los Osos, California. The Apache woman was giving therapeutic massages at a spa built atop a natural hot spring—perhaps one very much like the pool of heated water that Victorio and his people treasured, in the end, more than life. Lithe, quiet, and gentle, the planes of her face, the angles of her features, and the deep, watchful, calm of her dark eyes gave her an air of power—a coiled restraint. She was also funny, talkative, and enthusiastic about her profession, performing massages that melted through the muscled tensions at the surface to some deeper level of contentment. As a birthday gift, my wife and her sister underwent massages at the spa from the hands of Mira, the Apache woman.

Elissa was astonished at the sense of peace and health that the massage imparted. She was even more amazed at the end of the session when she took Mira's hands and discovered they had grown hot to the touch.

"Your hands are so hot," she exclaimed.

"Oh, yes," said Mira, smiling in an almost secret way. "It's the power of the massage."

"That's like Lozen," said my wife, who'd listened to me talk repeatedly about the great medicine woman and warrior of the Apache whose palms heated when she faced in the direction of her enemies.

"Who?" said Mira.

"Lozen. You know, Lozen," stammered Elissa, wondering if she'd gotten the name wrong or mistook Mira's tribe.

"Who is Lozen?" asked Mira.

So Elissa told her. Mira listened intently, in that moment connecting her own Power to heal and soothe with the long chain of Power and grace connecting her people to the very beginning of things. That is when I realized that Lozen's full story must be told—and not as a footnote to someone else's tale.

Of course, it is strange I should feel so compelled to do the telling. I'm a "White Eye"—the Apache term for white people—and the inhabitant of another century, another world. It is presumptuous of me to come here, with her story in my hands.

But against all reason, I believe Lozen would understand.

She understood the caprice of Ussen, her people's highest deity.

After all, didn't Ussen love the Apache best? Didn't he give them all the great gifts: the best land on earth, the most wisdom, the greatest strength, the strongest love of nature, the ability to endure, the sunset, the sunrise, the agave, the bow and the arrow?

But didn't he also make the White Eyes? And didn't he offer the gun to the Apache, who at first turned it down, on account of the great noise it made? Would not such a weapon frighten all the game and offend the rocks? Who would use such a thing? So Ussen gave the gun to the White Eyes, who had no reverence, or spirit, or grace, but knew only how to multiply their kind and how to make things. To them, Ussen gave the gun.

The Apache understand irony. They lived its full bitter measure. They have put it in their stories. They have learned that the way of things can never be fully understood. They have mastered the shrug.

If Ussen gave the gun to a people so unworthy of the gift, then perhaps there is more sense than we can see now in putting Lozen's telling in my hands.

PROLOGUE

▼▼▼

On the Rio Grande

September 1880

Lozen stood on the northern bank of the Rio Grande with Eclode and watched the People hurry south—not doubting the path on which her feet had been placed, but wondering at it a little. The women and children dwindling from her sight were mostly Chihenne—Lozen's own Red Paint People.[1] They trotted through the sand, not looking back to where Lozen stood on the riverbank. Not looking back to where the soldiers came on horseback behind. Not looking back to where the keen-eyed scouts, Native American Indians enlisted by the White Eyes, held the soldiers to the trail of the Chihenne.

The Chihenne warriors, with their Mescalero allies, were mostly cast out ahead and behind the women and children. Lozen knew that Victorio, her brother and the last hope of a free people, would remain far to the rear in the place of greatest danger. Normally, Lozen would ride alongside Victorio—using the Power the God Ussen had given her to warn him when his enemies approached too closely. He relied upon her ceremony, her judgment, and the tingling of her palms.

But then Eclode's time of birthing had come.[2] Lozen had taken on the responsibility of returning the Mescalero woman to the reservation—although it was a journey of many weeks along their back trail where soldiers now swarmed like ants whose hill has been broken open. It made sense she should take Eclode back, if for no other reason than to keep the goodwill of the Mescalero warriors, who had accompanied Lozen's band. Eclode wanted to go back to the reservation, where her baby would be safe and she would not need to jump up and run into the darkness whenever a raccoon made a noise in the night. So Lozen had said she would take Eclode home.

Even so, this was not the chief reason Lozen stood now on the riverbank watching the Chihenne flee into uncertainty. In truth, Lozen walked along a path she could not see, but only feel with her feet—as she had always done.

So she turned now with her rifle, her knife, and a cartridge belt and led Eclode back along their trail, away from the river, toward the soldiers and the scouts who were coming on quickly. As she walked, she looked for a place to turn aside where they would leave no gossipy tracks leading away from the main trail to whisper their secret to the careful ears of the scouts. But she had not gone far when she saw a faint smudge of dust. It might have been a playful twist of wind or a cow and her calf or a wolf chasing an antelope—but she knew it warned of the soldiers coming on quickly. She knew the time they had to hide was running with a dry rasp through open fingers. So Lozen turned aside and hid shortly before the soldiers appeared, riding warily along the trail, led by the scouts. Eclode made no sound, even when the labor pains came upon her, for the soldiers passed by so closely Lozen could have hit them with a stone.

Lozen shifted her Winchester into position, as one of the scouts reached the place where Lozen had turned aside from the trail. She watched him intently, knowing where he would stop, stoop, and turn to look in their direction if he saw their tracks. She decided that if he looked at them, she would shoot him—and then run to the south to lead the soldiers and scouts away from the girl, whose baby was coming on as though he could not wait another hour to be out in the world. Maybe the baby did not realize how dangerous the world had become in the small space left to the People between the White Eyes and the Mexicans.

But the scout did not look up when he reached the place where they had turned aside. He went on past it, trotting, his eyes overwhelmed by the clear trail of the women and the children who had gone on this way. So Lozen turned back to Eclode, to help her in the birthing, since the time had come. Lozen sang healing songs, her voice a whisper lest it carry on a treacherous breeze to the ears of the scouts. Ussen had given Lozen great Power in healing. She usually applied it to the wounds of the warriors, since she had always gone on the raids although she was not married and had no husband to help on the war trail. But, of course, she was Lozen, and Victorio's sister, the woman warrior who sat in council with the chiefs.

She had no special ceremonies for childbirth. Still, Lozen knew prayers and songs and the use of herbs that would ease this birth—so she tended Eclode. She helped Eclode squat, holding on to a branch of the tree, so the child would come more easily. She did not have the water with the herb in it that would ease the birth, but she had the four small pieces from the inner leaves of the yucca that she fed to Eclode, one after another.[3] Lozen massaged Eclode's stomach, pressing down to ease the child out and into the world. When the baby finally came, she reached down to take him, as Eclode strained, making no sound. When she had the baby fully out, Lozen moved quickly. She cut the cord with a piece of black flint the length of her thumb, then tied off the stub of the cord with a piece of yucca string. The baby came into the world suddenly, looking around and whimpering a little, but not crying much, as though he knew his enemies were near—so Lozen knew the baby would be strong and of a good disposition. She did not have the grease and red paint she normally would have smeared over the baby's body, but she took sacred pollen and ashes from a bag on her belt and spread it to the four directions, beginning with the east. Then she took the baby and wrapped him in a piece of a blanket Eclode had brought with her. She held the baby to the four directions, beginning once again with the east, saying the prayers that would ensure strength and a long life. Lozen then returned the baby to his mother, savoring Eclode's smile and the baby's strength. Lozen gathered up the afterbirth and the umbilical cord she had cut away and wrapped them carefully in another piece of the blanket. She said prayers over the bundle, so the child would be strong and live a long life. Then she left Eclode for a short time to find a fruit-bearing tree in which to hang the bundle. She found a tree and then hesitated, wondering whether the scouts coming along behind might see the bundle if she put it there in the branches as tradition demanded. She hid the bundle in the tree as best she could anyway, knowing that if she tried to bury the afterbirth coyotes might dig it up and give the boy bad luck all his life. Then she prayed four times, saying to the tree, *May the child live and grow up to see you bear fruit many times*.

When she returned, Lozen found the baby nestled against his mother, not crying—which was good because Lozen could still feel the presence of their enemies. The scouts came back soon, working along the trail. Lozen watched them with her rifle held ready, her fingers red with the afterbirth. But the scouts once again walked past the place where Lozen and Eclode hid. One of the scouts, a Chiricahua, nearly looked in their direction as Lozen's finger tightened on the trigger of her rifle. But he did not quite look at them, nor quite hesitate. She decided he had either not seen them or had decided not to tell the soldiers.

Soon, Lozen and Eclode and the baby were left alone, in a land full of enemies, a long way from home—at least, a long way from Eclode's home. Lozen no longer had a home, just the yearning for the Sacred Mountain that was once home, where Ussen had laid his gifts and his burdens on her. She could only remember the hot springs where she had been happy and where the rocks, grass, and trees knew the Red Paint People—as the wind knows the hawk and the streambed the water.

Lozen let her mind rest for a moment on the memory of the hot springs, steaming in the darkness as the stars wheeled past in the sky like one of the old stories that took all night to tell. She struggled once again to see the hidden logic in how Ussen had ordered things. Why had he given them to the Sacred Mountain, the hot springs, the pines, and the grasses if he intended to let the White Eyes have them? Why had he made the White Eyes so powerful, so numerous, and so relentless—although they knew none of his prayers? Why had he made the People run like hunted deer out onto the plain on weakening legs? Why had he given her the gift of Power, if Power could only delay death a little? But she could not hold to these thoughts for very long. Such questions came like hunger when the parfleche is empty, pushed aside unsatisfied. Most things could not be understood, but merely endured. Does the rabbit understand the snare, or the hawk the updraft? So she turned her attention back to Eclode and the baby and their return to the reservation through a hard and thirsty country—with soldiers guarding all the water holes.

It was good that Lozen turned her thoughts away from Ussen's intentions.

For the test of her faith had only begun. It was best that she had not the Power of foresight, considering what lay ahead and what loved names she must never speak again. Lozen was to live the rest of her life in the deep shadow of the decision to leave her brother for the sake of Eclode. That choice was the high, rocky ridge of her life. Once she crossed it, everything changed. Had she known, how could even Lozen—the shield of her People—have walked the bitter path upon which Ussen had set her feet?

▼▼

CHAPTER I

The Mid-1830s

Near Ojo Caliente, New Mexico

First, there was White Painted Woman—who some people called Changing Woman.

She lived, in the beginning, in a dangerous world.

Maybe it was after a big flood that drowned all the People who came before, people who prayed to the wind and the lightning but who didn't know anything about Ussen, the Creator. Maybe it was after a flood that covered the world, right up to near the top of White Ringed Mountain[1] where the receding waters left a white ring you can still see today.[2] Many of the animals escaped the flood, even Turkey, whose tail was caught in the rising flood-waters and so remains tipped in white. But the only person who escaped was White Painted Woman, who went to the top of White Ringed Mountain and waited there for the waters to go down again.[3]

When White Painted Woman came down from the mountain, she found the world was full of monsters and dangerous creatures. So White Painted Woman prayed to Ussen, Life Giver, for guidance. And a spirit came to her and said, *Lie down on your back and take off your clothes out there. You must have a child by the rain. Let the water fall on your navel. That boy, when he is born, you must call Child of Water.* So she did.

Then she had twins. One she called Child of Water, because his father was lightning and rain. The other child she called Killer of Enemies.[4]

It fell to White Painted Woman to protect her children from a fearsome giant, who came every day to her camp—looking for children to eat.

A Spirit had told her, *Don't let the giant seize your children, for he is surely going to kill them. There is only one way to save your children: You must dig a hole under your fireplace and put the babies there, out of the way of the giant. When Child of Water is old enough, make a bow and arrow for him so he can kill this giant, along with the eagle and the buffalo and the antelope. When the child is old enough to shoot the arrow, let him and Killer of Enemies go out hunting.*[5]

So she dug a hole under the fire where she could hide her children. Every day she waited and cried and thought how she could protect them.

One day when Child of Water was nursing, he began to cry. She quieted him as quickly as she could, knowing the giant would hear him. Quickly she put Child of Water back under the fire.

In just that moment, the giant came.

He said, *Ho, ho, ho, ho! I heard a baby cry here a while ago. Where is that baby?*

White Painted Woman looked directly at the giant and said, *I am here all alone.*

But the giant replied, *I heard a baby crying.*

White Painted Woman, who was clever and brave, said, *I am very, very lonely for a baby. I am all alone and imitated a baby crying.*

Let me hear you cry like a baby, said the giant.

So she cried just like a baby.

The giant did not quite believe her, but there was nothing he could do, so he went on his way, very suspicious.

So White Painted Woman continued to care for her children, praying every day with all her heart that Ussen would keep them safe, and anxious for them to grow old enough to use their bows.

After a long while, she brought out Child of Water again to play with him. She cleaned him with a piece of cloth, but in her rush to return her child to his sanctuary, she threw the cloth right down beside her.

No sooner was the baby back than the giant returned. He saw the cloth she had used to clean the baby, with a greenish-yellow smear on it.

There must have been a baby here, said the giant. *There is its excrement on this cloth.*

White Painted Woman, thinking very quickly, answered, *I am very lonely for a baby. I am trying to make that look like a baby's excrement.*

Show me how you did it, said the giant.

So she went to the stalk of a sotol, which is long and hollow and sometimes full of bees. She broke open the stalk and took out the honey and put some of that honey on the cloth and showed it to the giant who could see it looked just like a baby's excrement. So she got the better of the giant once again.

But then the giant looked down at the soft ground beside the fire where he saw the little baby's tracks and he said, *Ho, ho! A baby's tracks!*

White Painted Woman, still thinking more quickly than the giant, said the same thing again: *I am very, very lonely for a little baby and I made those tracks myself.*

Show me how you made those tracks, said the giant.

She quickly made the track with the outside of her hand and put the toe marks on it with her fingers. It was just like a baby's footprint. So she fooled the giant once again.

In this way, White Painted Woman protected her children until they grew old enough to pull back the bow. She survived because she knew when her enemy was approaching and could always think more quickly than the giant. Then she sat down and made bows for her children, singing over them so they would have Power. She gave each of the children a bow, which she had blessed.

One day, Killer of Enemies and Child of Water went out hunting and killed a deer. The giant came right away to take their meat and to eat them as well. But Child of Water challenged the giant to a fight, matching his arrows made of gama grass against the giant's arrows made of pine trees. The giant fired four times, but each time the giant fired, Child of Water took a piece of blue stone he found at his feet and put it in his mouth. When he blew on the giant's arrows, they shattered and fell harmlessly at his feet.[6] Child of Water then shot his four small arrows, each one shattering one layer of a four-layer coat of stone the giant wore. The final arrow pierced the giant's heart. Then Child of Water and Killer of Enemies went back to their mother, who had remained in the campsite worrying for them and praying. When she heard their story, she was so happy she began to dance and pray and sing.

She sang, *What a happy day it is, to be bringing in such good news.*

Then White Painted Woman gave the high, long cry still heard at the girl's puberty ceremony, which was the first time this was done on earth, even before White Painted Woman and Child of Water made human beings.

After that, Child of Water killed the giant buffalo, with the help of Gopher, who was the first gopher when animals talked as people, and who in his being expressed the Power that would animate all gophers to come. That was why animals in the future would still have Power that could help people who knew the proper prayers and thought in a proper manner. Child of Water killed the monster eagles, from whose feathers he made all of the birds. With the help of Lizard, he slayed the antelope that killed with its eyes. Each time Child of Water came safely home, White Painted Woman danced and sang. She taught him hunting magic, warning him not to mention the ordinary names of the animals while he hunted them.

So White Painted Woman and Child of Water and Killer of Enemies made all of the People. Child of Water made the Indians and gave them the bow and arrow, game to hunt, wild things to eat, and all the best places to live. Killer of Enemies gave the White Eyes the gun, corn, and cattle. Then White Painted Woman and her sons left, perhaps going up into a cloud or up on the Sacred Mountain. They left behind the Gan Mountain Spirits to protect and guide the People, but they themselves went away, as Ussen had gone away, coming back sometimes only in dreams.

▼

Every woman is a daughter of White Painted Woman, including Lozen, who was born within sight of the Sacred Mountain near Ojo Caliente where the People began.[7] Her father was a leading man of his band, as was his father before him.[8] And her parents, uncles, aunts, and all those who had responsibility for her set her feet early on the path. They held her to the four directions, offering her life to Ussen, seeking a blessing on her.

They fashioned with ritual care the cradle board in which she remained until she could crawl. The shamans carefully selected and blessed the oak for the buckskin-covered frame and the yucca stalk for the crosspieces bent into half-moons and the canopy of red-barked dogwood stems, and the ash wood for the footrest and the bedding of wild mustard. Then they prepared amulets to dangle from the frame: a bag of sacred pollen, turquoise beads, and bits of wood split from a tree by a bolt of lightning. They held a feast when the cradle board was ready, dancing in a great wheel. They marked the face of the baby with pollen as a blessing and prayed she would live to outgrow the cradle board.[9]

She grew up in the usual way. Until she could crawl, she rode in the cradle board her mother either wore on her back or hung in a tree while she worked. When Lozen was seven, she began to ride horses, and her parents noticed early on that Lozen had a way with them. First she learned to jump up to grab a handful of the horse's hair so she could climb up the horse's front leg. Then she began to practice jumping onto a horse from the ground, first setting the horse near a hill so she could run and jump onto his back. She soon became one of the best riders in the band, able to control her horse with only her knees and a rope tied around the nose.

She loved the rough games of the boys. All the girls of the band underwent hard physical training from the age of about eight, rising before daylight and running to the top of the mountain. After all, each of their lives depended on their legs and their lungs and their endurance—for they sprang from a band of warriors surrounded by enemies. And even though few women went with the warriors on raids, the People relied utterly upon them for survival. For the women gathered and prepared most of the food, made most of the clothing, and produced most of the things that enabled the People to survive. If their enemies attacked camp, the women gathered up the essential things and ran away with them.

The elders did not neglect the physical training of the girls, knowing they faced as many dangers as the warriors. But even though Lozen learned everything expected of her as a girl, she also took a keen interest in the warrior training of the boys.[10] Perhaps it was due to her position of leadership that she did this.

Perhaps it was because she wanted always to keep pace with Victorio, her brother, who seemed marked for great things. Or perhaps it was because these things were simply in her nature. In any case, she made slings of willow branches to flick bits of mud at birds. She made herself a bow and arrow and played with the boys in the endless target practice games. She rose before anyone and ran always with the leaders. She never fell to the back of the group when they ran, where the men who trained them waited with switches to inspire the slowest of them. She was small, so she could not overcome the larger boys in wrestling and feats of strength—but she was fast, clever, and nimble. She often won the footraces, the games of tag, and the endless sessions of hide-and-seek. When they staged mock battles with stones or arrows without arrowheads, she dodged the arrows fired at her so skill-fully that she was often among the last standing. She could creep about the camp with such care that even the seasoned warriors could not find her.

It was good she learned these things, for the times in which she lived were like the early times of White Painted Woman, when monsters infested the earth and no place was safe.

At the time of Lozen's birth, the leader of the People was a tough, grizzled, canny warrior named Juan Jose Compa. The Chih-enne lived then mostly in the Animas Mountains.[11] Some bands of Mexicans had come peacefully into the territory of the People, offering gifts and friendship if Juan Jose would let them establish a small settlement called Santa Rita, where they busied them-selves digging in the ground like ants. The warriors watched the Mexicans warily from the surrounding hills, wondering at the way they spent themselves in the digging. The Mexicans had made slaves of Indians from other bands and drove those slaves cease-lessly to work in the caves in the earth.

The Chihenne warriors were of divided council about whether they should tolerate the Mexicans in the heart of their land. Some of the young war leaders said the Mexicans were not to be trusted and it was disrespectful to let them dig in the earth, which was the mother of them all. The Mexicans were crazed for the golden metal, which was forbidden to the People by Ussen because it resembled the sun, which was an aspect of Ussen himself.

Mangas Coloradas, a respected war leader, felt this way. He towered over all the other warriors with a skill, reach, and cunning that made him untouchable in a knife fight. But he also had a great skill with words, which he could command like warriors in an ambush. But in this argument about the truce with the earth grubbers in Santa Rita, Juan Jose held sway—using the force of his personality and the edge of his reasoning to cut through the opposition. Juan Jose argued that the People must make peace with some bands of Mexicans or they would be hunted every-where. He insisted that the Mexicans at Santa Rita would keep the peace because they wanted only what they could dig out of the earth. Moreover, the warriors could profit by trading horses and cattle and other things with the Mexican band at Santa Rita. In this manner, they could obtain guns and ammunition—and whiskey and mescal, which were much more potent than the sweet, mild tizwin the People made for themselves. This last ar-gument convinced many warriors, who like Juan Jose loved the mescal of the Mexicans.

No one had much concern when the Mexicans at Santa Rita invited the People to a fiesta. One of the men there was a good friend of Juan Jose, a White Eye named John James Johnson. He had come from the north, where some said there lived another race of people as pale as a grub under a rock. Often these people bristled with hair on their faces, like beasts. So Juan Jose led many of the People to Santa Rita where the Mexicans had barrels of mescal and piles of presents. At first the warriors were wary, watching the Mexicans and the rough-looking White Eyes who came with James Johnson. But the gifts and the mescal soon soothed their fears, so that when Johnson threw the covering off a pile of gifts in the center of the plaza, many people crowded forward, even warriors.

But then the Mexicans and White Eyes uncovered some metal tubes mounted on wheels, which immediately belched smoke and fire and bullets. In an instant, the plaza was filled with the dead and dying. Juan Jose ran to Johnson, calling to him to stop the shooting. But Johnson pulled out his own gun and shot Juan Jose, which was the first example Lozen saw of the friendship of a White Eye.

Lozen and Victorio and other people not already dead ran from the square, dodging through the Mexicans and Johnson's men, who were shooting even the women and children. Mangas Coloradas and a few of the warriors who had held back from the whiskey out of wariness fought back to give people time to run before retreating themselves. Then Johnson and the Mexicans fell upon the bodies of the dead and dying to cut away their hair, taking it like an animal's pelt. Some said the Mexicans sold the hair of the people they murdered. This was a thing abhorrent to the People, who feared the dead and the malevolent chindi spirits that lingered after a death.[12]

▼

Mangas Coloradas took charge of the survivors. He called upon relatives in other bands to help take revenge on Santa Rita. The People believed in revenge, for it demonstrated to Ussen their worthiness and made their enemies afraid to kill them. Usually warriors raided in groups of half a dozen for horses and cattle and goods, going quietly and killing no one. But when any man had been killed, his women relatives called on the other warriors to take revenge. Then they gathered up a hundred warriors and killed as many people as they could from the band, or the town, or the people of the murderers.

Mangas Coloradas undertook this sacred duty of revenge on the Mexicans. First he set out parties of warriors to ambush the trappers who hunted for beaver alone or in small parties in the mountains. Then he set out war parties to wait for the pack trains of mules bringing supplies to Santa Rita. When the Mexicans in Santa Rita noticed that the supplies had stopped coming, they sent out parties of miners to discover what had happened. The warriors killed these men as well. Sometimes they brought prisoners back to camp. Lozen was still a little girl, but she was old enough to learn what would happen to an enemy. The warriors tied their hands together, then set them out in the middle of the circle of spectators. Then the wives, daughters, and mothers of the murdered people killed the men. Sometimes they crushed them under their horses. Sometimes they cut them to pieces with knives. Sometimes they beat them to death with clubs. Lozen watched how it was done, remembering everything. Soon the Mexicans in Santa Rita saw they were trapped, just as Juan Jose and his People had been trapped in the plaza. So they abandoned Santa Rita and marched south. Many started out, but only a few left the land of the Chihenne alive.[13]

So the Chihenne had purified their land of the Mexicans, ending the desecration of Mother Earth and driving them away. The warriors continued to go south for horses and cattle, but the Mexicans only rarely dared to follow the raiders back to the shadow of the Sacred Mountain.

Looking back, it can be seen that this was the last good time— the last free time.

The White Eyes were coming, already, from the east.

CHAPTER II

▼▼

Coming of Age

Ojo Caliente, 1840s

At first, Lozen was like many other girls. Even though she loved to run ahead of the boys, even though she had a way with horses, even though she could shoot a bow better than most—still she was a girl like any other. She gathered the firewood, waited to eat until her father and her uncles were finished, and spent long hours with the women preparing the food. She chewed sinew, tanned buckskin, gathered food, hauled the heart of the agave to the roasting pits, and carried water from the springs.

But a short time before she came of age, before she began to bleed, and before she underwent the Sunrise Ceremony in order to take on the aspect of White Painted Woman, a strange and wondrous thing occurred that set her apart and changed her heart.

There came from the east a strange warrior so stern and powerful that the Chihenne called him the Grey Ghost. They saw him several times, a warrior of great stature who rode alone and could not be approached. Once three warriors saw him riding up a canyon, pursued by Mexicans. The warriors gained the attention of the Grey Ghost and signaled to him the location of a hiding place. He hid there until the Mexicans gave up looking for him and then came to the Chihenne camp to stay for a time. The Grey Ghost learned enough words to talk to Victorio and said he came from a tribe that lived far toward the rising sun. His People had sent him out to find a place where they could live safe from the White Eyes. Everything Grey Ghost said filled Victorio with dread, for Grey Ghost said the White Eyes were like the leaves on the trees, too many to number.

Lozen was then only a girl who had not yet undergone the Coming of Age Ceremony. She was already beautiful, strong, and sleek. Many of the warriors eagerly anticipated her ceremony. Some of them already hoped she would accept the ponies they would tie in front of the wickiup of her father in hopes she would take them as her husband. But Lozen's eyes turned toward Grey Ghost, who pierced her heart as if he'd ridden upon her with a lance. Even so, she only watched him and blushed and turned her eyes away. The People are restrained in these matters, careful not to inspire bad talk. So Lozen, who had also the weight of responsibility to protect the good reputation of her family, only yearned for her ceremony and hoped Grey Ghost would turn his eyes toward her when it was finally proper for him to do so.

But then one day a strange wagon came into the land of the Chihenne. Twelve men rode beside it as guards and, although they all spoke the language of Mexico, they were not Mexicans. Another man drove the wagon and beside him sat an old woman. Inside the wagon they carried a beautiful young woman. When the wagon and its strange escort passed through the land of the Chihenne and continued west, Grey Ghost went with them. Lozen thought perhaps the woman and the men had come from his People in the east, so he would finish his quest. But Grey Ghost moved from mystery into mystery, in the unfathomable way of the world.

Lozen watched him go, not speaking. But her heart had set on

Grey Ghost, as wet buckskin takes the shape of the frame on which it is stretched. She did not seem interested in other men after that, but kept her heart like an empty cave, haunted by echoes.[1]

Who can say what thoughts shaped Lozen in the space Grey Ghost left behind? Perhaps Ussen set her heart on this impossible warrior so she would not take a husband and instead become a warrior and Victorio's strong right hand. Or perhaps it was Lozen who put her heart aside, so she would not become a wife to some other man. Or perhaps it was only the strange turnings of love, which no woman can say truthfully she understands.

Certainly through the long winter nights around the campfire, Lozen listened carefully to the stories of her People about women, and how they should behave. She heard the many stories about faithless wives—most of which ended with the wronged husband killing the lovers. She heard the story about the woman whose husband was away so much that she pleasured herself with a cactus from which she had cut off the thorns. Her husband then mocked her and sent her away when the cactus broke off inside of her so a shaman had to come to get it out. She listened to the story about how Coyote, the trickster spirit, was about to make love to a beautiful woman when he noticed she had teeth in her vagina. So he tricked her and put a rock in her vagina instead of his penis. The rock broke off the teeth in the woman's vagina, so the woman said, *Hereafter I shall be worth a lot. I am worth horses and many things now*—which is why men now bring horses and other gifts when they want a girl to marry them. She listened also to the story about how Coyote saw a beautiful girl playing the rock-and-stave game. Coyote was so smitten that he convinced Gopher to dig a hole under the girl so he could sneak underneath her and stick his penis up out of the ground to have intercourse with her. But when she felt him poke her, she jumped up and hit his penis with a rock, which is why Coyote's penis has a sheath.

Lozen also thought long about the story in which Coyote married his own daughter, or the time Coyote tricked his mother-in-law into reaching inside a hollow log so he could come up behind her and have intercourse with her without her knowing it was him.[2] She understood from these stories that marriage and a woman's role could sometimes be a snare that held a woman in one place.

But she also understood that the People could not survive without the work of women. They were all the children of White Painted Woman, who had protected Child of Water and taught him. Women in many ways had an honored place in the round of life. The men owed all of their work and loyalty to their wives' families and so honored and protected their wives. Sometimes women went on raids with the warriors, usually women with no children who would tend to their husbands' needs as they traveled. It was true that a man had a right to kill his wife or cut off her nose if she proved unfaithful, but a woman was also free to end her marriage to a man who was unfaithful or beat her or did not provide well. A woman could leave a marriage simply by putting her husband's things out of the wickiup. Even if she did this, she still kept all of the gifts her husband had given to her family and most of the household goods, which were produced by her labor. Women did more work than men did, but they were respected and lived surrounded by their families.

Still, Lozen found herself drawn to the rough games of the boys. She went with the boys when they played their war games, and she thought often that she would like to become an apprentice to a warrior—like Nana. Nonetheless, she also learned the things a woman must know: how to weave baskets and prepare buckskin and make moccasins and gather roots and prepare food and the hundreds of skills by which the People made a good living from a hard land.

She also learned the names of all the places around about Ojo Caliente and on up the Sacred Mountain. Each hill, outcropping,

spring, stream, cluster of trees, and canyon had a name given to
it by the First People.[3] She traveled along with her mother, her
father, her uncles, and Nana whenever she could, hoping they
would tell her the stories of the naming of each place. Each story
taught a lesson, usually about the consequences of bad thinking.
She especially loved the little bluff alongside a stream called Their
Shades Filled Up With Shit. Nana told her the story about that
place, saying:

> It happened here at Shades of Shit.
>
> They had much corn, those people who lived here, and their
> relatives had only a little. They refused to share it. Their rela-
> tives begged them but still they refused to share it.
>
> Then their relatives got angry and forced them to stay at
> home. They wouldn't let them go anywhere, not even to defe-
> cate. So they had to defecate at home, instead of walking a long
> ways off as was their custom. Their shades filled up with it.
> There was more and more of it! It was very bad! Those people
> got sick and nearly died.
>
> Then their relatives said, you have brought this on your-
> selves. Now you live in shades of shit! Finally, they agreed to
> share their corn.
>
> It happened at Shades of Shit.[4]

Nana taught Lozen the names of many such places, so that
everywhere she went in the land that knew them, she was reminded constantly of the right behavior and of the ancestors who
had passed down their wisdom and their spirit to her. She passed
often near the hill called Two Old Women Are Buried or the small
flat called They Are Grateful for Water or the mountain face
called Lizards Dart Away in Front or the slope called She Carries
Her Brother on Her Back or the cornfield called She Became Old
Sitting or the butte called Trail to Life Goes Up or the bend in

the stream called Water Flows Inward under the Cottonwood Tree.[5]

Each place-name taught her something—like the place named Big Cottonwood Trees Stand Here and There:

Long ago, the Pimas and the People were fighting. The Pimas carried long clubs made from mesquite wood, heavy and hard. Before dawn the Pimas arrived at that place and attacked the People there, while they were asleep. The Pimas killed people with their clubs. One old woman woke up, and heard her People crying out. The old woman thought it was her son-in-law because he often picked on her daughter. The old woman cried out, *You pick on my child a lot. You should act more pleasantly toward her.* Because the old woman cried out, the Pimas learned where she was. The Pimas came running to the old woman's camp and killed her with their clubs. Only one young girl ran away from there and hid beneath some bushes. She alone survived.

It happened at Big Cottonwood Trees Stand Here and There.[6]

Many of the stories taught her the importance of listening to her elders and respecting the Power that lay coiled up inside all things. For instance, she learned well about what happened at Line of White Rocks Extends Up and Out:

Long ago, a girl lived alone with her maternal grandmother. Her grandmother sent her out regularly to collect firewood. She went to a place above her camp. She could get there quickly by climbing up through a rocky canyon, but since many snakes lived there, her grandmother told her always to go another way.

Then the girl went to collect firewood. The day was hot, and the girl became thirsty. Then she thought, *This wood is heavy.*

I don't want to carry it too far. Then she started to walk down the rocky canyon. There were loose rocks where she walked, and she slipped and fell down. The firewood she was carrying scattered everywhere! As she started to pick it up, a snake bit her hand.

My grandmother told me this would happen to me, she thought.

By the time the girl returned to where she was living with her grandmother, her arm and hand had become badly swollen. Her People worked a curing ceremony over her. Later, when she was once again healthy, the girl went to her grandmother, and said, *My life is still my own.* Now she knew how to live right.

It happened at Line of White Rocks Extends Up and Out.[7]

If someone in Lozen's band were showing disrespect for their elders, or the Power of snakes, then an elder might mention Line of White Rocks Extends Up and Out, so that the person showing disrespect would instead think about that place and understand. Because everyone knew all of the stories, they could make almost any point by bringing up the right places—all without ever offering a direct criticism to wound a person's pride.

Nana explained to Lozen that places could stalk you, hunting down wrong thinking and wrong action. The places themselves could correct one's thinking. In this way, the places that each had their own Power would shape the thinking and the behavior of the People, just as the elders might instruct children. Nana said she must learn all of the place-names she could and remember each story. When she rode with him from place to place, she could hear him murmuring the stories as they passed so the places would work on him, for a person must seek the wisdom that sits in places. Nana explained that Lozen must go to these places and sit there a long while and listen. The places would know she was listening and they would help her to smooth out her mind, to let go of fear and emotion and ego and self-importance. Only places could impart the calm, focus, and attention that came with wisdom. Each person must strive for smoothness, resilience, and steadiness of mind, which came only through long study and thought. Wisdom, in turn, revealed the narrow pass through which a person must travel to find Power. A person who learns wisdom from places clears obstructions from her mind, so her thinking is smooth and clear. A wise person might foresee disaster, fend off misfortune, or avoid conflicts with other people, and she would surely live a long life that would stand as a blessing to the People.[8]

Lozen yearned for wisdom so she might serve her People. So she eagerly sought the names of every place she encountered and traveled constantly about Ojo Caliente and up and down the Sacred Mountain, repeating the names of each place and sitting quietly for hours at a time to let the wisdom of those places soak into her. She marveled that Ussen had made these places for the People, giving the land itself the Power to bring them wisdom.

In this fashion, Lozen worked hard in the first thirteen years of her life to find a place for herself among the People, her anticipation growing as the time approached for the Sunrise Ceremony that would mark her entrance into the responsibilities of a woman.

She made Nana tell her again and again the story of the woman who first learned the Sunrise Ceremony, an old medicine woman named Esonknhsendehe. One day she was on the Sacred Mountain keeping watch for enemies near a place where a great rock formation looks out over the valley. As she was passing by, the rocks formed the opening to a cave at the base of the cliff and there came a singing from inside the cave. Everyone else was afraid to go inside or even to approach the opening because of the enchanted singing. But the medicine woman resolved to go into the cave, for her Power was great. Each of her friends pleaded with her not to go, fearful she would not return. Nonetheless, she went alone into the cave. When she was gone, they heard songs and drums and experienced queer sensations and knew it was the spirit people making the sounds coming from the cave.

She was gone for so long a time everyone concluded she must have died inside the mountain, and so they left in sorrow and fear and stopped speaking her name out of respect. But one day she came back to them, calling out and carrying a lamp in her hand. They waited respectfully for her to speak about her experience in the cave, being too polite to question her directly. But she told them nothing about what had happened. Even so, her good deeds increased and her Power grew. After a time, she said that Life Giver had commanded her to climb a great cliff near their camp to pray.

That is impossible, my sister, said the People. *No man has ever scaled that precipice.*

Ussen has spoken. I obey, she said.

Let one man, or more, go with you, they said, seeing that she was only a woman who could not make such a climb alone.

But she replied, *Only Ussen can help me. Stay at the foot of the cliff and pray for me.*

So she climbed the sheer wall as they watched, marveling to see that a toehold appeared each time she needed it. As she neared the top of the cliff, she came to the opening of a cave that no one could see, perhaps a cave that had opened up as she climbed. She reached the opening, which was guarded by two huge bears. Beyond the bears she saw a pair of mountain lions, then two huge snakes, and beyond them two more creatures that no one will name. To enter, she had to pass between the rows of beasts. She was frightened, but she saw the path that had been set for her feet. So she bowed her head and walked calmly between the beasts. She continued to walk even after the door to the cave closed behind her. In the light that still suffused the cave, she could see dimly the rows of Mountain Spirits between whom she must walk.

What does our daughter seek? they asked.

That which will benefit my People, she replied.

We have the Power; each of us has a different Power. We will bestow upon you only one. Speak.

What Power have you?

That of healing. Others have other Powers.

All are good, said the woman, *but I seek that which heals sickness of spirit.*

Not until she reached the last Mountain Spirit did she find what she sought.

My daughter, said the Spirit, *do you realize what you ask?*

Perhaps not, Mother, replied the woman, *but in your infinite wisdom you know what will bring the greatest good to my People.*

I do, the Spirit replied. *If you had not been virtuous you would never have returned from the cave on the Sacred Mountain. If you had not been brave you would never have entered this place. What you ask I shall give. It is this: At times your People may have direct communication with the Mountain Spirits.*

How can that be? the woman asked. *We are Earth People.*

You are of earth, but you have reached this place where no other before you has been deemed worthy to come. We will come to you. Listen, remember, and obey: When your young girls have attained womanhood you are to make a feast for the worthy—the chaste. You will observe the rite of which I tell you. It is for the maidens, their sponsors, and the medicine men. It is to commemorate the sanctity of the gift of producing new life. The medicine men are to sing many prayers, at least one hundred seventy-four, during the four days of the ceremonial. You are to teach them these songs. While they sing, the maidens are to dance, and on the fourth night the singing is to continue until dawn. During this rite, the men will retire to a secret place and dress for their dance. There are to be four groups of four men each, for four is your sacred number. They will wear buckskin skirts, moccasins, and a mask surmounted by a high crown of sticks, painted with sacred symbols. No red is to be used. Their bodies are to be blackened and symbols painted upon chest and back. The men are to be accompanied by one or more clowns, with bodies painted white, and heads covered with masks. These will be boys learning the rites so that they may in time be admitted to the company of dancers. They are to serve the men, to return to them any wand that may be dropped by the dancers, and to relieve the solemnity of the occasion. Dance only at night, and show no sign of recognition of the dancers who impersonate the Mountain Spirits. Through the minds of the dancers, messages will be transmitted to the minds of the maidens who for four days will partake of the qualities of White Painted Woman. The maidens will tell the medicine men the messages they receive, and these must be obeyed, for they are for the benefit of the entire tribe. All who attend the dances will receive good.

All? asked the medicine woman, surprised. *The evil, too?*

All. Even though an enemy be present, he is to participate in the blessings.[9]

▼

Lozen listened to this story again and again, wishing she could have been the medicine woman who went into the cave and who found the courage to climb the cliff as Ussen bid. Lozen burned like a branch that is not consumed, hoping to be worthy of the message of the Mountain Spirits.

She also often begged Nana to tell her the story of Gouyan, who everyone respected as a wise woman and a strong fighter. Gouyan was just a girl when she married a respected warrior. But then a raiding party of Commanche killed her husband, whom she loved dearly. For Gouyan, mourning started with a great rage, so she swore to seek revenge for his death. She set out alone and followed the Commanche raiding party back to their own territory, where they celebrated their raid with a victory dance. Gouyan, who was beautiful and graceful as a lion, slipped into their camp and then took the great risk of going in among the dancers, hoping they would mistake her for a woman visiting from another camp. She looked for her opportunity to dance with the leader of the raiding party, dancing close up against him and flashing her dark eyes at him as though she ached for him. He was addled by her and by the liquor he had been drinking, and so he let her lead him away into the darkness, hoping she would lie down with him. Instead, she began to embrace him and then took the knife from his belt and plunged it deep into his chest. Then she cut away a piece of him and took his horse and rode quickly out of the camp before the other warriors discovered what she had done. She pushed on alone back to her camp, eluding their pursuit. The story of Gouyan's revenge for the death of her husband was still one of the favorite stories around the fire, and Lozen memorized every detail.[10]

So Lozen yearned for her ceremony. She spent many long hours with her sponsor, learning the songs, gestures, and rituals. She was anxious to do everything perfectly so she could bring the blessings of the Mountain Spirits and of White Painted Woman on her People, who needed those blessings so desperately. Her relatives began to collect the things they would need a year before the ceremony, knowing they must gather enough food to feed many people for the four days of the ceremony. They gave her grandmother and her sponsor the five flawless buckskins needed to make the ceremonial dress she would wear during the time she would partake of White Painted Woman. They decorated the per-fectly softened white buckskin with the morning star and the cres-cent moon and circles, rainbows, and sunbeams and colored the designs yellow—like pollen—by rubbing in yellow ocher. At each stage, they sang over the dress, and prayed to Ussen and to White Painted Woman.[11]

Her parents then obtained the blessing and the cooperation of a singer, who erected the sacred shelter, stretching hides over the four long poles, praying over the eagle feathers and sage and gama grass attached to the poles. The singer offered many prayers in the construction and so became connected to Lozen and to Lozen's family for all of his life, as though he were a relative. And each pole had a certain nature, as directions have a nature, and as colors have a nature. As they built the shelter, the singer shook his rattle and sang the dwelling song:

Killer of Enemies and White Painted Woman have made it so,[12]
They have made the poles of the dwelling so,
For long life stands the blue stallion.

Here Killer of Enemies and White Painted Woman have made
*   them so,*
They have made the poles of the dwelling so,
For long life stands the yellow stallion.

Here Killer of Enemies and White Painted Woman have made
*   them so,*
They have made the poles of the dwelling so,
For long life stands the black stallion.

Here Killer of Enemies and White Painted Woman have made
*   them so,*
They have made the poles of the dwelling so,
For long life stands the white stallion.

Each time the singer spoke the name of one of the supernaturals, the women made the cry of joy and applause with which

White Painted Woman greeted Child of Water when he came home to her after killing the giant. As the men finished the sacred dwelling, the singer cried:

> The home of the long-life dwelling ceremony
> Is the home of White Painted Woman,
> Of long life the home of White Painted Woman is made,
> For Killer of Enemies has it so,
> Killer of Enemies has made it so.[13]

When the time for the ceremony finally came, Lozen went into the special shelter built for her and there her sponsor washed her hair with yucca root soap before arranging her hair and dressing her—beginning with the right moccasin. Then, as Lozen faced the sunrise, her sponsor tied two eagle feathers in the long black hair hanging down her back, singing the old songs all this time. After she was dressed, everyone would call her White Painted Woman for the four days of the ceremony. They did this so the blessings promised would settle down over the People like soft rain and so the Mountain Spirits could offer guidance through these troubled times. Then the sponsor took yucca fruit with a cross of pollen on it and held it to the four directions. She motioned three times toward White Painted Woman before she put it in her mouth on the fourth. White Painted Woman was fed fruits and pinyon nuts, so that Lozen might have a good appetite all throughout her life. The sponsor spoke carefully, warning White Painted Woman that she must drink only through a tube, scratch only with the scratching stick, and stay in the sacred shelter for the four days of the ceremony and for four days thereafter. She must not talk much nor laugh nor wash, for if even the pollen on her hand should wash off, rain would come and spoil the good time. She must not even go to a spring or look up at the clouds, lest she summon rain. She must not become angry or curse any-

one or make fun of anyone, for Lozen's disposition during the four
days of the ceremony and the four days of meditation that followed would determine her nature for the rest of her life.

With the completion of the ceremonial structure on the first
day of the ceremony, White Painted Woman came forward and
knelt on the skin of a four-year-old black-tailed deer. Her attendant offered pollen to the four directions and then painted White
Painted Woman with it, marking her from cheek to cheek across
the bridge of her nose and along the part of her hair. White
Painted Woman then marked her attendant in the same way and
everyone formed a line leading south, so that White Painted
Woman might mark each of their faces with pollen in just the
same way—as a blessing. Sometimes, just this marking was
enough to cure sickness.

White Painted Woman lay down with her head pointing east
and her attendant came forward again to mold her, massaging her
from her head to her feet from the right side to the left so she
would be a good woman with a good disposition. As the old
woman rubbed White Painted Woman, she sang:

> *May this girl be good in disposition, good in morals.*
> *May she grow up, live long, and be a fine woman.*

Then White Painted Woman rose and watched as the attendant outlined four footsteps of pollen on the buckskin. White
Painted Woman took those four steps, going east, so she would
have good fortune and health. Then her attendant put a basket
containing bags of pollen and ocher, an elk-hoof rattle, a bundle
of gama grass, an eagle feather, and other things thirty paces to
the east and White Painted Woman trotted around the basket so
she might live a long while. Old men and young boys followed
her around the basket, praying as they ran, the old men hoping
for long life and the boys praying for anything good. Three more

times White Painted Woman ran around the basket, to bring blessings on the People.

Then Lozen's relatives came and threw fruit, nuts, and treats onto the blanket marked with the pollen footprints of White Painted Woman. Everyone rushed forward to grab up the gifts, laughing and scrambling in happiness and confusion. In this way was completed the cycle, as the fruits followed the pollen in the season of growth.

White Painted Woman then retired into the shelter prepared for her, while everyone joined in the games and the socializing— catching up on gossip, because the ceremony brought in people who had married and gone to live with other bands. The men gathered at the hoop-and-pole ground where they laughed and exclaimed and gambled great sums. They rolled the hoop out across the smoothed ground and threw the marked pole in such a way that it landed on top of the hoop when it finally tottered and fell on its side, scoring the throw by the markings on the pole. Meanwhile, the women gathered together to play the stave game, using three sticks painted black on the flat side and yellow on the rounded side that had been prepared by women who knew the proper ceremonies. They threw these sticks among forty stones arranged in patterns, scoring each throw according to which side landed faceup and where among the stones they fell. They could play as individuals or in teams and the games always inspired much betting and laughter.

As the shadows grew long in the afternoon, White Painted Woman emerged again and with her fire drill lit a fire in the ceremonial structure. Everyone then prepared for the evening cer- emonials and the appearance of the masked dancers—who would imitate the Mountain Spirits and so prepare their minds to receive the messages and blessings of the supernaturals from White Painted Woman.

The masked dancers dressed carefully, knowing mistakes could bring bad luck to themselves and to the People. Certain warriors learned the songs and the steps of the masked dancers, and of the Grey One, the clown. The shamans learned the proper way to dress the dancers, and the songs that must attend the preparation. The shaman sang:

> *In the middle of the Holy Mountain,*
> *In the middle of its body, stands a hut,*
> *Brush-built, for the Black Mountain Spirit.*
> *White Lightning streaks an angular path;*
> *I am the lightning flashes and streaking!*
> *This headdress lives; the noise of its pendants*
> *Sounds and is heard!*
> *My song shall encircle these dancers!*
>
> *Thus speaks earth's thunder:*
> *Because of it there is good about you,*
> *Because of it your body is well:*
> *Thus speaks earth's thunder.*

Everyone gathered in front of the sacred shelter as the fire rose, waiting for the masked dancers. Then they came in, moving one behind the other, dancing in a way that stopped the heart. They wore high moccasins and buckskin skirts colored yellow, held by a broad belt and hung with pendants. Their arms and chests and stomachs and backs were entirely painted, black, white, yellow, and blue, with narrow bands of bright color, or a design like a cactus, or a zigzag line, or a cross, or a four-pointed star. Each dancer carried a wooden stick. Each also tied to his elbow long buckskin streamers attached to fluttering eagle feathers. They wore masks made of buckskin with tiny holes for the eyes, painted black and yellow and blue, some with stars and designs and some a solid color. At the forehead some of the dancers wore abalone shell, some turquoise. At the top of the mask were colored sticks of split oak decorated with eagle feathers, turkey feathers, or green juniper, with pieces of wood hanging down so that they struck one against the other to announce the approach of the masked dancers.

The masked dancers came and danced through the village, stopping to dance for any family that had trouble or an illness or a wounded spirit. Lozen thrilled to hear the songs, the background chanting giving way to great bursts of melody in which the on-lookers joined. The songs suddenly hushed, then resumed, like an eagle bursting forth with a shimmer of feather and talon before veering back into the smooth cloud of chanted sound. Her parents had obtained the services of one of the most skillful singers, so everyone listened with delighted respect and waited for the cho-ruses they knew. The singer skillfully blended the different steps, the dancers joyfully and proudly adapting their movements to the shift of the song so it seemed they were its physical expression. A round of singing always started with a free-step song. This al-lowed each dancer to move according to his feelings. The singer first offered a free-step song:

> At the place called "Home in the Center of the Sky,"
> Inside is the home's holiness.
> The door to the home is of white clouds.
> There all the Gray Mountain Spirits
> Rejoicing over me
> Kneel in the four directions with me.
>
> When first my Power was created,
> Pollen's body, speaking my words,
> Brought my Power into being,
> So I have come here.

The singer watched to see when the dancers grew tired as they struggled for air through the tight-fitting buckskin masks, even though they passed sticks over their bodies to remove the fatigue. Then the singer shifted to a short-step song and the dancers slowed, dancing rigidly with studied posture and sharp steps. When the singer saw the dancers were rested, he shifted again to a high-step song, to the delight of the audience. The dancers formed a circle around the fire, facing away from it, and danced with violent grace, wild as a war dance—throwing one leg and then another up so violently they seemed sometimes to hover over the ground, held up by some Power. Everyone called out encouragement as the singer pushed the dancers to their limits. Once, two of the dancers smashed one into the other so violently one dancer dropped the wand he carried, which represented an aspect of the Power of the Mountain Spirits. Many people gasped, but the dancer knew better than to reach down and pick up the stick. Instead, he staggered about inside the circle as though stunned. The lead dancer, seeing the mishap, lined up all of the dancers in single file and they danced to the stick, paying respect to the wand from each of the four directions. When it was safe, the lead dancer picked it up and returned it to the masked dancer who had dropped it.

Meanwhile, the singer went to White Painted Woman, who handed him the rattle he had entrusted to her earlier in the day. He extended toward her an eagle feather, which she grasped in her right hand as he shook the rattle and walked slowly backward singing:

> They move her by means of the finest eagle feather,
> By means of it White Painted Woman walks into her home.

White Painted Woman walked around the fire in the ceremonial dwelling, moving always to the right in the sacred way, and sat before the fire. The singer also sat and lit a cigarette, chanting barely audible songs. As everyone listened in reverential silence, he sang a sequence of songs that represented the journey of the girl from the holy home through a long and successful life. The songs contained flowers and beautiful things so each of these might be realized in the girl's life. The songs described everything that grows on the earth, even each of the grasses and their stages of development and seasons of growth. Each of the songs called for a different dance step, mostly the shuffling-step songs that required White Painted Woman to stand and dance with her arms upright from the elbows, palms outward, her feet close together, moving from left to right and right to left, pivoting on her toes and heels. Then the singer would switch to another, easier step, in which she would dance in place with her hands on her hips. The songs continued all through the night. White Painted Woman knew that if she grew too weary she could kneel and rest as the song continued. But the hypnotic rhythm of the song, the repetition of her motion, and the singer's voice wove such a spell she could scarcely feel her feet. She drifted as in a dream as the soothing beauty of the songs washed over her like the water of the hot springs—warm as blood, as the womb, as the fire's perfect moment.

The songs continued hour upon hour, night upon night:

The spruce home of White Painted Woman is built of long life,
By means of a home built of this she has gone inside,
By means of her Power of goodness White Painted Woman has
       come to her,
By means of it the words have gone inside.

I come to White Painted Woman
By means of long life I come to her.

I come to her by means of her blessing.
I come to her by means of her good fortune,
I come to her by means of all her different fruits;
By means of the long life she bestows, I come to her;
By means of this holy truth she goes about.

I am about to sing this song of yours,
The song of long life.
Sun, I stand here on the earth with your song;
Moon, I have come in with your song.

Sometimes the singer would put in a smoking song. Then the men who were sitting just outside of the structure singing and drumming for the masked dancers would pause also to smoke—rolling the sacred tobacco in oak leaves and blowing smoke to the four directions and joining sometimes in the smoking song:

The time for smoking has come.
With the sun's tobacco let all be made pleasant.
From here on let good constantly follow,
From now on let many old men and old women rejoice;
Let them come back to many ceremonies like this;
Let all the girls be happy;
Let them know many ceremonies like this;
Let all rejoice;
Let all the boys rejoice;
Let them attend many ceremonies like this.

When the singer had finished the ceremonial songs for the evening, the masked dancers retired and the fun began, with songs and social dances. Then any singer could come forward with old songs, or songs of his own composition. Everyone had their favorites so they called out, cheered, teased, and laughed for the singers and the songs they liked best. The social songs were full of romance, mischief, and humor, and many a married couple who had lived a long life together would still smile and exchange shy glances when the song by which they had wooed one another came up. All through the night people danced in a circle, usually with the girls dancing around the inner circle and the boys dancing around the outside circle—sometimes one by one, sometimes as couples. When they danced as couples, the boys each had to pay the girl a gift. Many offered as fine a gift as they could possibly afford, knowing it spoke of his regard for her and that people would notice the value of the gifts and so judge his strength and generosity. So the singer cried out with laughter in his voice, every inflection creating a shift in emphasis that could turn the meaning of the song on its head, make a play on words, or suggest another meaning that was indelicate and delightful.

> *Young woman, you are thinking of something,*
> *Young woman, you are thinking of something;*
> *You are thinking of what you are going to get:*
> *That man of whom you are thinking is worthless!*

They made jokes: *She married an old man, with big buttocks.*

They made light of infidelity: *He asks me what happened, to his wife!*

They teased the love struck: *Wait for me, at the high bluff over there.*

Or they sang about love:

> *I see that girl again,*
>   *Then I become like this*
> *I see my own sweetheart again,*
>   *Then I become like this.*

Maiden, you talk kindly to me,
  You, I shall surely remember it,
I shall surely remember you alone,
Your words are so kind,
  You, I shall surely remember it.

Some songs struck a note of wistful longing:

My sweetheart, we surely could have gone home,
  But you were afraid!
When it was night we surely could have gone home,
  But you were afraid!

Some songs struck a note of mocking reproach:

Man from a distant land, why do you talk to me?
Why do you talk to me?
Why do you talk to me?
What have you done for me?
But just talk to me?

And so the dancing, singing, eating, drinking, fond looks, lowered eyes, high steps, old stories, new tales, and all of the ways by which the People remembered themselves continued right to the dawn. The second night went the same way. And the third night the same way, so that all the loves, longings, friendships, gossip, judgments, knowledge, and dreams that connected all of the scattered bands honored Lozen, who had become an aspect of White Painted Woman. In all her life to come, she would know she was of the People and beloved by White Painted Woman so she could be relied upon and as fitted to her place as the grass is to the earth.

On the fourth night, the ceremonial dancing and singing did not stop in the late evening but went on, song after song, to the dawn. The singer then completed the sequence of songs White Painted Woman left for the People to remind them of the journey of life and the cycles of the earth. He sang as White Painted Woman moved back and forth in the shuffling step:

White Painted Woman commands that which lies above,
Killer of Enemies commands,
By means of long life they command.
From the mouth of the chief bird
Yellowness emerges by means of it,
By means of it yellow emerges from your mouth.

The words of Killer of Enemies, good through long life,
Have entered you;
They have entered you by means of your necklace;
Your necklace has gone into your body,
For its Power is good.

White Painted Woman's Power emerges,
Her Power for sleep.
White Painted Woman carries this girl;
She carries her through long life,
She carries her to good fortune,
She carries her to old age,
She bears her to peaceful sleep.

By means of this ceremony I have gone to White Painted Woman,
I have gone to the source of long life created of goodness.
White Painted Woman, her grasses are striped with yellow,
Killer of Enemies spoke thus;
White Painted Woman, her grasses are much striped with blue,
Killer of Enemies, his grasses are much striped with red.

White Painted Woman has reached middle age by means of it,
She has reached middle age by means of it,
By means of it she has entered long life,
She has reached middle age by means of it.

He made the black staff of old age for me,
He made the road of the sun for me;
These holy things he has made for me, saying,
"With these you will grow old."
Now when I have become old,
You will remember me by means of them.

Then the masked dancers went out among the people, urging each of them into the dancing area. They went to every wickiup, to be sure no person missed the dancing, even people who were in their beds and trying to ignore the ceremony. The masked dancers went to each girl, to find out with which boy she wanted to dance. The dancers then pulled each fellow out so he would dance. And they danced on to the dawn, in joy and holiness, knowing White Painted Woman had come back down among them in Lozen's form, knowing the Mountain Spirits watched them and sheltered them and spoke to them through the minds of the dancers. By this they knew they were still the People in the shadow of the Sacred Mountain, in the place where the world began, all together like the circle of dancers, a circle in a circle, in the circle of the firelight. Then, just before dawn, the singer finished the songs of life:

You have started out on the good earth;
You have started out with good moccasins;
With moccasin strings of the rainbow, you have started out;
With moccasin strings of the sun's rays, you have started out;
In the midst of plenty you have started out.

So White Painted Woman, who was an aspect of Lozen, faced east and knelt on the hide. Everyone cleared the space between her and the rising sun so not even a dog could pass there. Then the singer faced also to the east and sang the last four songs. He put pollen on his face and on his head and on her face and on her head. Then he took the mixture of water and white clay the attendant had prepared and painted on her face one line of white and one of red. He turned back to the east and dipped his right forefinger into the red paint, holding it up, singing the Red Paint song. With a splinter of wood he traced a sun symbol on the palm of his left hand in pollen, red ocher, and specular iron ore. And he sang in this manner:

> Now I'll make long life of the sun's rays,
> Now I'll make long life of the sun's pointed rays,
> I'll make peaks extending outward.
> The rays of the sun and long life are made of pollen,
> The points of the sun and long life are made of specular iron ore,
> The points of the sun and long life are made of specular iron ore,
> The rays of the sun and long life are made of blue paint,
> The rays of the sun and long life are made of blue paint,
> The rays of the sun and long life are made of red paint,
> The rays of the sun and long life are made of red paint,
> The rays of the sun and long life are made of white paint,
> The rays of the sun and long life are made of white paint.

Then, holding up his hand so the first light of the rising sun would fall upon his painted palm, he sang:

> That which comes has come well out,
> In here it has come.

Again he faced the girl, touching his hand to her body here and there, moving sunwise. He rubbed the symbol he had painted on his hand into her hair as the rays of the rising sun reached her. He also tied a piece of turquoise on her forehead with a string. He thrust the eagle feather by which she had been led each night of the ceremony into a bundle of gama grass and used the stems and the feather to adorn White Painted Woman with white clay, first the right side and then the left side of her face, then her arms, then her legs. The people crowded forward and the singer marked each of them as well. When everyone who wished had received this blessing, the singer used the eagle feather to guide White Painted Woman to place her feet in the footsteps outlined in pollen. Then she ran again around the basket, which had now been set a long way off. She ran so lightly she thought perhaps she had not touched the ground at all. She felt she could have run all the way to the top of the Sacred Mountain and back down again without breath. Everyone who watched her running admired the way of it, thinking that even Lozen had never run so well—graceful as a prayer.

Finally, she returned to the ceremonial shelter where she remained for four more days, while the great gathering occasioned by the ceremony broke up, many visitors returning to their bands.

Lozen remained in prayer, like a dream.

And when the full four days of meditation had passed, she got up, taking nothing but a waterskin, and went up to the Sacred Mountain.[14] She found a place that seemed right to her and sat alone, not eating, barely moving, hoping for a vision. She hardly knew how long she remained there, but the light came and went and came again. The hunger nibbled, then gnawed—but she put it out of her mind, testing her discipline. After a time, the hunger gave up on her and left her to her thoughts. She began to put aside her thoughts, working to prevent her mind from racing after any one thing, but simply sitting with her mind clear. Sometimes she despaired—hearing only the sound of the wind in the trees, the crying of a distant raven and furtive movements in the grass. No vision would come to her. She was not worthy of visions. She was only a prideful girl, who did not understand her place, who yearned for something she was not fit to possess. She had not the virtue or the courage of the woman who went alone into the cave and climbed the cliff and passed between the bears and the lions and the Mountain Spirits to ask for a gift to help her People. But then Lozen saw that despair itself was a form of pride, so she let it go as well, as she had let go of the hunger and the thirst and the complaints of her body.

She knew she took a risk, coming so openly to seek Power— the gift of White Painted Woman. Usually, Power must make the first move. Power must seek you—sometimes coming as a voice, sometimes as an animal, sometimes as a glimpse of a supernatural. Power pervades all things; it is the animating force in everything—the life force. In this sense, everything is alive, even the rocks and the wind. Power has many aspects and appears to each person differently, so you might say, this mountain talks to me or this tree or this horse. But Power is dangerous and can break you, even when it does not mean to do so, like a child playing with a butterfly of gossamer and powder. Some people fear Power and refuse to answer when Power calls them. Others go too fast or use Power wrongly. Sometimes they go crazy. Sometimes they make mistakes and offend their Power so the Power turns against them. Sometimes they are not virtuous enough and they turn the Power against others—like a man who does not share his meat— and so they become witches. Sometimes the Power grows jealous or bored or merely cruel and demands payment or sacrifice. Sometimes people start out using Power to help their People, but then Power demands payment—saying this man or that one will have to die. Sometimes Power makes the one it chooses trade the life of another in order to live longer—maybe a wife or a brother or a son.

Even so, Lozen sought Power. Not for herself, but for her People—as the woman who went into the cave had sought it.

And so, finally, Power spoke to her. She saw visions. A horse came to her and spoke to her, saying she should have Horse Power. The horse carefully and tenderly taught her a song:

> *The sun's horse is a yellow stallion;*
> *His nose, the place above his nose, is of haze,*
> *His ears, of the small lightning, are moving back and forth,*
> *He has come to us.*
> *The sun's horse is a yellow stallion,*
> *A blue stallion, a black stallion;*
> *The sun's horse has come to us.*[15]

This song would give her Power over horses and an understanding of them and the ability to heal anyone who was affected by horse sickness or injured by a horse. She also saw other things, and heard other voices—things about which she did not speak again and that she did not describe nor question nor ever forget. These were private matters between Lozen and her Power. But as she sat on the Sacred Mountain in a long dream, her Power taught her a song—saying it was a song to be used only to protect her People. The song was given to the People through her—as the message of White Painted Woman comes through the minds of the dancers and through the mouth of the girl in the ceremony. So Lozen was given a warrior song—an Enemies Against song so she could locate enemies. Her Power also gave her the ability to heal. And in this vision and in this song and in the murmuring of her Power, Lozen saw the path that had been set for her. These were a warrior's gifts—to see the enemy, to handle horses, and to heal wounds. She knew that what her heart had whispered to her already was true after all and she must go with the warriors. Perhaps that was why Grey Ghost had been sent to her, although she was too young and so could never have the one thing on which her heart had been set.[16] Perhaps that was so she would not love any other, nor become a wife, nor have children and so have no reason to shy away from the war path and her responsibilities to her People and to Victorio.

But who can say? Power passes understanding and the world works itself out in ways that make no sense but cannot be altered.

So Lozen came down from the mountain, weak from hunger but filled with her vision. She sought out Nana who understood many things and Victorio who understood her so well. She told them those things her Power had said she might reveal. And they agreed she should take the training of a warrior, going as an apprentice on raids, even though girls did not normally take the training and women did not normally go with war parties unless they traveled with their husbands.

She told Victorio and Nana she had been given a ceremony to locate the enemy. She had been told she must stand in a clear space and sing the song she had been given. If an enemy was near, she would feel his presence in the heat on her palms when she faced in the direction from which the enemy would come. The greater the heat of her hands, the closer the enemy. She sang the song thus:

> *Upon this earth*
> *On which we live*
> *Ussen has Power.*
> *This Power is mine*
> *For locating the enemy.*
> *I search for that enemy*

Which only Ussen the Great
Can show to me.[17]

In this manner, Lozen set out on a lonely path—set apart, wondered at, and eventually revered.

And her Power was right.

Her People had great need of her, for they had not enough warriors, and not enough Power, and not enough luck. For everything was about to change and death would ride double with her for the rest of her life.

The White Eyes had come.

CHAPTER III

▼▼▼

The Coming of the
White Eyes

1852, New Mexico

Some years after Mangas Coloradas and the warriors drove out the Mexicans, the sentinels reported parties of White Eyes, well mounted and well armed and dressed alike. Mangas Coloradas and the other headmen watched them carefully for a time, wondering whether these strange men were enemies or allies. Some said the Mexicans and the White Eyes were enemies, so Mangas Coloradas thought the People and the White Eyes might be friends—united by their hatred of the Mexicans. This was the great gift of Mangas Coloradas, to think in layers and to lay far-seeing plans. That is why he married each of his daughters to the important leaders of other bands—including a strong Navajo chief and Cochise, who was the leader of the Chokonen. These Chiricahua lived in the Dragoon and Chiricahua Mountains to the east and their warriors often raided with the Chihenne. So Mangas Coloradas amassed more influence than any other chief among the Mimbres because of his diplomacy, eloquence, Power, and absolute courage in war. Where other leaders thought only of the present, Mangas Coloradas thought into the days to come, remembering details, just like the blue jay that returns in the winter to the pinyon seeds he hid in the summer.

So Mangas Coloradas approached the White Eyes and learned they indeed were fighting a war with the Mexicans. He offered to show them all of the secret trails by which the White Eyes could overcome the Mexicans. The White Eyes smiled and thanked him but said they did not need help.[1] Mangas Coloradas thought on that. He saw clearly the danger posed by these new people, who were more like the Mexicans than they were like the People. He knew the People had survived in their long war with the Mexicans because they could fight and then withdraw into their own country, where the Mexican soldiers feared to follow. But now the White Eyes were coming from the east, like the Commanche, but with good guns and strange ways. So Mangas Coloradas resolved to pray and find some way to avoid making enemies of the White Eyes.

Some while later, more White Eyes with their soldiers came back and camped near the mines the Mexicans had abandoned at Santa Rita. Again, Mangas Coloradas approached them—determined to make them his friends and allies rather than his enemies. He would not let his warriors touch anything that belonged to the White Eyes, who let their horses and cattle wander about. At first, the White Eyes were friendly and everything seemed good. They gave presents to the headmen, such as the splendid clothing they gave to Mangas Coloradas, who enjoyed dressing in an impressive way. Sometimes he wore the gleaming silver helmets of the Mexicans, with great black feathers. He especially liked to wear red, which was a powerful color, and sacred. He happily wore the finely made dark coat they gave him, with its gleaming silver buttons on top of a long garment all in red that reached from his feet to his neck.

But soon things began to go badly. Although it seemed the White Eyes were friendly, Mangas Coloradas visited their camp wearing the splendid new clothes and noted that many of the soldiers were laughing at him for reasons he did not understand. So he gambled away the fine clothes and watched the White Eyes more carefully.

Then one of the White Eyes seized two Mexican boys who had been adopted into the family of a respected warrior. Mangas Coloradas and the other headmen went to the White Eyes' head nantan and demanded the return of the children. But the nantan said the White Eyes had signed a paper with the Mexicans that required them to return to the Mexicans any captives held by the People. Mangas Coloradas protested that *he* had made no agreement with the Mexicans, who held captive many children of the People. Would the White Eyes make the Mexicans give back the captives they held? But, of course, they would not. Instead, they offered to pay the family for the two boys. The warriors opposed this, but they could do nothing without starting a fight. Mangas Coloradas accepted the payment, but he did not forget.

A little while later, a Mexican killed a warrior in the camp of the White Eyes for no reason at all. Mangas Coloradas and the other headmen demanded the Mexican be turned over to them, but the nantan refused, saying the murderer must be given a trial in the fashion of the White Eyes and punished according to their laws. Mangas Coloradas said the People had their own justice and the Mexican owed a life. The nantan offered to pay the family of the dead man, as though the warrior was a mule who had been shot. The nantan lectured Mangas Coloradas and the others, saying they must stop their attacks on the Mexicans and instead plant crops and live like the White Eyes. The payment and the injustice only made the warriors angry, so Mangas Coloradas said he would no longer protect the horses and cattle of the White Eyes. In a short while, the warriors had taken all of the livestock of the White Eyes, who left soon after—all going on foot.[2]

Still, many miners who had come along behind the soldiers

stayed and reopened the diggings of the Mexicans. Other White Eyes came along after them, scaring away the game and searching through the hills for the metals that made them so crazy with greed.

It did not take long for the warriors to begin fighting with such people. The White Eyes had no reverence and no respect and could not be trusted. They swarmed over everything. First one or two would come, but then they'd arrive in mounting numbers, like locusts descending on a crop.

So the war with the White Eyes began slowly, with the theft of a horse herd here, the killing of some cattle there, then the killing of a warrior, a miner, or a soldier and the debt of blood mounting. Mangas Coloradas tried to maintain peace, seeing the People could not long survive if they had to fight both the Mexicans and the White Eyes, like a rabbit run to earth by two hawks. But he knew he would lose his influence if he prevented the warriors from striking back when they had been wronged. Younger, more aggressive leaders always pushed for more direct action and Mangas Coloradas knew warriors would follow whomever they pleased. Leaders had only influence, not command.

Victorio usually followed Mangas Coloradas, although he had assumed a leading position in his own band. Nana, who had been leader when Victorio was a boy, had given up the position to Victorio with a deference and respect that immediately impressed the other warriors. Many felt Nana must have been directed by a vision to give the leadership to Victorio. Nana had great Power, especially in locating ammunition. He also had great endurance, like a man with Goose Power.[3] Victorio quickly earned the respect of the warriors in his own right. He was tall and striking. Some said he was the perfect warrior, like Child of Water.[4] Tall and imposing, he had farseeing, piercing eyes that could cut through you or dismiss you, for Victorio had Power in war and in the handling of men. Even warriors from other bands followed him in raids, seeing he was bold but not reckless and seemed to have good luck. Lozen usually rode with Victorio on these raids, having distinguished herself in the three raids of her apprenticeship and gained the respect of the warriors. Soon the other warriors noted that she also had Power, which every raiding party values. Some of the warriors saw that Victorio often talked to his sister before making a decision. They all knew he relied on Lozen's Enemies Against Ceremony when they were pursued or uncertain.

The other leaders also attended to the advice of Mangas Coloradas, although they remained independent and resentful of the restrictions he imposed. Delgadito Largo was second in influence to Mangas Coloradas and was a strong ally of the great chief. Cuchillo Negro, named for the blackened handle of a knife because he was hard to see and lethal in a fight, was more eager for war, but the others restrained him. Loco had begun to gather a following as well. Loco was a fierce warrior who was scarred by the claws of a grizzly bear he killed with only his knife. He was a careful, dangerous, clever man, given sometimes to outbursts of anger, as though he had partaken of the nature of the bear that had marked his face. Loco saw the great danger posed by the White Eyes and often supported Mangas Coloradas in urging restraint on the warriors.

But even leaders as well regarded as Mangas Coloradas and Loco could not hold back the warriors for long. Both the White Eyes and the People were warlike people—full of pride. Among the People, the leaders could only persuade, not command—so the advice of a chief could not overcome the demands of honor and vengeance. The warriors claimed the right of revenge whenever some White Eye did them or their families wrong. Unfortunately, the White Eyes constantly provided such provocation— especially the prospectors and scalp hunters who passed through the territory of the Chihenne, ignoring the advice of the soldiers. These White Eyes often killed warriors or attacked peaceful

camps. The warriors would then take their revenge against whatever White Eyes they encountered—in keeping with the long tradition of revenge against the Mexicans and rival bands. So the
warriors of a band whose women had been killed would look for
the killers but settle for ambushing a passing wagon train or a
prospector's camp. Other warriors felt called upon to kill White
Eyes who wandered over the Sacred Mountain or profaned it with
their digging. And whenever the warriors killed some White Eye—
even if he needed killing—the soldiers would seek revenge of their
own. So the fighting gradually escalated.

Soon the White Eyes sent out a new nantan, who brought word
the soldiers wanted to make peace. The leaders wondered whether
this new nantan could be trusted, for they did not yet know how
to judge White Eyes. Among the People, everything depended
on the character of a man. But who could know how it stood with
the White Eyes? The nantans said they could not make decisions
themselves and were bound by the promises written down on
paper—which seemed almost like witchcraft.

The chiefs had a talk with the nantan, who said the Great
Father in Washington wanted them to live in peace in their own
land and would give them gifts and food if they would not attack
the White Eyes anymore. Moreover, the Great Father would send
soldiers to protect them from the other White Eyes. Then the
nantan said they must also not go anymore into Mexico on raids.
This was too much, even for Mangas Coloradas. He knew the
People could not feed their children, gather the gifts necessary
for the ceremonies, or live any longer as warriors if they stopped
raiding on both sides of the border the White Eyes had made.
Besides, a great debt of blood still lay between the People and
the Mexicans.

So he said, *Are we to stand by with our arms folded while our
women and children are being murdered in cold blood as they were
the other day in Sonora? The Sonorans invited my people to a feast*

and manifested every show of kindness toward us. We were lulled into security by their hypocrisy. People drank and got drunk, and then the Sonorans beat out the brains of fifteen with clubs. Are we to be victims of such treachery and not be avenged? Are we not to have the privilege of protecting ourselves?[5]

The leaders and the warriors in council debated the agreement for a long while. They understood they could not long survive a war against the Mexicans and the White Eyes at the same time— for then they would have no refuge to which they could retreat when hard-pressed. They felt they must gamble on peace with either the White Eyes or the Mexicans—and most finally agreed they should test the promises of the White Eyes, for they already well understood the treachery of the Mexicans. Moreover, the White Eyes promised to provide rations if the bands remained camped in certain areas—which might lessen the need to continue raiding. So eventually, Victorio, Mangas Coloradas, Cuchillo Negro, and the other leading men made their mark on the paper and told their warriors to stop attacking the White Eyes, even when provoked. But they did not stop the warriors from raiding into Mexico, because they had not the authority, and because the White Eyes had no say in their war with the Mexicans. Besides, the Mexicans attacked camps of the People immediately after that treaty was made, so it was clear the White Eyes had no way to make the Mexicans stop the war.

Mangas Coloradas put all his powers behind maintaining the peace with the White Eyes. He urged the headmen to move their bands close to the agency and the soldier post. Soon, nearly one thousand people had gathered there, most of them from Mimbres bands. The White Eyes insisted they must remain in this small area, saying they would send the soldiers after the bands who wandered too far. Of course, with so many people gathered in one place they could not rely on hunting and so were forced to depend on the food the White Eyes gave them as payment for land that had once been theirs. But the promised supplies did not come often and many parties of warriors continued to raid down into Mexico so their children would not starve. Mangas Coloradas and the other headmen urged their People to plant crops, as the White Eyes advised. But the land the White Eyes left them was not good for growing the crops and the patches of corn were too small. The People got so hungry they ate the green corn, stalks and all, so they never had enough seed for the next season. The White Eyes sent a man to show them how to grow corn, but he didn't show them very much. Instead, he came in the night with barrels of whiskey from Mexico to sell to the warriors, who had little to do except drink the whiskey and remember when they could go where they pleased.⁶ Soon they began to fight one another, too drunk to contain their anger and frustration. The headmen went to the nantan to complain that the whiskey was making trouble, but nothing changed. Some people said the White Eyes intended to kill the People slowly with whiskey, disease, and starvation—keeping them trapped with promises, like an eagle in a cage of sticks.

Finally, the Great Father in Washington sent a new nantan they called Steck, who seemed a good man. Steck spoke directly, and saw the suffering of the People and the difficulties of the headmen who wanted peace. Steck called together the headmen to appeal to them to prevent war, in spite of all the troubles. He spoke in this manner to them:

The Great Father sent me to say that if you will continue to do well, he will help you. It is bad to be at war. The road to war is always red with blood—full of women and children weeping and starving—but the road to peace is easier to travel, and on it you will find safety for yourselves and plenty to eat for your wives and children. You know this is so. When you are at war you must hide in the mountains. When you are at peace, you come in and trade and talk with the People without fear of being molested. You must not

*steal or rob anymore or I will have nothing to do with you. If I hear
that anyone does steal, they must be punished. The Captains must
look to this. The People, when one of his men is killed, don't ask
for the man who killed him but instead kill the first American they
meet. The Great Father wants to be at peace. But it is not because
he is afraid for he has more soldiers than you can count, they are
like the grass on the prairie or the leaves on the trees. Take my advice
and stick to your world, you have promised to be good men and don't
forget your promise.*[7]

The headmen nodded, and grunted the "Hou" of assent, seeing
that the nantan had a good heart. They decided to make greater
efforts to restrain the warriors, to see if Steck could keep his
promises. Perhaps Steck had the confidence of the Great Father,
who had sent him to them upon hearing of their troubles and
upon learning that the men he had put over them could not be
trusted. Steck traveled to all of the bands, going fearlessly among
them. He seemed to feel for them and did not hold back supplies.
Steck came even to the headwaters of the Animas River that
flowed into the Rio Grande where Victorio, Nana, and Lozen were
camped. He stayed with them to show them how the White Eyes
planted their crops.

Steck urged them to sign a new treaty, saying it would convince
the Great Father to help them and the army to protect them. But
Mangas Coloradas, who had grown wary of the paper promises of
the White Eyes, opposed the treaty. He said the only sure thing
in the treaty was that the People would give up most of their land
and that only a little bit of the land they would have left could
be farmed.[8] So Mangas Coloradas made excuses for not coming
when the other headmen made their mark on the paper.

Still, most of the chiefs did everything they could to keep the
peace, knowing they were trapped between the Mexicans and the
White Eyes. Delgadito suggested Steck set up a fort to protect
the bands from the settlers who sometimes attacked them. That

way, the soldiers would see that the Chihenne and the Mimbres were not the ones who were doing the raiding. Delgadito even warned Steck when one group of Mimbres raiders left to take horses from the settlements of the White Eyes. The soldiers overtook the raiders and killed three warriors, which caused some warriors to speak against Delgadito and he lost influence with many of them. However, he said that all of the People would suffer and many women would mourn their husbands and children their fathers if they did not keep peace with the White Eyes.

Even so, a short time later soldiers attacked Delgadito's camp. Delgadito had gathered together his people to greet a party of about sixty soldiers, but to his astonishment the soldiers started shooting, killing one woman and one child and wounding four others. Everyone ran away at first, but then Delgadito and his subchief approached the soldiers and pleaded with them to stop. The soldiers said it was a mistake, but few of the warriors believed them.[9]

After that, some of the warriors retaliated. They found a white man hunting alone and killed him. This killing caused a great deal of trouble because the man was the agent for the Navajo and an important man. Some warriors raided near some of the settlements, taking horses and livestock to which they felt they were entitled because the soldiers had killed peaceful women and children and had never done anything to make up for the killings they claimed had been a mistake.

Finally, the soldiers gathered together an army from several forts and went out all around the reservation, killing peaceful bands whenever they found them. Mostly, they killed those who had left the reservation—although warriors had to leave the reservation to hunt so their children would survive. Sometimes the soldiers came right onto the reservation.[10] They attacked Cuchillo Negro's band and even killed a chief who argued strongly for peace. Some of the chiefs tried to stop the war, but after the soldiers fired at one party coming to them with a flag of truce, most of the bands fled the reservation. The great disaster Mangas Coloradas and Victorio and the other leaders had tried hard to avert seemed to have come upon them anyway.

Victorio took his band down into Mexico, where they had long maintained a peace with the city of Janos. The Chihenne often camped near Janos and went into the city where they could sell the cattle, horses, and goods they captured on their raids against other Mexican bands. But then the Janos Mexicans seized a group of People visiting that town and sent word they would hold their prisoners until Mangas Coloradas returned some stolen livestock. The Mexicans put poison in the food and in the whiskey so many People sickened and died.

Seeing he could not live safely in Mexico nor fight a war with the Mexicans and the Americans at the same time, Mangas Coloradas sent back word to Steck saying he wanted to return to the reservation and live in peace. So most of the bands returned to the reservation, living quietly near the agency with little to eat and few weapons. Even here, the Mexicans came with a band of men and attacked a peaceful camp, killing many women and children—chasing down those who fled and hacking them to death with machetes. The soldiers came out from the fort and stopped the Mexicans after all the fighting was done, but then let them go. Everyone could see the promises of the White Eyes were useless. Even so, the chiefs pleaded with the warriors to keep the peace. What else could they do? In a single year, they had lost one out of every five of their fighting men to violence and disease. In every wickiup, the women were keening, their hair cut short in mourning.

Victorio, Nana, and Lozen could only try to keep their band out of the way of the fighting. They learned to live as warily as the antelope, which takes a single bite and then watches for enemies as he chews. They relied on Lozen's Power. Often she stood, chanting the song her Power had taught her on the Sacred Mountain and turning in a circle as the warriors watched, drawn tight like a bowstring. Whenever her palms grew warm, they packed up the camp and moved out of the path of danger. Victorio chafed at the restraint he had imposed on himself and on his warriors in his effort to convince the White Eyes he wanted peace. He was a true warrior, full of pride and strength. It galled him to move always to the side. Worse yet, more miners returned to the diggings the Mexicans had abandoned long ago and began to root in the earth after the sacred metal.

Still, Victorio held back his warriors, using his Power to restrain them rather than to rouse their courage for battle. He set his mind on simply holding onto the Sacred Mountain and the hot springs where the People had begun and the deep canyons graced with cold streams and tall trees. He knew that all of those places, with all of the stories of their naming, guided and soothed and protected the People. Those places imparted wisdom, Power, and vision, helping the People hold on to the old ways so they would remember who they were. He could not see how they could survive as a People with prayers and grace and courage if they lost those places that knew them.

So Victorio prevented any attacks on the miners or the stagecoaches that passed regularly through his territory. He did not even protest when the soldiers established a post near Ojo Caliente. Nor would he let his warriors attack the settlers who came and took some of the best places the Great Father in Washington had promised to the Chihenne. Victorio did not want to give the White Eyes an excuse to take the rest of their land away from them. Victorio had already heard rumors Steck wanted to remove them all to a reservation further from the settlements and the miners. He heard that Steck had even gone to the Dragoons and to Apache Pass to meet with Cochise and give him presents to convince him to move as well.[11]

But it was no use. It was impossible to keep peace with the White Eyes, who had no honor and seemed not to recognize their own promises, even when put down on paper. No matter how hard they tried, Victorio and Mangas Coloradas could not prevent trouble. One day a band of miners from the Pinos Altos gold mines in the heart of the Chihenne territory got together and attacked a peaceful camp of women and children who had killed and eaten a mule. It didn't matter that the Chihenne had permission from the mule's owner. The miners killed four people and took fifteen women and children prisoner. Then they went to the Mimbres Valley, led by a man named Tevis—the very man who had given them permission to kill the mule in the first place.[12] The White Eyes found the band of Elias, a Chihenne headman, who thought Tevis was his friend. The miners ran right into Elias's camp, killing anyone they could. When Elias cursed them in the English he had learned from his "friend" Tevis, they killed him too. He could only curse in English because the People have no such words, for no one would ever think to use the holy name of Ussen as a curse. The miners killed four people in the attack and the survivors ran down into Mexico, sending word to the other bands that the White Eyes had started up the war again.

This time, Victorio heeded the warning. He and Lozen sent word they would go to war again. Nana also said he would fight, so the other warriors followed along. Victorio sent word to Mangas Coloradas, but that great chief refused to go to war—insisting they could not fight two wars at once. Moreover, Mangas Coloradas said he would try to convince miners at Pinos Altos to go somewhere else, which might save the peace.

Surely, he could reason with the White Eyes, said Mangas Coloradas. The world Ussen had made was great and stretched on beyond sight. Surely there was room enough for both the White Eyes and the People.

CHAPTER IV

▼▼▼

War

1861

Mangas Coloradas went among the White Eyes at Pinos Altos, making friends as best he could. He had grown old in the service of his People, but he still towered over other men and carried himself with dignity and Power. Moreover, he could still draw together more chiefs and warriors than any other leader. He believed the survival of the People depended entirely on solving the riddle of the White Eyes. So he went to the White Eyes he knew and said he could tell them about other places they could find the metal Ussen had forbidden to the People. He told first one, and then another, that he could take them to a new place where they could dig if they would leave Pinos Altos.

But one afternoon when he came back into Pinos Altos, a group of miners seized him. Although he could have killed any one of them alone, he was helpless against their numbers. They dragged him to a scaffold, so at first he thought they intended to hang him. In truth, it was worse. They tied him to the timbers and whipped him like a dog. He hung on the timbers, not making a sound, as the whip opened up his back. But the humiliation made a deeper mark than the whip, which could only cut his flesh and draw his blood. They whipped him until they grew tired then left him there and went away laughing. His sons came in the night, cut him down, and took him to a hiding place where he remained until his back healed—but the humiliation festered like a rancid wound.

Now he saw Victorio was right and it was better to die like a warrior than to live like a whipped dog on the scraps of the White Eyes. So Mangas Coloradas sent word to Cochise, who was his son-in-law, that he was going to war with the White Eyes. He learned the White Eyes had broken faith with Cochise as well. Cochise had for a long time been the most feared and respected of war leaders and many other bands thought his Chokonen were like wild men. Nonetheless, the Chokonen were the westernmost division of the Chiricahua and therefore brothers to the Chihenne. Grave and fearless, with an aura of great Power and authority, Cochise had such Power that he could almost command his warriors like a White Eye nantan. He relied on the force of his will rather than the eloquence of his speech and the subtlety of his plans, as did Mangas Coloradas. Cochise had fought the Mexicans a long time, but he had been friendly to the White Eyes, for he knew the Mexicans were helpless against him so long as his refuge in the Dragoons remained safe. Cochise let the White Eyes set up forts for their soldiers on the edge of his territory and even tolerated buildings in Apache Pass for the stagecoach that went through Chokonen territory. He even urged his warriors to bring wood to the stage station and visited the station himself, speaking in a friendly way with the men who stayed there.

But one day a rude young lieutenant barely out of baby grass brought soldiers to Apache Pass and asked to speak to Cochise under a flag of truce. Cochise went to the nantan's tent, bringing his wife, his son, his brother, and a few others. But the nantan called his guards and accused Cochise of kidnapping a boy from a nearby ranch. The nantan said he would hold Cochise and his family prisoner until Cochise returned the boy.

But Cochise knew nothing about the kidnapped boy, who was half-Mexican and half-Apache. In truth, the boy had been taken by a Coyotero band. No one knew it then—but the boy would one day be called Mickey Free and would make a great deal of additional trouble for the People and for Lozen. Cochise said he wanted no trouble with the soldiers and so would try to find out who had taken the boy and to obtain his return. But the nantan called Cochise a liar so Cochise turned suddenly, pulled out his knife, cut through the wall of the tent, and ran past the astonished guards. Many shot at him, but his Power protected him and he ran through the bullets and up the hill—still holding the cup from which he had been drinking in the tent. After Cochise had reunited with his People, he returned to the station with his warriors and seized as prisoners the men living there. They ambushed a wagon at the entrance of Apache Pass, killed the Mexicans in it, and took more prisoners. Cochise tried to exchange his prisoners for his family, but more soldiers came to get the nantan out of the trap he had made for himself. The soldiers hung Cochise's brother and the other warriors they had taken prisoner, but they released his wife and son, Naiche. So Cochise killed his prisoners as well and rode away, determined to make war on the White Eyes.[1]

▼

Now the Mimbres and Chihenne and Chiricahua and the other fighting people were united, regardless of the consequences. They attacked isolated ranches and laid so many ambushes the White Eyes soon stopped sending stages. Their combined forces laid siege to Pinos Altos, ambushing anyone who left the settlement. Once they even mounted an attack on the mines themselves, so the miners would realize that even their numbers could not protect them. After a time, the miners gave up and Pinos Altos was once again deserted. Even the soldiers grew fearful and weary. They could chase the fast-moving raiding parties, but they could not catch them unless the warriors turned at a place where they had all the advantage of terrain, numbers, and surprise.[2]

Soon, to the delight of Victorio and Lozen and all of the other leaders, the soldiers abandoned their forts and marched away. The settlers and the miners, seeing the soldiers leaving, also fled. They remained in only a few places like Tucson and Santa Fe. But most of the land returned to the control of the People so that everywhere the warriors held victory dances. They gathered openly as they had not dared to do in many years. The young men recounted their exploits in the boisterous ceremonials and the old men sent up prayers of gratitude to Ussen. The women cradled their babies and dreamed about the times to come when they might sleep peacefully in their beds, see their children grow up, and not wait for the inevitable death of their husbands.

Lozen, in that small space of victory, thought perhaps she might become like other women, now that the survival of the People did not depend on her gift of Enemies Against Ceremony. She had earned the respect of the warriors, who accepted her in their front ranks and respected both her Power and the way Victorio turned to her for counsel. Still, she was also a woman, who had been an aspect of White Painted Woman herself. The warriors might protect the People for a day, or for a battle, or through a long, dark time—but only the women could ensure their survival. Only the women could cast the People ahead into the days to come. Only the daughters of White Painted Woman could make life and bring it forth and cherish it and nurture it. Perhaps when Lozen had done her duty to her People and used the gift of Power, she might bring forth life and be like other women.

But that was not to be, for Ussen had not finished with her. She must walk the path on which her feet were set to its stony and barren end, even as she had once walked in the footprints of pollen and dreamed of a long life filled with beauty.

Soon enough, the White Eyes returned.

▼

They came first from the east, into the land of the Mescalero who had always been friends and allies to the Chihenne. They wore different clothing than the soldiers who had come before. This time they did not offer to talk, but killed every one they encountered. Some of the headmen put a white flag on a stick and went up to the soldiers, but the soldiers shot them down. Some said the White Eyes were fighting a war among themselves. Leaders like Mangas Coloradas wondered whether the Chihenne and the Mescalero could make friends with one side by fighting against the other, but it was very confusing and hard to know which way to turn.[3]

But it did not truly matter.

First the soldiers who came from the east killed the People wherever they could find them. Then came more soldiers from the west, blue coats like the ones the warriors had fought before, coming first into the land of the Chiricahua. Cochise sent out scouts to watch them as he laid his plans, determined not to let the White Eyes take back what he had won at such cost. Cochise sent word to his father-in-law, Mangas Coloradas, who promised his help and who in turn called on Victorio, Nana, and the other headmen of the Chihenne and Mimbres. The Chihenne came with one hundred warriors, including Victorio, Lozen, Nana, and the others. Cochise brought perhaps one hundred warriors of his own, including the already feared and respected Juh of the Nednhi, and also a rising Bedonkohe war shaman named Geronimo. Lozen took careful note of Juh, a stocky, powerfully built warrior with a gift for strategy, a fierce Power over men, and a stutter. He was built like a bear, with a hard, flat face like a slab of granite.

He was among the most warlike of the leaders, living with his Nednhi in the untouchable heart of the rugged Sierra Madre deep in Mexico. The Nednhi were feared and respected by all the other bands and their ranks included warriors who had been cast out of other bands. Geronimo was very much like Juh, an eager warrior with great Power and a bitter hatred of the Mexicans, who, in a treacherous attack, had killed his wife, mother, and children. Geronimo had Enemies Against Power so bullets could not touch him and so he knew about things before they had a chance to happen. He was stocky and strong, but not so heavyset as Juh. Geronimo was not eloquent in council, but he was so cunning, wary, and single-minded in his purpose that he could win others over with the force of his mind and the persistence of his will.

Cochise had arranged everything with care. He knew the soldiers coming from the west would leave Tucson and follow the abandoned stagecoach route. They would come to the last spring in the Dragoon Mountains and then hurry the forty miles across the waterless Sulfur Springs Valley to Apache Pass, where the spring provided the only water they could reach for a day's ride. First Cochise would send warriors to determine the strength of the soldiers. Then he would prepare fortifications in Apache Pass so they could trap the soldiers when they tried to reach the spring.

At first, it seemed Cochise's plan would work perfectly. One band of warriors went into the soldier camp in a friendly way, counting men and horses. They came away safely, after killing several soldiers who walked too far from camp. Cochise then set the warriors to building rock walls on the side of the canyon leading to the spring at a place where narrowing of the canyon would force the soldiers under the guns and bows of the warriors on the hillside. The soldiers came on just as Cochise had hoped, sending ahead a small force and thereby giving the waiting warriors the advantage of surprise, terrain, and numbers. However, several eager warriors spoiled the surprise by making a try for the pack train coming along behind the main body of soldiers. When the soldiers rushed for the spring, the hidden warriors rose up from behind their stone fortifications and drove the soldiers away from the water, killing several. The warriors settled down to wait, knowing that Ussen's sun was their ally and thirst would drive the soldiers forward.

But the soldiers had a surprise for the warriors. They brought up two long metal tubes on wheels. As Lozen watched the soldiers roll them into place, she remembered that terrible day when she was a little girl and the scalp hunters had thrown the cover off the guns on wheels that had killed so many of her People. Sure enough, the soldiers began firing the wagons, the giant bullets landing on the slope and exploding with a great thunderclap that scattered bits of metal and rock in all directions.

One of the sentinels shouted a warning that some of the soldiers had fled back the way they had come, to bring more soldiers.[4] Mangas Coloradas took several warriors and rode to cut off those soldiers, but the White Eyes were too far ahead and got out of the pass ahead of the warriors—except for one soldier whose horse Mangas Coloradas brought down with a good shot. The warriors jeered, seeing that the other soldiers kept on running, leaving their friend to his fate. Then the warriors closed in on the soldier, who took cover behind the body of his horse and began shooting so rapidly it seemed he must be three men. Mangas Coloradas nonetheless tried to move in on the soldier, who shot him in the chest. Dismayed, the other warriors got their wounded chief safely away, leaving the brave soldier alone.

After this, the Chihenne lost interest in the battle, knowing they could do nothing against the wagon guns. The warriors briefly tried to stop the soldiers from reaching the spring, but heavy fire drove them off the hillside. The Chihenne then took Mangas Coloradas to Janos, where they knew a doctor of great skill. They argued among themselves, some saying it would be better to trust

Lozen or someone else with Power in healing wounds. But others said they should also use the healing Power of the White Eyes, as this was a White Eye bullet. Some said the White Eyes' doctor couldn't be trusted—even the Janos doctor—and that he might poison Mangas Coloradas instead of healing him. So they went into Janos and told the doctor that if Mangas Coloradas died, they would destroy the town and everyone in it. The doctor, of course, took good care of Mangas Coloradas, who did not die from his wounds as many expected. Perhaps it was not because of the doctor, though, but because of the songs that Lozen sang over Mangas Coloradas.[5]

But some said Mangas Coloradas never returned fully to himself after the wound. It took him a long while to recover his strength. And even after he was recovered, he said it was no use to fight the White Eyes and the People must make peace or be destroyed.

Of course, after the fight at Apache Pass even Cochise, Victorio, and other leaders who had favored fighting agreed it was no use to attack large bodies of soldiers. Sometimes, the warriors had won great victories against the Mexicans in such circumstances. But the White Eyes had too many soldiers, too well armed—especially if they brought along the wagon guns. After the warriors withdrew, the soldiers went through the pass and continued east. Some said they were still fighting each other as they passed through to Santa Fe. In any case, they came back later and built a fort on the high ground in Apache Pass overlooking the spring.[6]

The war continued, but the People now had little hope they could once again drive out the White Eyes who had returned in greater numbers than ever and seemed determined to kill everyone they could catch. They killed Delgadito, Cuchillo Negro, and other leaders, as well as many warriors, women, and children. Cochise and his Chiricahua remained mostly in the Sierra Madre in Mexico or in the Dragoon Mountains in Arizona, where they could see their enemies coming from forty miles off and thus avoid any fight they could not win. Juh and his Nednhi retreated into the Sierra Madre, plundering the Mexicans and sometimes coming north across the border. Victorio and Nana moved back and forth between the mountains near Ojo Caliente and mountain ranges in Mexico, relying heavily on Lozen's Power to keep them out of the way of their enemies. Geronimo and the Bedonkohe shifted back and forth, remaining sometimes with Cochise and sometimes with Juh, for the Bedonkohe now had so few warriors they could not survive alone.

Mangas Coloradas saw that the People had become as leaves on the cottonwood in the season of Earth is Reddish Brown. They could not long endure. He heard the White Eyes had sent out a group to talk peace near Ojo Caliente and resolved to see if he could stop the war. He met with the council of chiefs, seeking their advice. Victorio, Nana, Geronimo, and others all urged him to stay with them and not place his life in the hands of White Eyes.[7] But Mangas Coloradas was adamant. Some said he had a vision and must fulfill it. Some said he was an old man who had not the strength to lead the warriors and so now wanted to throw away his life. But Mangas Coloradas said he had to take the risk for the People, who were dying in all their secret places—hunted by the soldiers, and by hunger.

Mangas Coloradas took his family and his closest followers to Santa Rita. He left his family camped nearby and went alone to meet with the White Eyes. But the White Eyes proved true to their treacherous nature. They seized Mangas Coloradas and delivered him into the hands of the soldiers. The nantan told the men guarding him that he wanted Mangas Coloradas dead, and then he left the great chief with the guards. That night, the guards heated their bayonets in the fire and put the hot metal against the feet of Mangas Coloradas. He accepted the torture in silence until at last he rose up and said to them, *I am not a child that you can play with me*—so they shot him. They threw his body into a ditch. The next morning they cut off his head, boiled it in a pot, and sent it to the Great Father in Washington.[8]

The soldiers then went to the camp of Mangas Coloradas's family who waited for news of the peace talks. They killed a dozen people and used their scalps as ornaments for the bridles of their horses. They found another group nearby, who did not yet know of the killings. So the White Eyes gave them food and, while they were eating, opened fire—killing nine.

Lozen, Victorio, and their band were cast into mourning and despair when they heard the news of the murder and mutilation of Mangas Coloradas. Many among them cut their hair short in respect for the chief whose name they could speak no longer. Many people said you had to live in the Happy Place forever in the same condition in which you were killed, so it was a terrible thing the soldiers had done to the great chief.

Victorio and Nana now moved their bands constantly, staying in the mountains and going back and forth to Mexico—ever hungry for the revenge Ussen had commanded as their duty to their chief. Many warriors after that time mutilated the bodies of the White Eyes they killed, so the White Eyes would be deformed in the next life as well. Many people felt what had been done to Mangas Coloradas as though it were done to one of their own family and thereafter took their revenge on any White Eye they could—even killing the prisoners in the painful way Mangas Coloradas had been killed. Sometimes when they caught a White Eye, they tied his feet to a tree branch and hung him upside down over a fire so his death would be slow and terrible. But usually they simply killed all the men, any women who were difficult or weak, and children too old to be trained. They usually mutilated the bodies only after death.[9]

But mostly Victorio, Nana, and Lozen labored to keep their People out of the way of the White Eyes. They hid in the mountains near Ojo Caliente, especially the San Mateo Mountains. When the soldiers pursued them there, they could move quickly from one side of the mountain to another along trails too steep for the soldiers' horses. If the soldiers pressed too closely, or if Lozen's ceremony warned them their enemies were coming from several directions at once, they would move south into Mexico, slipping past their pursuers. They killed anyone who saw them, to smother word of their passing. But mostly they tried to survive, stealing what cattle and horses they could and remaining unseen whenever possible.

Then Victorio heard rumors Agent Steck had come back, so hope fluttered in him.[10] But he also heard rumors that the hated Carleton had already broken the Navajo and the Mescalero.[11] They said Kit Carson, who had been considered a friend by the Navajo, led the soldiers against them—even into the canyons they had long defended against any enemy. Kit Carson also led soldiers against the Mescalero, who were the brothers to the Chihenne. Because the Mescalero lived further north they could not retreat so easily into Mexico and so they did not last long against the soldiers. Carleton told Carson to kill any warrior, even under a flag of peace. Sometimes Carson did this, but sometimes his heart was softened toward the Mescalero because some of them had been his friends. Also, Carson knew the Mescalero had no heart for fighting, but only stole a few horses and cattle to prevent the starvation of their women and children. Many of the soldiers followed the orders to kill anyone they found, but some bands found they could surrender to Carson if they approached him carefully. So Carson sent Chief Cadete, a Mescalero leader, and some of the other leading men to Santa Fe where they appealed to Carleton to stop the war.

Cadete spoke to Carleton in his manner: *You are stronger than we. We have fought you as long as we had rifles and powder; but your weapons are better than ours. Give us weapons and turn us*

*loose, and we will fight you again. But we are worn out. We have
no more heart. We have no provisions, no means to live. Your troops
are everywhere; our springs and water holes are either occupied or
overlooked by your young men. You have driven us from our last and
best stronghold, and we have no more heart. Do with us as may seem
good to you, but do not forget we are men and braves.*[12]

But Carleton would not let the Mescalero remain in their own
land. Instead, he sent them to Bosque Redondo, a place that could
support a few bands but not the hundreds of tattered and hungry
women and children of the Mescalero.

Then Carleton set Carson and the soldiers on the Navajo, who
were rich and numerous and who often fought the People, although Mangas Coloradas had allies among the Navajo. Carson
took a strong force of soldiers all through their land, destroying
their crops and herds and making hunger his strong ally. Soon,
the Navajo had no choice but to surrender. So Carleton put the
thousands of Navajo at Bosque Redondo as well. There, the Navajo and the Mescalero alike sickened and died—cold and hungry
and hunted by disease. The Navajo and the Mescalero fought
among themselves, like camp dogs on a trash heap.

▼

Lozen heard about all of these things through the fugitives and
raiders who came to their camp and enjoyed the hospitality of the
People. The Chihenne remained in hiding, doing only what they
must to feed their people. Although they knew the soldiers would
turn on them when they had finished with the Navajo and the
Mescalero, they felt relatively safe in the mountains that knew
them so well. They even maintained their contacts and friendly
relations with people living at Pinos Altos and Mesilla. They knew
traders there who would give them bullets and guns and other
things in return for the horses and cattle they obtained in Mexico.
Lozen and Victorio and the other leaders talked often about what

they should do and agreed they should accept any peace that allowed them to live near the Sacred Mountain, but that they must never let themselves be herded like sheep onto the killing ground of Bosque Redondo.

Sometimes, Lozen went into Mesilla and Pinos Altos to gather news. She reported that the people seemed friendly, so Victorio, Chief Rinon, and Salvidor, a son of Mangas Coloradas, took fifty-nine warriors to meet with Steck and ask for a treaty. They promised to prevent all attacks on the White Eyes if the agent would give them land of their own. They would be guided by his advice in everything, considering him like their father. It galled Victorio to speak in this way to a White Eye, but he thought Steck was an honorable man who would stand behind his promises. Steck promised to do everything possible to make a treaty and give them a reservation, but his promise was never fulfilled.[13]

A little while later, Carleton sent a nantan to Pinos Altos to meet with Victorio and Nana and say they must go to Bosque Redondo.[14] Victorio refused, saying, *My people and I want peace. We are tired of war. We are poor and we have little for ourselves and our families to eat or wear. It is very cold. We want to make peace, a lasting peace.* But he was also resolved not to die as Mangas Coloradas had died because he trusted the promise of the White Eyes, nor would he lead his People to their deaths in a place the White Eyes had designed only for the purpose of killing them.

So the Chihenne continued hiding in the mountains, sending out small parties when they needed supplies. Once, Lozen went with a band of warriors who crept close to Fort Craig. Lozen, whose Apache name meant "dexterous horse thief," was respected for the Horse Power that enabled her to go right in among her enemies and bring away their horses. So she took a leading role when the small group of warriors hid near the fort to watch how the soldiers handled their horse herd. The warriors hid for a long time, watching for the weak place in their routine, like the fraying of a string of rawhide. The warriors had only bows, so they did not dare risk an open fight with the soldiers. Then when the soldiers' horse guards were not paying close attention, Lozen and the warriors slipped in among the horses and ran them off—stealing the whole herd so that the angry soldiers had to follow them on foot.[15]

They escaped without any loss and were honored with a joyful victory dance when they returned to the camp. The People gathered around in a circle as the singers called out the names of the warriors who had distinguished themselves—Lozen foremost among them. Each warrior danced out into the firelight and the women made the cry of applause, like the cry White Painted Woman had made after Child of Water killed the giant. Each warrior acted out his actions in the battle, swelling with pride to have taken away the soldiers' horse herd and protected their People. Lozen went out when her name was called, but she did not dance long. The applause embarrassed her and made her uneasy. She worried always that the warriors would resent her or the People would say it was unseemly for a woman to act the part of a man. So she did not push herself forward, nor speak in the council unless Victorio or Nana asked directly for her opinion, nor make herself large in speaking and in the retelling of her deeds. Only the gifts of Ussen made her successful in raiding and stealing horses and anticipating the presence of her enemies, so she feared what her Power might do and what people might think if she took the credit that belonged to her Power. Besides, her role was to support and serve Victorio, in whose hands the fate of the People had been placed. She did not wish to do anything to undercut his leadership, so she offered her counsel to him privately and gave him credit in all things before the warriors.[16]

So the Chihenne remained free even as other peoples yielded to the overwhelming power of the White Eyes. Soon, Victorio heard Steck was no longer an agent and so was glad he had not put trust in the word of even that White Eye.[17] Still, the headmen knew they must hold themselves ready to make peace when they could. Loco, who had a following of twenty warriors, maintained his contacts with White Eyes he knew, telling them the Chihenne would come in if the soldiers would give them a reservation. The Chihenne had learned that even the Mescalero could not bear to stay at Bosque Redondo and so had fled to hide in the mountains. Even many of the Navajo had gone home, hoping the soldiers would not come after them.

Then finally, there came another agent—this time a soldier called Drew—who sent word he would make peace.[18] So hope and fear came for them, two hunters after the same prey.

CHAPTER V

▼▼

A Fragile Peace

1869

The new agent came to speak with Loco, who had so grown in influence among the Chihenne that his standing rivaled Victorio's. The two chiefs argued long in council about what they should do. Loco spoke with eloquence and Power, saying the warriors could not long resist the White Eyes. If they continued to fight for their own land, the White Eyes would wear them down, as wolves wear out even the strongest elk with long chasing. Loco said they should make an agreement with the White Eyes while they still had enough warriors to force a good bargain. Every year, there were fewer warriors and more White Eyes. They all knew it was true. They had all seen the soldiers coming out of their forts like ants and knew how quickly new settlers and miners filled the places of the ones they killed, replenished from an inexhaustible storehouse. So Loco had fear and truth on his side of the argument. But in each conference, Victorio and Nana pointed out something else they all knew: White Eyes could not be trusted. They all remembered Mangas Coloradas, though they did not speak his name. The soldiers had killed so many peaceful people;

their promises offered nothing more than a pause in the battle, a blind behind which they prepared the next ambush. Victorio said the People could neither know the will of Ussen nor understand the thinking of the White Eyes. They could only fight as men and die as warriors, rather than letting the soldiers boil their heads in a pot. Most of the younger warriors supported Victorio, because they longed to prove their courage and had not so much to lose. But most of the older men who held sway in council sided with Loco, for they knew any victory against the White Eyes was temporary. So the talk went back and forth in the camps and in the councils of the headmen.

Loco went first to the new agent, who seemed a good man, and came back saying he thought they might trust this man. He convinced Victorio, Lozen, Nana, and the others to meet with the agent near Canada Alamosa, a town where many people were friendly to the Chihenne—especially the many traders who exchanged supplies for livestock the Chihenne took in their raids.[1] Victorio brought with him a force of forty warriors posted on every high place during the conference to warn of any treachery.

Agent Drew spoke for peace between the Chihenne and the White Eyes, saying he knew the Chihenne often got the blame for things done by others. The leaders all liked the agent's talk, but they noted he had no gifts to show his goodwill. He said the White Eyes wanted peace but he could not make an agreement until after he talked to the other nantans and to the Great Father. So Victorio and Lozen and the others went away, feeling a little better, but still doubtful.

Agent Drew set up his headquarters near Canada Alamosa and many bands camped nearby. Victorio and Lozen stayed in the mountains where they could not be surprised, but Victorio told his warriors to not raid among the White Eyes to see if Agent Drew could give them the peace he promised. Soon, perhaps three hundred people were camping near Canada Alamosa, doing no harm. They were heartened when Agent Drew defended them against unjust complaints and against parties of Mexicans that sometimes tried to attack their camps. Unlike other agents, Drew was himself a soldier nantan, so the soldiers followed his orders. Of course, you could never tell with White Eyes. The White Eyes often fought among themselves, like headmen jealous of each other's influence. The agents often argued with the soldiers, each accusing the other of stealing supplies. They also heard rumors Agent Drew was fighting with some of the Canada Alamosa traders—even Thomas Jeffords, who was a friend of Cochise.[2]

But just as they began to trust Agent Drew, he died in a perplexing way. Drew led fifteen soldiers after some Mescalero who stole some horses, but he got lost in the mountains. The soldiers separated to find water. Some made it back and a search party finally found Drew, but he'd had no water for four days and died before they could get him home.

Lozen wondered at the news. How could a nantan simply get lost and die of thirst? And how could a people so helpless nonetheless crush the People? None of these things made sense. But she could only acknowledge the strangeness of the world. She had listened long enough to the stories intended to explain these things—how Child of Water had made the People and how Killer of Enemies had made the White Eyes and the Mexicans in the times when the animals were like tribes of people. The Supernaturals had put out gifts and the People had chosen the bow, which Child of Water had used to slay the giant. But the White Eyes and the Mexicans chose the gun. Then Killer of Enemies stole cattle from the Crows and gave those to the White Eyes as well. Everything had worked out like a Coyote story, full of loss and irony. Now the People could be defeated by soldiers so weak that even their nantans might get lost and die of thirst in a place where a boy could live alone indefinitely with only a knife.

Things grew even more confused after the death of Agent

Drew. The leaders prevented their warriors from raiding among the White Eyes, but the Mexican traders at Canada Alamosa warned the Chihenne that the new agent would end all trade and make the People live only on the agent's paltry rations. The traders also talked against the agent's translator. Victorio was wary, thinking perhaps the traders only wanted to protect their sale of whiskey—which was the cause of a great deal of trouble. Both Lozen and Victorio urged their followers to drink mostly the sweet, mild tizwin fermented from corn and served on ceremonial and social occasions instead of the strong liquor of the White Eyes that caused so many fights. Lozen said the same thing, seeing that the whiskey also endangered the women and children. Living free, a wife could easily put her husband's things out of the wickiup and send him back to his parents' band if he struck her. But now they had to remain in camps near the agency where the whiskey sellers plagued them, so violence inside the families increased.

Gradually the problems escalated—with the People divided between the traders and the new agent, Agent Hennisee. The Mexicans who ran Canada Alamosa came into open conflict with the agent and the soldiers who supported him. First soldiers tried to seize many barrels of whiskey from the homes of some of the leading Mexicans. But then a large band of armed Mexicans chased the soldiers out of town. Then the Mexicans arrested the agent. The Chihenne watched these events in wonder and consternation, not sure which side to favor. They did not trust the traders, but they trusted the army far less.[3]

So when Agent Hennisee called together Victorio and other leaders of the six hundred people camping near Canada Alamosa in the Season of Large Fruit,[4] they came warily. Hennisee said he would not give them any more rations until they returned the horses and other property stolen from the translator and the settlers. Victorio and the others promised to look for any stolen horses, but they feared they would be drawn into the fight between the agent and the Mexicans. Agent Hennisee also said he would meet with all of the bands to set up an official, permanent reservation. Some twenty-two chiefs with about eight hundred followers were camped now near Ojo Caliente and Canada Alamosa, including Cochise and his Chokonen.

In the meeting with Hennisee, the leaders spoke with dignity and pride. Cochise rose up with such Power that everyone within hearing could feel it. He said he had been at war for ten years and although his warriors had killed many whites, he had not enough men left to provide for the women and children. He said he desired peace and would talk straight and wanted the government to talk straight with him. If the government would feed his People and give them clothing, in a few months all the Indians of his tribe would be at peace. He had come to see what Canada Alamosa was like, so he could decide whether to bring his People to that place. Victorio agreed, saying that if the White Eyes let them live peacefully at Canada Alamosa, within one moon twelve hundred people would come.[5]

The agent talked pleasantly, but he promised only to go back to the Great Father in Washington and explain everything. He said the government would set up a reservation, but the chiefs and the warriors must be patient and do no harm to anyone while they waited word.

So the warriors went back to their camps, both doubtful and hopeful. Soon more than one thousand people were camped around the agency. The chiefs did their best to prevent raiding, although war parties continued to slip away into Mexico. But the rations the White Eyes issued left everyone hungry all the time, and with so many people gathered in one place they could not rely on hunting. Many hungry people took the green corn out of the fields of farms nearby.

And so they waited. Victorio kept all his warriors in readiness, half expecting soldiers to come suddenly to kill them. He noticed the White Eyes had begun to build a settlement at Tularosa, which was a high, cold place bad for crops and people. Meanwhile, Nana took a portion of the band to live on the Mescalero Reservation to determine whether it would be a good place for the Chihenne. Nana, Victorio, and Lozen had long ago learned the lesson of the warpath—to prepare layers of plans and alternative esapes. So Nana went to the Mescalero Reservation to make sure the Chihenne had a place to run if the White Eyes sent their soldiers against them at Canada Alamosa.

Lozen prayed each day, rising before the sun to thank it for returning. The People had need of her healing ceremonies, as hunger and disease stalked them like winter wolves. She did not drink the whiskey the traders always brought into the camps, but she could not influence many warriors to follow her example. She sought the advice and guidance of her Power, but she felt frustrated and frightened for her People.

Then two things happened.

Some Chiricahua visitors brought news the White Eyes had massacred a band of women and children camped peacefully near Camp Grant. The White Eyes, along with some Pima Indians, clubbed to death and mutilated 150 women and children in Eskiminsin's Arivipia band when most of the warriors were away hunting. The soldiers afterward said they were sorry this thing had happened, but they did nothing to hold the White Eyes responsible.[6]

And then the White Eyes sent the Chihenne a new agent in the Season of the Ghost Dance.[7] So Lozen and the other Chihenne waited once again to learn their fate. Would the White Eyes let them live in their own land? Or would the People be left to choose only the manner of their death?

Chapter VI

The Mirage of Peace

1870

At first, the arrival of the new nantans changed nothing.

Agent Orlanda Piper spoke soothing words, but he said the government had not decided what to do about a reservation. Many thought the White Eyes had decided to move them to the Mescalero Reservation, far from the slopes of the Sacred Mountain and the rejuvenating water of the hot springs. Victorio and Lozen talked with the agent who tried to reassure them, but they did not lean on the thin reed of his promises. They had been held in place by such promises for two years now and wondered whether this was just another trick to hold them together for killing. So Victorio held his warriors in readiness, waiting for an attack. Again and again, the agent came to demand the return of horses and cattle the Chihenne had not taken, so Lozen suspected the White Eyes sought an excuse to attack.[1]

Lozen tried to hold herself from fear and despair, remembering that patience was a warrior's weapon. But it was so hard to predict or understand the White Eyes, like a dream full of meaning all jumbled upon waking. If you put your trust in one man of good character, they soon took that man away. Sometimes it seemed the soldiers were protecting the People against the thievery and hatred of other whites. But sometimes it seemed the agents were protecting them from the soldiers. Sometimes the Mexican traders seemed their best friends and sometimes it seemed the agents wanted to protect them from the traders. So Victorio moved his band into the mountains where they could not be surprised.

Finally, another agent came directly from the Great Father in Washington—a man named Vincent Colyer who had the power to establish a reservation. Victorio stayed away but Loco took Colyer to Ojo Caliente, where the Chihenne longed to live peacefully. But Colyer said there was too little farmland and too many settlers at Ojo Caliente. This made little sense, for the settlers came without permission and the land at Tularosa was not good for farming because winter came so early there. Clearly, the agent just wanted to give the best land to the settlers and move the Chihenne away from the traders at Canada Alamosa.[2]

After Colyer went back to the Great Father, Agent Piper told the headmen they must move to Tularosa. Even Cochise came to the conference. But the leaders all refused: Tularosa was too far, too cold, and not their country. They said the agent could give their rations to the wolves, but they would not live at Tularosa. The White Eyes sent out another nantan who tried to convince the headmen to go to Washington to talk with the Great Father, but they suspected a trap.[3] Cochise said he would not go, but the agent could take a picture of him to Washington. Then the nantan went away, leaving everything unsettled. After that, many Mexicans living at Canada Alamosa warned the Chihenne that the soldiers would kill them all if they went to Tularosa. But Victorio consulted his Power and prayed a long while. Finally, he agreed to go to Tularosa and came back resigned to the necessity of moving there. Perhaps the agent was right and they could never live peacefully so long as they clung to land that the White Eyes wanted. So they would take this risk and test the promise of the agent.

So the People began moving slowly and sorrowfully to Tularosa—including three hundred in the bands of Loco and Victorio plus several hundred Mescalero. Tom Jeffords, who was a friend of Cochise, and Nathaniel Streeter, a White Eye who had lived among the People and had even fought alongside them, went along, so Victorio felt a little more secure from treachery.

They reached Tularosa full of discontent and fear. The nights were cold, the water was bad, the crops were scanty, and many people fell sick. The old stories said the First People had lived here, but they been drowned in a flood because of their foolishness and conflict. The medicine men said no good would come of living in such a place, but Victorio and Lozen held the People there, playing for time. Perhaps the new agent would eventually relent and let them return to the Sacred Mountain and the hot springs and the places they loved. Lozen prayed for that each day, for in Tularosa she did not know the stories of each place and so they could not smooth her spirit and teach her wisdom, as a potter shapes a clay bowl.

Then the Great Father sent General Otis Howard to settle everything. General Howard was a strange man who had lost one arm in the war among the White Eyes and now talked in a great voice and sometimes fell to his knees to pray. This frightened some people, who thought he was witching them. Others said he was praying to the Creator for guidance. This seemed hopeful, as a wise warrior must always seek the Creator's guidance. This lack of reverence, humility, or spiritual sense was one of the most disconcerting things about the White Eyes—but this man seemed different. Moreover, General Howard talked straight and listened carefully—saying he wanted the headmen to explain to him clearly why they did not like Tularosa.

He called everyone together for a council at Tularosa, including Victorio, Loco, Nana, the other headmen, and also the agents.[4] Howard said, *I want the Indians to tell me all of their wants and needs and I will put it down on paper and tell it to the President in Washington.*

I will speak the truth, let the fault be where it may, replied Victorio. *We are dressed very badly and have no shoes, and I hope that those that are well dressed will look out for those that are not. We do not feel contented here, and want to go to Canada Alamosa where the sun shines upon us and we feel well and where the council is our own. I have always talked well and always done well and I have done what was told me to do, but I want to go to Canada Alamosa which is my country. God is pleased because we are here today and are telling the truth. The wind, sun, and sky are smiling upon us. The People are my children and if you will take us back to Canada Alamosa we shall have many children born to us and they will not die as they do here. There are but few of the People here, but if you will take us back to Canada Alamosa we shall have many with us, and we shall increase. While we were at Canada Alamosa, our women were with us and we slept with them and they gave birth to many children, and all were contented. I do not want to do all the talking. I want General Howard to talk too.*

Howard replied, *I want first to hear all your complaints of this reservation so that I can lay them before the President in Washington.*

The People are all leaving here, said Victorio. *The sun and moon and all the world here is getting old and they cannot get mescal, pumpkins, grapes, and all kinds of fruits which they can get at Canada Alamosa.*

Loco then spoke in agreement. *Everything Victorio has said is right, and what I would say, but I want to talk a little because I have now met a man I like to talk with. We have always lived in the Mimbres Mountains, were born there, and brought up there and we made peace there and our food stays better upon our stomachs there. We want to go back to Canada Alamosa, which is our home.*

Victorio then spoke again. *Every word you say we drink in, for we think you have had a good father and a good mother and have been well brought up.*

We have the same Father in heaven over all of us, said General Howard.

Then Gordo, who was also a chief, said, *They have taken me first from my own country to Canada Alamosa and now they have taken me away from there, and I will stay and not leave these people. All want to go back, even children.*

We mean no disrespect, added Victorio carefully, *but that Piper—the agent—is getting old and he had better go home and see his children, and take care of them.*

Said General Howard, *You have said you were promised the Canada Alamosa by an agent of the government. Will you tell me who promised that reservation to you?*

We were promised by Lieutenant Drew, Victorio replied, *that we should always live at Canada Alamosa.*

Gordo then explained why they did not want to stay at Tularosa, seeing that General Howard perhaps understood about spirit things. Gordo said, *There used to be a lake here where the marsh is now and the horses died and thousands of the People were about here, but they did not dare go near the lake and the mules and horses used to groan and the whole place was bewitched and now we cannot stay here. We could then go down as far as the mesa and live if we prayed, but if we went beyond we died. The whole place was bewitched and we cannot stay here.*

But General Howard replied, *The water has been examined by the doctor and is good. I drink it every day.*

The water makes all the People sick, insisted Victorio. *Whether it does other people or not, we want to leave it.*

General Howard replied that some Americans had started living at Canada Alamosa and so he must convince the government to buy the land back before the People could return. But he promised to go back to the Great Father to get the necessary money and they should remain at Tularosa until they heard from him.

We don't want to remain here at all, protested Victorio. *How many thousands of dollars will it take to buy Canada Alamosa?*

I cannot tell you, said Howard.

We would like to nominate their agent, added Victorio.

But General Howard replied, *We cannot change the agent, who will give you all the good things that are proper for you to have. Victorio knows the difference between good men and bad men.*

Even among animals there are some good and some bad; there are not always some good ones, there are some bad, agreed Victorio.

After that, Victorio and Loco went with General Howard to Canada Alamosa to show him it was a better place. He agreed and promised to tell the Great Father to put the reservation there, for it would cost the government more to haul their supplies all the way to Tularosa than it would to buy the land at Canada Alamosa. They wondered at this, surprised they had found a White Eye man who would listen, but still they were afraid to let their hopes rise like Hawk on the wind.[5] When Howard asked how he could find Cochise to convince the Chiricahua to live at Canada Alamosa also, Victorio arranged for General Howard to go see Cochise with two warriors who were relatives of Cochise.

After Howard left to find Cochise, Victorio, Nana, Lozen, and the other leaders settled down to wait for him to fulfill his promise. They tried to keep the warriors quiet so the whites would have no excuse to break the promise, but bands not living on the reservation made difficulties. After each incident, Nana, Loco, and Victorio reassured the soldiers the Chihenne were keeping their promise.[6]

Still they waited. One moon passed into another and new nantans arrived, so the chiefs could not rely on anything they had been told. Lozen could not understand why the White Eyes were always coming and going. How did they expect their warriors to follow them? It was like going on a raiding party with strangers instead of relatives.

So Victorio and Lozen struggled to calm the warriors, who reared like horses in a thunderstorm. Victorio's following grew as warriors brought their families to his camp. In the winter, seven hundred people lived at Tularosa, but in the summer half of those people went to Mexico and other places. Victorio's Power had drawn a large following, for the White Eyes feared him. Victorio used all of his influence to prevent trouble with the Americans, but he did not prevent the warriors from raiding in Mexico. He knew they needed this chance to feel like men and the People needed the supplies.

Once, an excitable agent named Levi Edwin Dudley came straight to Victorio and complained that one hundred warriors had left the reservation to raid.[7] Victorio said the warriors were just trying to find food and asked again when they could go to Canada Alamosa. Dudley said they must wait for Cochise and insisted Victorio stop the raiding party. So Victorio rode off to turn back the raid, turning Dudley's words over like a bone from a medicine bag. Perhaps the White Eyes had already decided to throw away Howard's promise.

In the Season of Ghost Dance the soldiers shot a woman at Fort Tularosa.[8] She had been hanging around at the fort, joking with some warriors, when one of the nantans interfered, talking to the warriors in an insulting way. The warriors pointed their guns at him to brush him away and he complained to the chief nantan, who was drunk. When the officer came back, the soldiers started shooting. But the only person they hit was the woman they were supposedly trying to protect, and she died after the White Eye doctor cut off her arm.

Victorio and Loco kept their warriors from retaliating, but the anger mounted up like summer thunderheads. Sometimes a warrior would shoot an arrow toward a White Eye, just to see him jump. One band—including Victorio's nephew—stole some horses and clashed with the soldiers who chased them. Victorio refused the agent's demand that he help hunt down the band, but the soldiers caught them without any help. The soliders held thirty people as hostages—including Victorio's nephew—so Victorio decided to keep the peace a while longer.

Agent Dudley said they must move to Fort Stanton and live on the Mescalero Reservation, but Victorio refused. They knew the White Eyes did not make decisions easily, as skittish as deer in their thinking. So Lozen said the People must be like hunters on a game trail, relying on patience and stillness.⁹ So they must silently resist until the White Eyes changed their minds, waiting through the bad agents and the weak promises until the White Eyes grew tired of the argument. The nantans were accustomed to giving orders, not the long talk of the council where the talking continued until everyone agreed.

Just as Lozen predicted, Agent Dudley began to talk about a reservation at Canada Alamosa for the Chihenne, the Mescalero, and even Cochise's Chokonen.¹⁰ Lozen and the other leading Chihenne did not know what to make of this. They heard Cochise was gravely ill—perhaps witched—and no one knew what would happen among the Chiricahua if Cochise died. They worried that war leaders like Juh and Geronimo might make a lot of trouble if they came to live at Ojo Caliente without Cochise to restrain them.

Cochise died in the Season of Many Leaves,¹¹ and the People mourned the passing of so great a man in this hour of great need. Even the Chihenne felt his passing, remembering when Cochise and Mangas Coloradas had led a free people. Cochise had been like the great heart of the agave plant, which joined all the bristling leaves. Who would hold the People together now? Many of the Chiricahua followed the leadership of his son, Taza—a brave warrior with great Power. His brother, Naiche, was tall and beautiful and brave, but he had no Power and little ambition. Both promised their father they would keep the peace, for Cochise understood that no one could hope to fight the White Eyes anymore. But Taza had not the influence of his father. Strong, angry leaders like Juh, Geronimo, Skinya, and his brother Poinsenay broke away, living apart and raiding in Mexico.

▼

Then, unaccountably, Agent Dudley said the Chihenne could move back to Ojo Caliente.[12] No one could make sense of it. They did not know whether to celebrate or to prepare to flee. Some said Ussen had changed the hearts of the White Eyes. Some said it was a trap. Some said the Chiricahua and the Mescalero would all be moved there as well, so it would end up being worse than Tularosa. Nonetheless, Lozen, Victorio, Nana, and Loco traveled the seventy miles to Canada Alamosa with perhaps 400 people, including 175 men of fighting age. The soldiers rode along to protect them from any attack by other White Eyes along the way.

Lozen let hope blossom—a small flower, close to the ground. Perhaps they had worn down the White Eyes, as you might train a horse with the persistence of your will. Perhaps they might live now at peace in their own land, having passed the test set for them by Ussen.

So they lived quietly around Ojo Caliente under a new agent, a man named Shaw, who continued to steal their rations and sell them. Traders and merchants gathered around the reservation like vultures, with wattled heads of naked greed.[13] The traders moved among the scattered camps of the People, mostly selling whiskey. Sometimes Lozen wondered whether the real plan of the White Eyes was to kill them with whiskey and disease. Still, Victorio,

Nana, and Loco held the Chihenne in place, glad at least to be living in their own country. Even when no rations came for weeks, the headmen urged the warriors to remain with their families and not raid.

They spent a full round of seasons living this way, happy to be in their own land, struggling to restrain the pride of the warriors, and wondering when the soldiers would come. Victorio had a wife and five children, so he knew what a return to fighting would cost him. Washington,[14] his son, was a respected warrior who supported his wife and children and also three children who had been orphaned. Nana had a wife, seven children, and another orphaned boy. Many families now lived that way. In the good times before the White Eyes, most warriors had only one wife. But now many men married the wives of their dead brothers or took in the children of dead relatives. For instance, Loco had three wives, three children, and twelve other people living in his household who had no warrior to provide for them.[15]

Still, the rations dwindled and the troubles mounted. Often, the settlers blamed the Chihenne for raiding done by Mexicans, bandits, and other Indians. Weeks went by without any rations and the headmen debated whether they should defy the agent and send out raiding and hunting parties. Lookouts warned of the approach of a large number of the black, curly-haired buffalo soldiers coming from Santa Fe. Victorio had never relaxed his vigilance, for the White Eyes were unpredictable and might turn on the People at any time—especially now that the settlers were blaming the Chihenne for things they hadn't done. So Victorio gathered together all of his warriors and gave even the women and children the old muzzle-loading rifles so the soldiers would see the Chihenne were prepared to fight. Victorio met with the buffalo soldiers' nantan—a White Eye—and explained the Chihenne had received no rations in four months. He said they had given up most of their land and done no harm, but they would not sit in their camps and watch their children starve. They must go to war with either the United States or Mexico and he would rather make war on the United States because the Americans were rich and the Mexicans were poor. If the Americans would not abide by their promises, the Chihenne would make peace with Mexico and begin raiding in the United States. Victorio said he could not retain any influence if he continued to try to restrain the warriors when their children were crying.[16] After that, rations began again, this time coming from the army instead of the agent—for the agent had been stealing their rations. Often, the agents and the army were like warring bands and the division between them made everything much more difficult and confusing for the People.

But trouble continued to gather, like wolves at the edge of an elk herd. Much of the trouble started on the Chiricahua Reservation, where the leaders had turned one against the other after the death of Cochise. Taza and Naiche tried to keep the peace, but Poinsenay, Juh, Geronimo, and others made trouble. They killed some whiskey sellers and then fought with Taza who set out with his warriors to punish them.

Eventually, White Eyes made the Chiricahua move to San Carlos and gave their land to the settlers and miners. Taza, bound by his promise to his father, moved many of his people peacefully—although San Carlos was hot, barren, and diseased. Some said Ussen had left San Carlos just like he found it so everyone would appreciate how well he had fixed up every other place. But many Chiricahua slipped away, including Geronimo and Juh.[17] They went down into Mexico to the Sierra Madre with Juh's Nednhi band. Some settled on the Chihenne reservation while others raided on both sides of the border. Soon, the soldiers began blaming the Chihenne for the raids.

In the Season of Large Fruit, soldiers and their Navajo scouts attacked Lozen's camp.[18] The camp guards gave a warning so

everyone escaped, but the soldiers destroyed the village and supplies. When Victorio protested, the agent said the soldiers had
been following the trail of some raiders and had attacked Victorio's
camp by mistake. So Victorio moved his village to the mountains,
but trouble hunted them there as well. Settlers attacked the village, running off the horse herd. Again, the agent explained it was
a mistake, although he never returned the stolen horses.

Lozen saw they were trapped now, like a deer surrounded by
wolves. Even if their own warriors remained in camp, they could
not escape the blame for what others did. Nor could they turn
aside their Chiricahua relatives seeking sanctuary. Besides, she
knew the White Eyes would throw aside their promises like an
empty sack when it suited them, as they had done to Cochise's
people.

In the end, Geronimo gave the White Eyes the pretext they
needed. In the season of Little Eagles, Geronimo came to Ojo
Caliente with one hundred horses and stories of raiding on both
sides of the border.[19] Lozen listened to his stories, both admiring
his strength and Power and fearing the trouble he could draw
down on the Chihenne. She understood how easy it was to fight,
especially if your Power urged it. Holding back was harder, for it
wounded the pride.[20] Of course, as a woman these things came
more easily to her than to the warriors called out to dance in the
circle of firelight. She better understood that the true value of a
warrior lay in protecting the little ones and the weak ones. She
understood the strength of cattails that lie down before the wind
and spring back up afterward. So she loved Victorio for the way
he held himself back from his prideful yearning and she feared
Geronimo for the way he hurried forward into danger. But she
did not speak openly against Geronimo, for every warrior must
choose his own course and Geronimo was Bedonkohe and so not
responsible to the Chihenne. Besides, she had long ago decided
not to push herself forward in council. So she spoke little and

listened much, standing ready to support her brother into whose hands the People had been given by the same Power that spoke to her all those years ago on the Sacred Mountain.

But, of course, she was right. Geronimo did bring the lightning.

Agent John Clum, whom people called Turkey Gobbler because of the way he puffed himself up, came with one hundred scouts from the San Carlos Reservation—mostly White Mountain warriors who had never been close to the Chihenne or to the Chiricahua. Clum hid most of the warriors in the buildings at the agency and then asked Geronimo and Naiche to come in for a talk. When they did, he took them prisoner, chaining them in a horse corral.[21]

Turkey Gobbler next sent for Victorio, Nana, Loco, and the other leading men of the Mimbres. They listened carefully, balancing his qualities in their minds like a throwing knife. He said they must leave Ojo Caliente and come to live at San Carlos; the settlers, soldiers, and everyone else at Ojo Caliente had turned against them so it was no longer safe for them there. It did not matter that Geronimo and the other Chiricahua had caused the problems; to the White Eyes all Indians were the same. They must move or the soldiers would hunt them down. But if they came to live at San Carlos under his care, they would have charge of their own affairs on the reservation: Their own warriors would keep order and their own headmen would decide things. He would make sure they got their rations and help them plant their crops and raise cattle, so they would make money and support themselves like White Eyes.

The leaders protested that their People had done nothing to cause the government to retract General Howard's promise of a reservation in their own country, but they could see it was no use and Turkey Gobbler could only follow his orders. No one wanted to move to San Carlos, so far from the sacred springs and the Sacred Mountain and the songs of the Gan Mountain Spirits. San

Carlos had a bad reputation and was perhaps only another way to kill them with disease and longing.

Some said they should run away, as many Chiricahua had done when the White Eyes closed their reservation. Lozen knew this was what Victorio longed to do, but leadership had tethered him like a hawk tied to the ground. Soldiers had gathered all around the reservation, eager to kill them. If they broke for Mexico now, many would die before they could reach the Sierra Madre. Moreover, they could never win this war. Even Cochise and Mangas Coloradas had made their peace and in the years since then the White Eyes had swarmed like winged ants after the summer rain while the People had dwindled like puddles on the playa.

Some said Turkey Gobbler was a good man, although he was young and loved the sound of his own voice. Many White Mountain warriors said he was truthful and fair and treated them with respect. He often quarreled with the soldiers, insisting they stay off the reservation. Nor did he steal their rations as other agents had done. The Chihenne considered this information carefully. Most White Eyes had no heart and no honor and more regard for their cattle than for the People. The life of an Indian woman or child meant nothing to them and you could not rely on their words for the length of time it takes a feather to fall to the ground. Only a few were true men—like General Howard and Jeffords. So perhaps Agent Clum was such a man, although he was young and did not understand how little he knew.

The talk in the council went back and forth a long while, the way the wind moves a sand dune one grain at a time. Finally, they came to a decision. They would go with Turkey Gobbler, but first they would hide all of their good weapons in caves. They would see how things stood at San Carlos. Perhaps Agent Clum would be a man who could keep his promises. But if San Carlos proved a trap, they would return for their weapons and cached supplies. If they fled now, too many would die. If they picked their moment, they had a better chance of reaching Mexico. Most of the leaders agreed with this plan, but others slipped away during the night. No one said anything about this, or tried to stop them. Each family must make its own choice.

More than four hundred people went with Turkey Gobbler and his scouts to San Carlos.[22] They traveled slowly, encumbered by wagons in which Geronimo and the other prisoners were chained, riding in proud silence. Everyone wondered whether the White Eyes would hang him when they reached San Carlos and Lozen and Victorio debated as they rode along whether they could risk staying there if Clum hanged Geronimo. Along the way, four babies were born. The births were hurried but joyful and they paused for the songs that would help ensure a long life in even so dark a time. But along the way eight people died of the spotted disease. Their bodies were hidden away and their few pitiful possessions burned as their relatives cried out, keening as they cut short their hair. Lozen prayed and grieved and rejoiced and wondered at the numbers: four babies born, a sacred number; and eight people dead, so even in the journey they lost two for every life gained—a bad omen.

So she prayed. Not for intervention, for Ussen did not meddle in the small doings of human beings. She prayed rather for strength and Power to help the People through this long dark time. Now they must walk unflinching between the bears and the snakes and the monsters down into the darkness, armed only with their courage, listening only to the distant singing of the Mountain Spirits—faint as a sigh.

CHAPTER VII

▼▼

San Carlos—
Escaping the Trap

1876

Lozen prayed for strength and San Carlos demanded it.

The People had to camp near Camp Goodwin, a fort the soldiers had abandoned on the banks of the fetid, brackish, marshy Gila River. Malaria had run the soldiers off and the People began dying just as the soldiers had. Camp Goodwin was one of the worst places on the reservation, plagued by insects, disease, and lamentation. Many empty cradle boards, with their burdens of heartbreak, were left hanging in the stunted trees and thorned thickets around the camp.

Moreover, the Chihenne were surrounded by enemies. Bandits stole their horses. The warriors, with nothing to do but listen to the crying of their children, got drunk and fought—setting in motion more blood feuds. They even had to guard against bands not living on the reservation, including Poinsenay's Chiricahua. Some of the raiders with relatives among the Chihenne also would come into camp boasting, filling the frustrated Chihenne warriors with stories about raids in Mexico.

Turkey Gobbler seemed like a good man—although vain. He

quarreled constantly with the soldiers, insisting he could manage without any help from them. Some said Clum had caused the trouble by trying to get all the bands together at San Carlos so he could draw a bigger salary[1] and that he had poisoned Taza, the son of Cochise, when they had gone on a journey to see the Great Father in Washington. But others said Taza had gotten sick and pointed out that Turkey Gobbler had earned the respect of many White Mountain bands. Turkey Gobbler did not interfere with the leadership in the bands, used warriors to police the reservation, and let the leaders decide who should be punished when they made trouble. Lozen thought Turkey Gobbler could be trusted, although he was proud and quarrelsome.[2]

But in the end, Turkey Gobbler got tired of fighting with the nantans for control of the reservation and quit—although some said he was mad because the government wouldn't give him more money. Lozen had long ago learned that no White Eye could hold on to the handle of his promise, but losing Turkey Gobbler was like a blow in the stomach, for now they could not count on any of his promises.

So the Chihenne gathered in council once more. Disease had taken a heavy toll in the summer they had spent at San Carlos. Moreover, they now fought constantly with the White Mountain and Coyotero bands living nearby; quarrels, killings, and thefts swung back and forth between them. To make matters worse, the new agent cut the rations so hunger rode alongside disease. Moreover, Poinsenay's band was camped on the reservation, urging the Chihenne to break out and join them.

Lozen said little, sitting near Victorio, one of the few women who attended council. The warriors knew they would need her Power to flee through the layered ranks of their enemies. They talked a long while. Nana and Victorio spoke strongly for leaving. Nana was like the coals that have smoldered to a red glow, waiting only for a handful of dry grass. Finally, even Loco agreed they must return to Ojo Caliente to convince the White Eyes to give them back their own land. They had tried to live at San Carlos, but it was impossible. They would show the soldiers it was better to let them return to their own country than to fight a war that would cost the lives of hundreds of White Eyes. It had worked before, when they resisted going to Bosque Redondo or to the Mescalero Reservation. Perhaps it would work again.

▼

They made their preparations in secret, and late in the Season of Large Fruit[3] they took the horses they needed from the Coyotero bands camped nearby and fled the reservation with more than three hundred people. The Chihenne joined forces with some Chiricahua bands, including Poinsenay's.

Some Chihenne warriors killed a White Mountain chief as they fled to settle a score. Lozen worried the White Mountain warriors would therefore chase them as a result, but you could hardly stop a warrior from fulfilling his obligation to his relatives. They split into groups to confuse the trail with Lozen, Victorio, Loco, and Nana moving north and Poinsenay heading east. The soldiers and scouts caught up with the Chihenne at Ash Creek, capturing some horses, supplies, and thirty women and children. A few days later, soldiers led by Coyotero scouts caught up to them again. But the warriors took up good defensive positions and fought until dark, losing one warrior and eleven women and children. The rest slipped away in the darkness.

They relied heavily on Lozen's ceremony to avoid fleeing headlong into a trap. They knew the soldiers and the White Mountain scouts were clinging to their trail and that other soldiers would come out of every fort, like wasps from a broken hive. Small parties of warriors moved ahead and to the side, scooping up horses and cattle, watching for the dust that warned of approaching soldiers and killing anyone they encountered who might warn the soldiers. Normally, the warriors did not make war on women and children, and they often adopted children into the band. But when seeking revenge for the murder of their own families, they demanded payment in kind. The fury of their revenge had kept the People safe among a host of enemies for generations. Besides, when running ahead of the soldiers, their survival relied on remaining hidden. Anyone who glimpsed them or even saw their tracks would run quickly to the soldiers. So they could not afford to leave witnesses. Of course, some warriors had grown so crazy with revenge they even enjoyed killing women and children—but most knew it was a terrible necessity, one that haunted their dreams.

Victorio was everywhere as they swung around and moved south, usually with Lozen alongside. Sometimes she traveled with the women and children, to keep their courage up. Often at night when they camped, she joined the women in gathering food and repairing moccasins, so no one would criticize her for neglecting a woman's duties. Nana supported the spirit of his followers as well, tough as a gnarled branch of ironwood, using his Power to find ammunition. They fought several battles as they fled, standing their ground only long enough to give the women and children time to escape.[4] Lozen's Power kept them out of the way of large bodies of soldiers, so they usually had the advantage of numbers. Each day, they agreed upon a meeting place in case they had to scatter in the face of an attack. Sometimes, they had to leave behind old people and young children who could not keep up— as most of the People were on foot. The old ones would hide near a water hole, knowing Victorio would send someone back for them if he could.

After they reached the mountains near Ojo Caliente they knew so well, they slipped away from their pursuers. Victorio resolved to go again to the soldiers to plead for the return of Ojo Caliente. He knew he could win every battle and still lose the war—for he could not replace his warriors, while the soldiers welled up from the earth as though from a spring. So he sent word and arranged for a meeting with a nantan he almost trusted from Fort Wingate. They met at a place where Victorio could easily escape and spoke together in Spanish. The nantan spoke gravely, advising Victorio to return quickly to San Carlos.[5]

But we are in our own land, replied Victorio. *This is the place that was promised to me and mine so long as the mountains stand and the rivers are here. Look out the door. Are not both still there?*

The nantan replied, *They are, Victorio. Your claim is just, but I am a soldier and I must obey orders just as your warriors do when you issue commands. I understand why you are called the conqueror, and I admire and respect you. But I am just a soldier. Orders are that every Apache man, woman, or child found off the reservation is to be shot without being given a chance to surrender.*

But we are on our reservation, said Victorio.

It has been taken from you, said the nantan regretfully.

You are a good enemy, said Victorio. *It is good to know one honorable White Eye. You have been fair with me. I will be fair with you. I will not go to San Carlos. I will not take my People there. We prefer to die in our own land under the tall, cool pines. We will leave our bones with those of our People. It is better to die fighting than to starve—I have spoken.*

I have heard, said the captain. *There is one thing more I will tell you, even though it may cost me my commission. There is a reservation across the Rio Grande.*

I know, said Victorio, thinking of the Mescalero Reservation and of the close ties between the Mescalero and the Chihenne.

If you can get permission to take your band there, said the officer carefully, *you may have safety and security there.*

Victorio took those words back to the other leaders. Loco said in the end they must go back to San Carlos and had already lost too many people in useless fighting. The White Eyes would not relent, any more than a Gila monster could stop biting. But Victorio had decided he would not return to San Carlos, no matter what the cost. Still, he could not order anyone to follow him; he could only go his own way and let others choose for themselves. The other leaders were of different minds. So they sat in a circle to talk, Lozen taking her place beside Nana—the only woman so welcomed.[6]

All know the situation, said Nana. *Victorio has refused to return to San Carlos as ordered by the soldiers. We went once to that place on the Gila where our people died like flies. Our chief prefers death in battle to bondage and starvation. But I leave the decision to you, brothers, for no warrior is forced to fight. We are a free people. You all know that refusal to return to San Carlos means fighting—fighting to the death. If we refuse, there is an alternative. The cavalry has orders to shoot any Apache—man, woman, or child—seen off the reservation. We no longer have a reservation. But if our brothers, the Mescalero, will admit us, we may have refuge with them. Does anyone know of another possibility?*

No one spoke for a long time. Then spoke Sanchez, a respected warrior who had been a captive in Mexico and so had learned Spanish and all the customs of the Mexicans. *There is always Mexico. Sonora is a much better place than Chihuahua. Juh, chief of the Nednhi, is my friend. His stronghold is in the Blue Mountains that divide the two states. He has many hideouts in that lofty range. Many of you have visited Juh and know that I speak the truth. You know that he controls the divide and that without his consent nobody crosses the Sierra Madre. Juh's favorite retreat is an immense flat-topped mountain upon which there is a forest, streams, grass, and abundance of game. To the top there is one trail and only one. It is a zigzag path, leading to the crest. Along it huge stones are poised so that even a boy could send them crashing down upon the trail. Mexican troops tried it once. There are still bits of metal and bones at the foot.*

Nana replied, *My brother speaks wisely. That refuge is always open to us. I have been there and Juh has said it to me. It is for our immediate need that we consider Mescalero—not for a permanent home, but for a temporary retreat. There are many of our People in hiding in the Black Range. They are without mounts, ammunition, or blankets. If we go at once to Mexico we must leave them. Should we do that?*

Sanchez yielded to Nana's argument without loss of face: *There will be enough time when we have looked after their needs.*

Nana then spoke again, drawing together a consensus like the string at the mouth of a pouch. *There is a possibility that those at Mescalero may not admit us. In order to go to their reservation we must consult the headmen: Natzili, the head Mescalero chief, named for the buffalo; Magoosh, the Lipan chief from across the Pecos and San Juan, if he is still living. If they consent to our coming, there is still the agent. I doubt that he will refuse, for the more Apache he has enrolled on the reservation, the greater the opportunity of robbing them of the supplies furnished by the government in Washington. From that place comes only evil, and we have had enough of that. Still, we must make the attempt. If you agree, whom shall we send to negotiate with the ones in control?*

He asked each in turn, and each spoke Nana's name.

Lozen said, *It is fitting you intercede for us.*

Then it is decided, said Nana. *I may fail you. I can but do my best.*

So the bands split up. Some remained with Lozen and Victorio who hid in the mountains and continued to raid cautiously with about thirty-five warriors, going sometimes into Mexico to get ammunition and weapons. They hid caches of supplies for future use. Victorio hoped the soldiers might give them back Ojo Caliente or let them live peacefully with the Mescalero, but he would not put his life in the hands of the White Eyes nor sleep without sentries. As always, he sought peace and prepared for war. Others went with Nana to camp near the Mescalero, including Kaytennae who was a fearless warrior and the best shot in the band. Nana went openly to the Mescalero agent and enrolled sixty-three Chihenne there so they could draw rations. But most of the warriors remained in hiding, so they could come and go as necessary without being counted by the agent.

So they waited on the incomprehensible deliberations of the White Eyes. Each time Victorio sent emissaries, the nantans said they must return to San Carlos—and each time Victorio refused. Each agent and each nantan said they must follow their orders. So the People lived on rumors, like the suggestion that the government wanted to make them go to a place called "Indian Territory" where tribes from all over had been sent. This made Lozen remember Grey Ghost, and she wondered if his people had ever found a home—perhaps in that Indian Territory. But the memory of Grey Ghost seemed now like something that had happened before the First World drowned because of the foolishness of human beings.[7]

Victorio's band drifted closer to Ojo Caliente, taking care not to raid the White Eyes for the soldiers no longer hunted them. Lozen rejoiced to have returned home, saying the names of all of the places like a chant, riding from one to the other as though performing a ceremony. She sat again in the places where she had found wisdom, happy for the first time in a long while. Victorio sent Lozen to talk with the agent who remained at Ojo Caliente.[8] The agent seemed friendly and said they should camp nearby and he would give them food and blankets and clothing. He even suggested they might send for relatives at San Carlos. Hearing this, more bands gathered near the Sacred Mountain and the sacred spring where the world began, until 250 people lived nearby. The agent said they must turn in their guns and horses and await the decision of the government, so Victorio and the other leaders hid their guns and their horses and waited. The leaders consulted their Powers for guidance and exerted all their influence to keep the young warriors from provoking the White Eyes. They looked for signs, pondered their dreams, sent forth spies, and gathered rumors—but the White Eyes remained a mystery.[9]

Some of the leaders asked the Ojo Caliente agent to send them to Washington, DC to talk with the Great Father, but he sent for orders and never received word. So the Chihenne resolved to convince the White Eyes by their behavior to let them remain in their own land.[10] They planted crops, sought to make friends with the nantans, and did not raid. Victorio even told the agent they would live happily on half-rations if the Great Father would give them tools so they could plant crops at Ojo Caliente. The agent promised he would relay Victorio's offer. He seemed kind and encouraging, but no word ever came back from the Great Father.

▼

But after they had remained in that place doing no harm for nearly two years, Victorio heard word soldiers were coming to take them back to San Carlos.[11] Some said the government was angry because raiding parties had gone into Mexico. Of course, the headmen could not control every party of warriors. Nor could the People survive on the agent's stringy beef and moldy flour. But most said the White Eyes simply wanted to destroy the People with disease, idleness, starvation, and whiskey at San Carlos. Most of the warriors fled to the mountains before the soldiers arrived, so they could not be captured and caged. But they remained nearby in well-hidden positions, waiting to see what the soldiers intended.

Victorio and Lozen had gone off the reservation on a four-day pass to talk to Nana on the Mescalero Reservation. Nana reported that the Mescalero were friendly, but only a few young warriors would join the Chihenne if it came to a war. Nana said the Mescalero Reservation was not a bad place to live, although the agent was selling most of the rations. Every week wagons loaded with supplies left the agency and went into the town. Once, Nana sent a war party to intercept the wagons and take back the supplies. After that, the agent did things more carefully, knowing he could not complain to the army that the Chihenne had stolen back their own supplies.[12] Despite the agent's behavior, Victorio and Lozen decided they could not yet risk an open war. Instead, they thought they might convince the soldiers to let them live with the Mescalero if they could not keep Ojo Caliente.

But when Victorio and Lozen returned, they found everything in an uproar as the soldiers and agent had demanded a council to approve a return to San Carlos. Loco and his band had agreed already to go. Victorio met with the nantan and said they would not return to San Carlos, where the water was bad, their children were sick, and their enemies gathered. He implored the soldiers to let them stay at Ojo Caliente, or take them anyplace besides San Carlos. But the nantan said he had no choices, only orders. So Victorio and Lozen returned to the council, which split along the old divisions. Then in the midst of the council, they heard a woman screaming—a Mescalero woman who rode up the canyon warning them soldiers were coming to kill them. Everyone scattered immediately.

Loco insisted the soldiers would not harm them and so he sent word his band would go quietly back to San Carlos. Some 169 people set out as prisoners soon after, struggling through the mud and the storms and the snow—reaching San Carlos in the Season of the Ghost Dance.[13]

Lozen and Victorio resolved to remain in hiding in hopes the White Eyes would relent. They led a raiding party into Mexico to gather supplies, leaving the women and children in the mountains near the Mescalero Reservation where Nana's band still waited. When the raiders returned from Mexico, Lozen and Victorio with perhaps twenty-two followers camped in the mountains near Ojo

Caliente, and Lozen went down once again to talk to the nantan. He said he would not attack them while he sought permission for them to remain there.[14]

So once again, Victorio, Lozen, and their People waited. The nantan seemed like a good man, but they had begun to fear that even a good man among the White Eyes could not accomplish anything. The White Eyes were all like horses, broken in spirit with a metal bit in their mouths. They had no spirit. No heart. But like a herd of buffalo, they were irresistible in their mindless urge to run all together.

So they had no great hope when the nantan returned, although he acted as though the news was good. Victorio listened carefully to the translator, who said the Chihenne must return to San Carlos.[15] Victorio felt a great surge of rage and frustration and jumped to his feet. He shouted he would die rather than return to that place and bolted from the conference. He quickly gathered the women and children and set off again.

▼

Lozen and Victorio raided as they ran. They killed four herders and fifteen mules near Silver City, stopping only long enough to cut the meat from the mules. They also killed two other herders to prevent the word of their passing from escaping. Victorio consulted Lozen's ceremony often, changing course when she warned of the enemy's approach. They knew soldiers might come on them from any direction, led by the scouts. The soldiers overtook them in the Mogollon Mountains, killing two warriors and capturing most of their horses.

As they moved through the mountains, Victorio sent a runner to the Mescalero Reservation to see if Nana would join him. But Nana sent word that a great mistake had been made—perhaps by the translator. Actually, the nantan at Ojo Caliente had said the Chihenne could live at the Mescalero Reservation.

So Lozen and Victorio and their warriors headed back to the Mescalero Reservation in the Season of Many Leaves[16] to meet with the agent there, a weak, fast-talking man with a beard jutting from his chin like an animal. Victorio spoke strongly to him, tired of all of the tricks and evasions of the White Eyes. Victorio said if the soldiers intended to send his People to San Carlos, he would fight, but he would keep the peace if they were allowed to settle on the Mescalero Reservation. Agent Russell said the government had decided they could remain with the Mescalero if they stopped fighting.

So Victorio camped near Nana and sent word to the scattered bands, which soon began to gather on the reservation. About 140 Chihenne gathered there in the next four weeks, all hoping the White Eyes had finally changed their minds. Nana said the agent was a weak man who stole their rations, but they could rely on a rancher named Paul Blazer for food and supplies. Blazer was a good man—for a White Eye—who operated a trading post and sold cattle to the army. Perhaps beause he made money selling the army supplies for the People, he was friendly and anxious for them to remain on the reservation. So Victorio moved his camp to the Tularosa River across from Blazer's mill and ranch.

But when Lozen and Victorio went to draw their rations, the White Eyes said they must first get a ration card. But when they went to the Mescalero agent, he made them wait outside his door like children. Eventually the agent sent word he had no authority to feed them without ration cards, and that perhaps in a month they could get cards. Victorio shook his head, mastering his anger, saying, *A month is a long time to be hungry.*

Lozen and Victorio concluded they had once again walked into a trap of promises and so again made preparations. They sought allies among the Mescalero chiefs, but they found few among them willing to fight. Victorio talked also to Blazer, hoping he might explain why the White Eyes' promises drifted like dandelion seeds.

The agent promised food and refused to give it, said Victorio. *It was not to be a gift, but a payment made by the government for taking our reservation and for preserving the peace.*

Yes, I know, agreed Blazer. *But the cavalry has orders to kill all found off the reservation. You'll be killed.*

We'll not be killed, we'll be free, said Victorio. *What is life if we are imprisoned like cattle in a corral? We have been a wild, free people, free to come and go as we wished. How can we be caged?*[17]

Blazer had no answer. He could only shake his head. But he let Victorio take a cow out of his herd to feed his family until the rations came. So Victorio swallowed his pride and took the cow, and wondered how long he could stomach being pushed down into the dust.

▼

A short time later, they heard rumors a warrant had been issued for Victorio's arrest. Sanchez, who had the clothes of a Mexican cowboy he had killed, sometimes went into little towns to see what he could learn. In this way, he heard some people say the sheriff was planning to take Victorio from the reservation and hang him. Blazer said he had heard those rumors also. Alarmed, Victorio went with Kaytennae, now one of his most reliable warriors, to confront the agent. Again, the agent kept them waiting. When finally admitted, Victorio asked again about his ration card.

Does your word mean nothing? Victorio asked.

I am your friend, said the agent through the translator, smooth as the scales of a snake.

Does a friend refuse food to a friend? Victorio demanded.

But the agent did not answer. Instead, he turned his back on Victorio and busied himself with some papers on his desk. Victorio looked at his back, thinking of the men he had killed for less offense. Then he gestured with his chin toward the agent.

Kaytennae stepped forward and seized the agent's long beard and began dragging him about the office. The agent yelped like a dog that has been stepped on and begged the translator to make Kaytennae stop. But the translator was laughing too hard to speak and even Victorio smiled to watch Kaytennae drag the scrawny agent about the little room by his repulsive beard. When Victorio returned to his camp, he made sure everything was in readiness for when the soldiers came to arrest him.

Soon, word came to him that a judge, a prosecutor, and several others were coming to the reservation to hang him. Perhaps they would cut his head off and boil it in a kettle, as they had done to Mangas Coloradas all those years ago.[18]

They met in council and Victorio and Lozen said they would not wait for the soldiers to surround their camp, but would leave the reservation and fight for as long as they could. Perhaps the White Eyes would once again relent—capricious as a dust devil. Or perhaps they must now fight on to the death. It did not matter. At least they would die as warriors—rather than as the cattle of the White Eyes sundered from the places that knew them and the prayers that purified them. They could live a long while in the mountains, moving back and forth from Mexico to the United States. Nana gravely agreed, as did the other headmen. Lozen listened to the gathering of assent, caught between grief and pride. She felt a great sense of relief as the decision made itself clear in the council, knowing they would be free again. But sorrow gathered as well, because she understood what the decision would cost, as she was both a woman and a warrior. The men could yearn for the glory and clarity and Power—but the women and the children would pay the bitter price. Women understood death better than men, because they tended life's flicker—like a coal nourished through a winter night.

But now she had no choice to make: The choice had made itself.

It had sought them out, like Power: Now they must give themselves into its hands, though it might break them like dry sticks.

CHAPTER VIII

▼▼

War

August 1879

Now Lozen and Victorio and Nana called upon their Powers, each perfectly suited to this moment. They left quietly and quickly with perhaps seventy-five warriors and twice that number of women and children.[1] They sent out small parties to gather up the guns they had hidden and scoop up any horses they could find as they ran back toward their beloved Sacred Mountain. Lozen's heart rose up to be at last free and she rejoiced to see her brother's spirit also catch the updraft of action.

Sometimes Lozen rode with the warriors, but often Victorio asked her to ride with the women and children who respected her Power and felt safer from an ambush when she was with them. Moreover, he knew Lozen gave the other women courage—setting an example for them as a chief sets an example for his warriors. So she rode with the women as they left the mountains, protected by a flung-out screen of warriors. They moved quickly to the Rio Grande, finding it swollen with rain. They were all moving down into Mexico, knowing the American soldiers would be following their trail—led by the scouts. They hoped the Americans would not follow them down into Mexico and they would be safe there for a time. They fled from rendezvous to rendezvous, traveling in groups to leave a harder trail and meeting up again every few days at predetermined points until they reached the Rio Grande.

They eyed the swirling, muddy water fearfully. Blanco, a medicine man, was one of the only warriors with them then—for most of the men were scouring the countryside for supplies or providing a rear guard to prevent the soldiers from overtaking their families. Blanco sang a prayer to the river, an undulating sound made by tapping his hand over his mouth as he expressed his respect and gratitude. Then he threw some bits of turquoise into the water, which swallowed them, angry and dangerous.

Still, nobody moved.[2]

Then Blanco rode along the line, urging first one and then another to ride into the torrent. He was a medicine man with great Power, but they did not obey.

He chided them, saying, *When there is no danger, you forget Ussen, but when you fear for your lives you pray to him. You pay little heed when I tell you how to live; but when you face death you remember your feelings. Songs and prayers avail little those who have not lived according to the will of Ussen. You are in much greater danger from the cavalry on our trail than from the river. Is there no brave woman who will take the lead?*

The wife of Nana spurred her horse forward, but the horse turned aside and would not enter the river.

Then a commotion passed along the long line of fearful people, and they parted to let a single rider through. Lozen rode a powerful black horse, holding her rifle above her head. There was a glitter in her eye as her right foot lifted and struck the shoulder of her horse. He reared, then plunged into the torrent. She turned his head upstream and he began swimming.

The others followed her into the swift water, holding onto their horses, drawn safely across by her Power. Lozen waited on the far bank, urging them on. Seeing one horse washed downstream with its rider, Lozen plunged again into the river, her horse swimming strongly until she overtook the frightened woman. Lozen turned the woman's panic-stricken horse toward the bank and they safely reached the far shore. They rode back upstream to where the others were coming out of the water, wringing out their blankets and gathering their family groups together once more.

When they had all come safely across the river, Lozen performed her ceremony again—seeking traps in their path. She sensed danger on the route south—perhaps soldiers patrolling the border seeking to prevent them from escaping into Mexico. So she decided the women and children should change direction and seek refuge in the mountains where the soldiers were not yet seeking them. So Lozen rode to Nana's wife, saying, *You take charge of the women and children now. I must return to the warriors. Head for the Sacred Mountain in the San Andres and permit only short stops until you reach it. Camp near the spring and wait there until Nana comes. We can spare no men, but the young boys will obey your orders. Nana has told them you are in charge. Get the People mounted and start. I go to join my brother.*

So she rode until she found Victorio and the warriors, haunting the backtrail of the women and children to fend off the soldiers coming on from behind. They greeted one another in the joyful and affectionate manner of their People, passing along all of the news each had gathered since they had last seen one another. Then Victorio and the warriors followed her back to where the women and children were hidden, relying on her Power to warn them of the approach of their enemies.

San Andres was one of the four sacred mountains that defined the limits of the territory of the Chihenne. Coming to the Sacred Mountain was like a prayer, so she moved in a prayerful way, thought in a prayerful way, saw in a prayerful way, and heard in a prayerful way. Lozen felt her Power stir in her and everything

seemed suddenly clear and vivid, sparkling like dew on a spider-
web at sunrise. Lozen felt the Gan Mountain Spirits watching as
she approached the Sacred Mountain where they lived, where
White Painted Woman had gone, where every rock knew them.[3]
She could feel their attention, the way drums resound in one's
bones after a night of dancing. Upon reaching the Sacred Mountain, they stopped to pray and to give thanks before heading toward Canada Alamosa, where the enemy waited.

Lozen knew they could not stay ahead of the soldiers with so
many women and children if they did not find horses—and if they
did not somehow prevent the soldiers at Ojo Caliente from pursuing them on horseback. So she went with a group of warriors
to find the soldiers' horse herd. The warriors all counted on her
ability to warn them of an ambush and on her Power with horses.
She had many times earned her name—Dexterous Horse Thief—
and they had need of her skill now.

The warriors approached the herd cautiously, warned by
Lozen's Power that the guards were close by. They spread out
carefully around the herd, locating each sentry before they struck.
The warriors killed eight White Eyes in the first moments of the
fighting. Then Lozen and several other warriors each took a horse
and drove the herd before them, coming away with sixty-eight
horses—including the nantan's fine stallion.[4] They ran the horses
back to where they had left the women and children and then
the entire band of close to 225 Chihenne all hurried on once
again, knowing the soldiers could not follow them on foot.

In this lay the great strength of the People. A warrior could
ride a horse to death, covering forty miles at a run. Then he could
cut a meal from the dead horse and run another 40 miles on
foot—moving as quickly as a horse could trot. But the soldiers
could only overtake a dismounted warrior if they were riding fresh
horses. That is why the warriors remained as much as possible in
the mountains, knowing they could run up the hill in places where

horses could not follow and so elude pursuit, for the soldiers would not come after them on foot. The warriors spent their lives learning to climb and could scale a cliff no soldier would attempt. They could crawl up the rock like lizards, then lower ropes and draw the old people and children up after them. Only the scouts on their trail could follow them up such a cliff—the accursed scouts who had sold themselves for a pouch full of bullets.

They moved quickly now, with warriors thrown out on all sides to shield the main body of women and children. A few days after they took the horse herd from Ojo Caliente, they fought soldiers coming after them from Fort Bayard at a ranch just west of the Rio Grande. Lozen's Power warned them of the approaching soldiers, so they were ready. They fought for five hours from a good position, killing ten soldiers and losing no warriors themselves. Once again, they took horses from the ranch where they fought and from the soldiers as well.[5]

Now Lozen felt her Power rising. Victorio also had grown strong and had the ability to visualize the terrain of battles as if with hawk eyes from the air, so he knew where to place his warriors and where the soldiers would go. Nana drew on the Goose Power that sustained him and could ride without ceasing, only sleeping a little in the saddle. The young warriors, seeing this old man riding without pause, would do anything to keep up and match his stamina, so Nana's scouting parties could cover eighty miles in a day.

Sometimes it seemed to Lozen she had been born and nurtured for just this moment and so she wondered why they had for so long let the White Eyes grind them into the dust. But then she saw the struggle of the children and the old ones to keep up and she wondered whether they had blundered into a Coyote story, drawn toward disaster by their own foolishness. But mostly, she simply rode and prayed, listening to the murmur of her Power.

The soldiers and the scouts from Fort Bayard proved the most persistent, even after losing so many men in the fight on the ranch on the Rio Grande. Using the eyes of the scouts, the soldiers found the trail of the Chihenne a week later in Sierra Blanca Canyon near the headwaters of the Animas River. But Lozen felt them coming, so Victorio sent the women and children hurrying ahead and turned back with the warriors to prepare a trap for the soldiers. He told the warriors to shoot the soldiers' horses first, for they were much easier targets then the men riding on top. He reminded them that they fought not to kill soldiers but to slow the pursuit. They could do that just as well by killing the horses as by killing the soldiers, for dismounted soldiers could never keep up with even women and children. So they ambushed the soldiers in a canyon, firing at them from all sides. They fought all day, as the women and children fled on to safety. They killed most of the soldiers' horses and five men, for even when the men were in good cover the warriors could often hit the horses. Victorio let the soldiers escape in the darkness, having accomplished his purpose.

They moved on up along the Animas River, which flows down from the spine of the world that divides the rivers in the Black Range. Victorio selected each camp with great care and prayer. He usually chose high ground, with easily guarded approaches and several escape routes. Each night, they all slept with weapons and supplies close at hand so they could awake and flee at any moment. Each day the leaders made sure every person knew the rendezvous in case they were attacked and forced to scatter. And each day Lozen sang the song her Power had given her, standing alone in the circle of warriors with her hands outstretched as she cleared her mind of fear and fatigue and filled it with gratitude:

> *In this world Ussen has Power;*
> *This Power he has granted me.*
> *For the good of my People.*
> *This I see as one from a height*

Sees in every direction;
This I feel as though I
Held in my palms something that tingles.
This Power is mine to use,
But only for the good of my People.

As she faced the direction from which they had come, she would feel her palms tingle, then burn. All of the warriors watched as she did this, holding themselves in a prayerful way, knowing only Power could help them walk, dry, through the raindrops.

Once again, Victorio prepared the trap—setting the warriors in position for the ambush. Once again, the soldiers came on into the trap, as though directed by Victorio's Power. They fought a long time and it seemed they would be able to kill all the soldiers and get their ammunition. But then a second force of soldiers and scouts arrived, forcing the warriors to loosen the snare enough so the soldiers could escape.

Lozen watched the White Eyes scrambling backward, leaving their wounded. Then one of the nantans ran back to help a wounded soldier, covering perhaps six hundred feet across open ground. The nantan picked up the wounded man and ran back across the open space. Lozen watched him with respect, half hoping no bullet would find him.[6] The warriors all admired how it was done and decided the nantan must have Power against bullets. It was one of their best fights, because the soldiers ran off so quickly the warriors captured their baggage train—and so gained more ammunition than they used.

The People moved on quickly, back and forth through the Black Range, which Victorio and Lozen both knew better than their own dreams. Still, soldiers seemed to come up out of the ground. Sometimes when she sang her Enemies Against song, Lozen's hands grew warm in every direction she faced, for their enemies were converging on them from all sides.

And she was right. The soldiers from Fort Bayard came on again, perhaps two hundred men led by a nantan named Morrow and scouts commanded by Lieutenant Charles Gatewood, also called Long Nose. Some of the warriors said Gatewood was both a good man and a bad enemy. He treated the scouts he commanded with respect and laughed easily, but he was fearless and quick and he would not give up a trail. Again and again, the Chihenne scattered to shatter their trail, only to see Gatewood's careful scouts pick it up and return to the pursuit, as though reconstructing a deer from a scattering of bones. Usually, the scouts moved ahead of the soldiers, who could not keep up. Once Gatewood's scouts surrounded the camp in the night, but the murmuring of Lozen's Power prompted them to slip away before first light.[7] Sometimes, her Power spoke to her in dreams. Sometimes she heard Power's soft voice in her ear. Sometimes Power spoke to her through the warmth of her palms or the twitching of a certain muscle in her leg. Then again, sometimes horses spoke to her with their eyes, so she could almost hear their voices in her mind. But even Lozen's Power occasionally fell silent. Once, the scouts found the camp and opened fire quickly, killing three people. Everyone scattered and the scouts captured fifteen horses and some supplies. Sometime later, the scouts hit them again in a deep canyon. At first, the warriors thought only a few scouts had found them and so advanced quickly to finish them off. The warriors called out to the scouts, mocking them, saying they should come ahead and come to dinner, and the scouts called back that they would be right over. But more scouts came up behind the first ones, including Gatewood, so the Chihenne retreated, leaving two of their best men dead.

From a distance, Victorio watched the soldiers as they camped in a vulnerable place, a canyon eight hundred feet deep with rocky sides and plenty of shelter for the attackers, who would also have easy lines of retreat. Warriors killed mounted guards on a bluff overlooking the camp and at daylight fired down first into the camp of the scouts and then on the main body of soldiers. They showed their disdain for the soldiers by taking off their breech-clouts and waving them in a gesture of contempt—hoping the soldiers or the scouts would get so angry they would come out from their cover. But the soldiers held their discipline and Gate-wood rallied the scouts and led them up the canyon against the warriors.[8]

Lozen thought perhaps they could ambush the soldiers on open ground and force them to retreat, leaving their baggage be-hind. But another force of scouts attacked them from behind, drawn by the gunfire. Fortunately, Victorio had chosen the ground carefully and the warriors withdrew along the edge of the canyon to another strong position. Even with the additional scouts, the soldiers could only withdraw from the canyon with difficulty. Vic-torio sent warriors to harry them all along their retreat. The battle was a great success, for they turned back the soldiers and allowed the women and children to escape without any loss of life among the warriors. The People counted success in these terms, instead of counting up their dead enemies as did the White Eyes. How-ever, several warriors were wounded—including Washington, Vic-torio's son who was therefore to Lozen like the son her Power had not allowed her. They made camp not far from the battle place, but Lozen sensed once again the approach of the troops and they fled—leaving behind beef not yet butchered.

▼

The leaders decided they must go down into Mexico, although they had been moving back and forth through their own country for two moons, beating the soldiers in every battle. But Lozen knew they were leaning too heavily now on Power and luck. Power might do wonderful things, but it must not be used carelessly, lest it be depleted or offended. Power would help only those who were smart, strong, and deserving. So they must give thanks for the help they had been given, but not take it for granted, like a man too lazy to hunt who loiters in his brother's wickiup. Besides, the constant fighting had used up their ammunition and horses so they must go to Mexico to get horses and cattle and rest, although it would mean crossing some dangerous places as they moved south. So Lozen sang fervently to locate the enemy as they swung wide through the mountains to avoid the soldiers chasing them—reversing course and heading south through the San Mateos and down the eastern face of the Black Range. They killed any White Eyes they encountered, taking horses and cattle from ranches, seizing a wagon train and killing eleven teamsters and making sure no one who crossed their trail would carry the word to the soldiers. Sometimes the killing troubled Lozen, especially when they had to kill women and children. But she hardened herself by thinking of the children the soldiers had killed and with the knowledge the soldiers would kill them all if they had the chance. The Chihenne had not wanted this fight, but the White Eyes had insisted on it and now they must do what was necessary.

As they moved south to Mexico, they encountered a large raiding party of Chiricahua, led by Juh and Geronimo.[9] They met in friendly fashion, although hard feelings remained between the Chihenne and the Chiricahua because raiding by Juh and Geronimo had given the White Eyes the excuse to close the reservation at Ojo Caliente. Moreover, trouble had grown up between them at San Carlos like stinging nettles and some Chiricahua now scouted for the soldiers who chased them. Still, Lozen's band needed every warrior, and Juh's sanctuary in the Sierra Madre remained a possible refuge for the Chihenne. So the Chihenne stopped in their flight long enough to hold a ceremony to honor and welcome the Chiricahua, dancing out their own exploits and calling Geronimo's warriors by name so they could also dance out into the firelight to boast of their battles.

Lozen admired Geronimo's pride, the justified arrogance of a warrior. And she noted the sense of Power he projected. Geronimo had great influence with Juh, one of the most feared war leaders. His Nednhi warriors were considered wild men, men who had been cast out by other bands.

▼

The next day they continued south with their augmented force, crossing the border into Mexico before slowing their pace, hoping the soldiers and scouts would turn back at the border. They suffered from thirst that threatened to kill many of their horses. Finally, they came to the edge of a steep river canyon where they stopped to rest, although Victorio took care to fortify the approaches to the camp and to the canyon. But just as darkness gathered, they heard the neighing of thirsty horses catching the scent of water, so they knew the soldiers had found them again. Warriors quickly ran to their positions and the women and children fled to safety as the scouts led by Gatewood came up against them. Victorio shifted his warriors into strong positions as the scouts bravely charged up the hill as darkness fell and the moon came out. The warriors kept them at a distance with good shooting, but just when it seemed they might turn the knife around and trap the scouts, more soldiers came up the canyon.

Victorio quickly shifted his warriors to new positions and Lozen again observed the care with which her brother chose the ground on which to fight. Victorio rallied the warriors, taking a drum to a hill where they all could hear him as he chanted in his high strong voice. The warriors all drew strength from Victorio's Enemies Against song, hoping the soldiers' bullets would be turned aside so they could move through the outstretched fingers of their enemies. They knew Victorio's medicine brought them safely through all these fights before, just as Lozen's medicine had moved them out of danger's path. So the warriors laughed and shouted their defiance. In lulls in the fighting, Victorio called to the scouts, urging them to join their brothers. He knew that without the scouts, the soldiers could never hang on to their trail, for the scouts had among them men of Power, who could see ahead to where the Chihenne would go. Victorio did not fear the medicine of the White Eyes, which was invested in the things they made and not in themselves. But in his dreams and visions and the evidence of his eyes, he knew they could not forever elude the soldiers who were guided by warriors of the People. So he called out to the scouts, some of them by name.

Come and join us, he called out, *and together we can kill the white soldiers and the black soldiers and live free.*

But none of the scouts came across the line. They were held by their promises to the White Eyes, by their fear for their families, and by the dried blood that lay between them and the Chihenne.

The soldiers pressed forward, sending the scouts around in a flanking movement. The scouts came up against the low cliff Victorio had selected with great care, but although they pressed their attack to within ten feet of where the warriors lay protected by the rocks, they could not force their way through. When both sides began to run out of bullets, the warriors threw rocks down the hill on the scouts, who could do nothing against them and so retreated reluctantly down the hillside. Lozen watched them retreat with a great sense of grief and loss. The scouts were the point of the spear the White Eyes cast now at the Chihenne, but what might the People have accomplished if they had fought all together instead of letting the White Eyes divide them one against the other?

The soldiers finally gave up the fighting when the moon was already moving down toward the long, graceful line of the horizon, dark against the stars. The soldiers had already been seventy hours without rest and water and their horses were nearly dead. Victorio let them withdraw, unwilling to risk any more warriors. They had only killed and wounded a few soldiers and a few scouts and lost one or two warriors in return. The Chihenne and the Chiricahua had the strong advantage of numbers in the fight and might have killed more soldiers—but Lozen knew there was little point in killing soldiers, or even the scouts. They might as well try to cut every blade of grass with a knife. They could kill ten soldiers for every warrior lost and yet lose everything. Better to save their ammunition and use the soldiers' retreat to slip away.

▼

Victorio, Lozen, and Nana led their People along with the Chiricahua on down into Mexico, into the Candelaria Mountains overlooking the important road leading from El Paso to Chihuahua. On the northern slope was a natural stone catch basin that held water even in the dry months, so the mountains were a favorite camping place. Because the Chihenne had gone through that area many times, Victorio tried to maintain friendships with the nearby Mexican town of Carrizal, sometimes trading the horses and cattle the warriors took from other towns. They had long maintained a wary, dangerous accommodation with the ranchers there, who knew that if they kept their horses and cattle in corrals the warriors would sometimes take the horses but rarely bother the ranchers. But when the ranchers kept guards on their cattle and made forts of their corrals, the warriors would kill the guards when they needed the horses.

Still, Victorio did not trust any Mexican and so sent Sanchez into Carrizal dressed as a vaquero. Drinking in the cantina, Sanchez talked to the servants of leading ranchers and learned of a plan to invite Victorio to a big fiesta and then kill the warriors when they were drunk. This was an old trick of the Mexicans, for often bands would make peace with one town or another so they would have a safe place to camp and somewhere to trade. Such agreements with Mexican towns often ended in betrayal, how-ever—on one side or the other. The news that Carrizal hoped to trick them to their deaths kindled anger in Victorio, which built hour by hour until it was like metal left all night in the fire. The next day, the people of Carrizal sent to Victorio's camp a Tara-humara Indian with an invitation to the fiesta. The People and the Tarahumara were long and bitter enemies, so Victorio did not trust that man's soothing words—but he did admire his courage for coming alone into Victorio's camp. The Tarahumara were strong enemies and a brave people. Victorio resolved to turn the visit of the messenger to his advantage and hid most of his war-riors, making it seem he had only a small force.

Victorio sent several warriors to steal the small group of horses grazing in a corral in front of Carrizal, saying the warriors should make sure they were seen and take no care to cover their trail. Then he prepared an ambush carefully. He found a small canyon with a good stream and posted a few warriors led by Kaytennae on the north side of the canyon overlooking a good place to drink. He posted the main body of warriors on the south side of the canyon in a cluster of rocks offering good cover. Victorio and Lozen went with a few others onto a mesa that overlooked the canyon and offered a good view of the approaches where they waited for the Mexicans. Lozen sang her song, until she felt their enemies approaching. Then Victorio used his signal mirror to flash a warning to the waiting warriors.

The eighteen Mexicans rode easily into the trap. They dis-mounted at the stream as Victorio had willed them to do. Kay-tennae waited until they were all within range before he began firing, shooting first at the horses. The Mexicans fired back, but seeing they had no cover by the stream they ran quickly to the rocks on the south side of the canyon, just as Victorio had in-tended. As they reached the rocks, Nana's men began firing. It ended quickly, the Mexicans running back and forth like antelope caught between two fires. Lozen watched grimly as the warriors moved among the bodies, collecting ammunition and everything useful. They did not bother to take the old, muzzle-loading guns some of the Mexicans carried.

One man, not yet dead, moved a little and groaned and a warrior ran him through with a spear. It had been that way for a long time between the People and the Mexicans, neither side taking prisoner any adult men. Carrizal should not have planned treachery, Lozen told herself. She turned and looked back toward Carrizal and knew more Mexicans would come after the first.[10] She talked with her brother and they decided they would wait to see who else would come down this game trail for human beings. Victorio directed the warriors to move the bodies out of the way and to once again set the trap.

After a time, another party of twenty Mexicans arrived, looking for their friends. Once again, the warriors on the north side fired so the Mexicans fled south toward the rocks where the hidden warriors came out from their places above and began shooting. This time, about five Mexicans managed to escape down the canyon—but the others soon had no place to go. The warriors took their time, making their ammunition count. One group of Mexicans took shelter in a space between two rocks, but the warriors fired down into them until they had made of the Mexicans a great pile of bodies. Another man wedged himself into a small space from which he could shoot at the warriors, but his legs stuck out into the open below the knee. So the warriors used his legs for target practice until his legs had been shot nearly off and his cries and groans fell silent.

▼

The People once again went on their way, knowing every hand was turned against them and they could not rely on the friendship of any town. They moved from mountain to mountain, killing anyone they encountered, afraid to remain in any place long, increasingly worn out by the constant movement and fear.[11] They accumulated supplies for the winter as they went. In a town called Galena, they killed two men and stole sixty horses. The next day they moved to San Lorezo, killing three men and capturing three hundred horses. They destroyed a wagon train, taking many supplies. But they could not take too many horses nor too many supplies, lest their force grow too large to remain hidden. Moreover, one by one they lost good warriors—even leaders. They won every fight and moved as though they owned the whole land, but they dwindled like a sandbar in a rising stream.

The Chiricahua split off as the summer subsided, taking with them a third of Victorio's fighting strength. The Chiricahua had only a raiding party, with not many women and children. They were after plunder and adventure and knew the whites and the Mexicans would not stop chasing the Chihenne so long as any were left alive. So the Chiricahua turned aside and Victorio let them go with as much friendship as he could, knowing he might have need of their help and of their sanctuaries in the Sierra Madre.[12] Later, they heard the trader Tom Jeffords found the camp of Juh and Geronimo and convinced them to return to the San Carlos Reservation. They went peacefully, telling Jeffords they had not raided with the Chihenne.

Victorio and Lozen moved the Chihenne, together with some Mescalero warriors and even some Commanche warriors, back north across the border into the United States. They needed American bullets for their American guns and the Mexicans were mostly poor, so the plunder would be much better among the White Eyes. Lozen knew that, unlikely as it might be, Victorio also still nurtured a faint hope the White Eyes would grow so weary of fighting they would let him live at Ojo Caliente. The White Eyes changed their minds so often you never knew what they might do. Moreover, he could not overlook even a small chance of an acceptable peace—for he knew their luck would eventually run out. Perhaps the White Eyes would decide it was easier to let the Chihenne have their own land than to chase them everywhere. The Chihenne had killed hundreds of people and taken thousands of horses and cattle and lost not a single battle in a year of fighting. Surely even the White Eyes, who were stubborn as gun metal, would see it made no sense to pay such a terrible cost to keep the Chihenne from living in a place for which the White Eyes themselves had so little use. So they moved back into the Black Range. But Gatewood's scouts quickly found their trail once again, leading Morrow's soldiers after them. Victorio remained ahead of them, relying as always on Lozen's ceremony, Nana's deep knowledge of the land, and his own Power.

They passed within fifteen miles of Ojo Caliente deep in the Season of the Ghost Dance.[13] Lozen's heart ached to see all the good places once again and she wondered how many more times in her life she would lift her eyes to the silhouette of the Sacred Mountain. She knew each meadow and cluster of trees, each spring and hidden seep. She knew the place where Coyote had played the game with the Ravens, who were taking out their eyes and throwing them down the hill and then chasing after them all in good fun. He nagged them to let him play as well, until they became irritated and resolved to play a trick on him. When Coyote threw his eyes down the hill, the Ravens ran away with them, so he wandered around a long time looking for his eyes—acting foolishily. She knew the names of each place, and spoke them in a sacred tone—prayerfully and with gratitude. Those places spoke back to her, smoothing her mind and offering her wisdom.

Each place had a particular name that described its appearance, and a teaching about something that had happened there. These stories taught right behavior—like Tsee Chiizh Dah Sidile, or Coarse-Textured Rocks Lie Above in a Compact Cluster, whose story went like this: Long ago a man became sexually attracted to his stepdaughter. He was living below Coarse-Textured Rocks Lie Above in a Compact Cluster with his stepdaughter and her mother. Waiting until no one else was present and sitting alone with her, he started to molest her. The girl's maternal uncle happened to come by and he killed the man with a rock. The man's skull was cracked open. It was raining. The girl's maternal uncle dragged the man's body up above to Coarse-Textured Rocks Lie Above in a Compact Cluster and placed it there in a storage pit. The girl's mother came home and was told by her daughter of all that had happened. The people who owned the storage pit removed the man's body and put it somewhere else. The people never had a wake for the dead man's body. It happened at Coarse-Textured Rocks Lie Above in a Compact Cluster.[14]

She also learned all the stories linked generally to sacred places—certain rivers or mountains. So she knew the plain between two mountains where Gopher had helped Child of Water kill Buffalo, one of the monsters that made it impossible for people to live in the world. Buffalo lived in the middle of a great plain where no one would approach him without being trampled to death. But Gopher told Child of Water exactly what he must do and then dug a tunnel to the place beneath where Buffalo lay on the ground sleeping. Gopher chewed away the impenetrable hair on a spot over Buffalo's heart—so Child of Water could crawl through the tunnel under Buffalo and strike him in the heart. Then Child of Water ran back down through one tunnel after another as Buffalo dug down after him. But Buffalo died just as he was about to dig down through the fourth and final tunnel.

Lozen also knew the place she had been born. Every time she passed it, she lay down and rolled herself in the four directions—to show her gratitude to the Life Giver and her reverence for the places that shaped her and protected her and taught her. She understood that the People could only remain themselves in the places that knew them and remembered them and shaped them—

for those places shaped her mind, making it smooth and resilient and steady.

Passing by these places filled her with a happiness very close to grief. A shadow fell across her heart in the moment of her joy, like looking into the face of a loved one after a dream has prepared you for his death, or like the memory of Grey Ghost, worn smooth by the fingers of her recollection. She kept these feelings mostly hidden, even from Victorio, because she did not want to weaken him with her longing. But she saw it in him as well. When they neared Ojo Caliente, he sent her alone and without the weapons of a warrior to see if the agent might yet surrender and give them their own land.[15] Lozen often spoke to the soldiers for Victorio, for the soldiers were less likely to take a woman prisoner. Lozen said they would give themselves up to the agent, but not to the army, whom they could not trust. The agent wished to speak to Victorio, so Victorio brought with him sixty warriors, well armed and well mounted. But the agent could make no promises, only urge them to surrender before the soldiers killed them all.

So the Chihenne lingered only a short time in the places they loved best, then went on their way. They relied on Lozen's Power to evade the enemy, Nana's Power to find ammunition, and Victorio's Power in the fighting—knowing the soldiers were hunting them, for the agent had made no promises. The soldiers caught up to them in the San Mateos a few days after they left Ojo Caliente, but the warriors killed a nantan and wounded two scouts without any loss to themselves. They doubled back to Ojo Caliente, then headed south down the east face of the Black Range. They split into two parties to confuse the pursuit and then reunited at the mouth of the Palomas River. Here they fought a new band of soldiers[16] before slipping away in the darkness, crossing the Rio Grande, and circling around to return to the San Andres Mountains.

But in a canyon in the San Andres Mountains, Morrow and

Gatewood's scouts caught up with them again. The scouts sought to keep them fighting until the soldiers could catch up, but the Chihenne divided into bands of fifteen that moved from cover to cover—trading ground for time as the soldiers drove them up the canyon. With nightfall, they scattered in the darkness, many now afoot, trying to shake the scouts before the soldiers could catch up. They escaped once again, but lost several warriors they could not replace.

Six days later, a fresh group of soldiers found them in a canyon in the San Andreas. This time, Victorio surprised everyone by calling on the warriors to charge the enemy. Usually, Victorio fought on the defensive, having trained his warriors to put up rock-walled firing pits with loopholes for their rifles in every camp. But this time his Power told him to attack the soldiers, who were a small force and tired from the chase. Victorio and Lozen led the attack themselves, for leaders of the People go first into danger, relying on example, the pride of warriors, and their own Power instead of hanging back in safety to issue orders like the great nantans of the White Eyes. So the warriors came along behind Victorio, laughing and jeering when the soldiers broke and tumbled away from them, leaving rations and blankets the Chihenne sorely needed.

▼

Having shaken off pursuit, the Chihenne moved back into the San Andres Mountains, hiding in Hembrillo Canyon on the east side of the range. They crossed a long waterless stretch as quickly as they could and finally came upon a spring. Every warrior knew the location of every water source in the vast territory through which they wandered, for it was their chief advantage over the soldiers—who knew the locations of the major springs and all the rivers and streams but not the seeps that yielded a trickle or the dry watercourses that could yield a mouthful of water in the bottom of a hole. The soldiers had learned to haunt the most reliable springs, so plotting a course from water to water was crucial in the low desert areas where they must stretch their physical limits. Smelling the spring, the horses strained to reach the water. But Nana cocked his head as though listening to someone talking, then looked in each direction, squatted down, and dipped his hand into the spring. He sniffed the water, shook it off his hand, and then said no one should drink it, nor let his horse drink. The warriors nodded, seeing Nana's Power had spoken to him. So they turned their horses aside with difficulty and turned their backs on the water—not one of them complaining. They reached Hembrillo Canyon after a long, thirsty time and the warriors rested there, as the women and children came in from the places they had hidden during the pursuit. From there, raiding parties went out to steal horses and ammunition from local Mexican ranches. They also sent out runners to the Mescalero Reservation, hoping more warriors might join them. The ranks of Victorio's warriors had grown as thin as the frayed blankets the agents did not bother to steal. He needed new fighters so he could continue to split off raiding parties and still have enough men to hold his positions and keep the soldiers from flanking him.

They had not been in Hembrillo Canyon very long when Lozen warned Victorio of the approach of their enemies. The women scattered and the warriors moved into strong positions overlooking the spring. Just as Lozen had foreseen, a force of perhaps seventy soldiers came into the canyon, hurrying toward the water and acting very strangely—wobbling on their feet as though sick. Victorio let them come close before he began shooting, driving the soldiers away from the water. The soldiers wavered, hardly able to run, and Lozen knew they had drunk from the spring Nana's Power had warned her People against. The warriors worked their way in around the soldiers, who were too weak to escape back down the canyon. The fighting went on for hours and many of the soldiers were wounded and a few killed. Victorio drew the snare tighter, waiting for thirst, his strong ally, to take its toll on the trapped soldiers.

But just when it seemed they would be able to kill all of the soldiers, gunshots resounded from behind the warriors. Morrow had found them again, led by Gatewood's scouts. So Victorio shifted the positions of his warriors, who were now themselves in the trap. They gave ground reluctantly, moving with calm courage from one good position to another until they had opened a line of retreat. The fighting continued all day, until the warriors slipped away, disappointed they had not been able to crush the lives of the soldiers put into their hands by Nana's Power.

They moved south quickly through the mountains, hoping the soldiers would be too tired and sick to follow. But Lozen sensed danger ahead of them as well and the screen of warriors Victorio threw out ahead and to the side warned them that another large force of soldiers was coming straight toward them. They had only a moment to scatter, each warrior, woman, and child melting into the grass and rocks and trees just as they had practiced all of their lives. Often, the warriors traveled with bunches of grass or branches tied to them to break up their outline. They all knew how to find a slight depression in the earth in which they could lie down beneath a bit of brush or grass. They had learned by reflex never to look over a ridgeline or the top of a rock without holding a branch before their faces so their eneimes would not glimpse the outline of a human head. Every one of them knew how to dust themselves with dirt or slide down into the smallest gully or rivulet and remain so motionless the soldiers could nearly step over them without seeing them. Some even had Power to make themselves invisible.

Now the soldiers hurried past them, so close Lozen could have picked up a stone and hit the nantan in the back. But no one made a sound, knowing that even if they killed many of the soldiers they would suffer heavy casualties fighting in such a place. But Victorio's Enemies Against Power cloaked them, so the soldiers' eyes slid over them, seeing nothing. They hardly breathed until the soldiers had ridden out of sight—perhaps hurrying to help their brother soldiers, not knowing the fight in the canyon had ended.

After this incident, Victorio saw his force was too large to hide together in a country so filled with soldiers. So he split his forces again, sending one group, including Lozen, to the Mescalero Reservation to recruit more warriors and get more ammunition. The rest moved through the mountains. He sent Washington with fifteen warriors to the San Carlos Reservation to retrieve some of the families of his warriors, for many warriors who had been fighting this long time without their families had grown heartsick and lonely and were talking among themselves about returning to San Carlos. He also told Washington he might kill the families of some of the scouts who had been chasing them, which might convince many of the scouts to go home to protect their families. Even if it did not, the Chihenne would have the small satisfaction of revenge.

They could see the shape of their deaths now, like the outline of an owl by firelight. They could elude the soldiers indefinitely, but not the scouts who turned up every time they stopped to rest, like a mountain lion waiting by the water hole. They had only the goodwill of Power to cling to now and that seemed not enough.

CHAPTER IX

▼▼▼

Power Turns

May 1880

The Chihenne who journeyed to the Mescalero Reservation had no trouble recruiting warriors, for the White Eyes had recently attacked the Mescalero. The agent, a man they did not trust, told the Mescalero to camp close to his headquarters so the soldiers would not mistake them for Victorio's men. But when they complied, seven hundred soldiers came quickly out of nowhere, taking all their horses and livestock and weapons and attacking any bands that hesitated to flee. Perhaps thirty warriors escaped the roundup, but the soldiers killed many others.

Lozen and Victorio listened grimly, glad for the small increase in their strength, but understanding how much they had lost now that the Mescalero Reservation was closed to them. The Chihenne were like the jackrabbit, run between two hawks. Still, they would not make it easy for the White Eyes.

Washington's return from the journey to the San Carlos Reservation brought more bad news. He had attacked a camp, thinking they were from the same band as the scouts who were chasing them. But it was actually a camp aligned with Juh. The news stirred fear in Lozen. They had not even known the Chiricahua and Nednhi had returned to the reservation, assuming they had gone down into the Sierra Madre. Instead, the Nednhi now had reasons to hate the Chihenne. Fortunately, Washington had come away safely, although he fought a short battle with the soldiers near Rocky Canyon in Arizona before rejoining Victorio in the mountains near Ojo Caliente.

▼

Reunited, the Chihenne camped uneasily, sensing their Power turning against them, like the heavy smell of rain in the air.

Then, just at dawn, shots rang out at the edge of camp.[1] Everyone jumped up immediately, seizing the weapons and the pouches of food they always kept close by in their sleep. The warriors took positions to slow down the scouts, who ran toward the camp killing anyone in their paths. The women and children fled the cross fire, only to run into the gunsight of more scouts on the other side of camp. They turned back, but found themselves under fire from a third direction.

Victorio saw they were surrounded, so he led his People to a pile of rocks on a small hill against the side of the canyon. Lozen ran along with the warriors, dodging the bullets that kicked up the dirt around her.

The scouts must have found them the day before or during the night, because they had spent some time surrounding the Chihenne. Lozen wondered why her Power had not warned her the enemy was near when she had prayed the night before. Why had her Power not used her dreams to wake her to the danger? Perhaps she had offended her Power by leaning too heavily against it, like a greedy guest who eats without courtesy. Perhaps she had stepped over one of Coyote's tracks, or committed some other offense.[2] Moreover, she felt responsible for the trap in which they now found themselves. Victorio might have picked a better place or put out more sentries if her ceremony had not reassured him no enemies were near.

For the Chihenne, this was the worst battle yet. They spent all day trapped in the rocks, shooting uselessly at the scouts and staring out at the bodies of the people killed in the first rush. Even Victorio was wounded, shot in the leg. Lozen attended him, singing as she burned the thorns off a nopal cactus pad, slit it open, and tied the sticky pulp over his wound. She sang quietly the songs her Power had given her, trying to clear her mind of the fear and the guilt and the doubts. Victorio made no complaint and she knew he did not blame her, but he did not need to blame her for she could do that herself.

Victorio quickly returned to the front ranks, hoarding his ammunition. Throughout the day, he called to the scouts, urging them to stop killing their own people. Some of them he knew. Some even had relatives among the Chihenne. He kept talking to them, wondering at the Power of the White Eyes over good warriors. The scouts shouted back; they joked, they bragged, they jeered him. Then the scouts said they would kill Victorio and called on the women to come out and go back with the scouts to San Carlos. Hearing this, Lozen called out that no woman of the Chihenne would come out there. Not one of them would desert their men. And should Victorio fall in battle, they would rather devour his body themselves than let it fall into the unworthy hands of the scouts.[3]

The scouts held the Chihenne in the trap all that day and throughout the night. The warriors probed for an escape, but the scouts had every bit of terrain covered. The night seemed endless and they each prayed to their Powers and prepared themselves for death. They knew the scouts were holding them until the soldiers arrived, who would surely come soon. Lozen could see that Victorio carried the same weight as she and blamed himself for selecting a camp that could be surrounded.

But Nana seemed undisturbed, accepting the approach of their death calmly and with dignity. They all gathered courage from him, as they always had.

They greeted the dawn with prayer, facing to the east. Lozen felt a great surge of courage in the light of her last dawn, savoring Ussen's final gift. Nana's voice carried to the sky, as finely grained and beautiful as ironwood smoothed by sand.

Then, to their surprise, the scouts withdrew. The warriors sent a few shots after them, and came out of their hiding places with delight and astonishment. They pursued the scouts back down the canyon, harrying them on their way. Lozen realized the scouts must have run out of bullets, because they had run on ahead of their pack train and ahead of the soldiers. No one could understand why the soldiers had not arrived while the scouts had held the Chihenne in the trap. Perhaps Ussen's Power had confused the soldiers.[4]

Still, they could hardly rejoice. Everywhere, people were grieving, cutting away their hair and calling out in dismay. The scouts had killed thirty-one warriors and twenty-four women and children—most of them in the first moments of the attack. A single fight had cost Victorio perhaps one-third of his fighting force. Now, without hope of reinforcement from the Mescalero or the Chiricahua and with so small a force of warriors remaining, they could hardly fight.

Heavy with foreboding and the seeming desertion of Power, they hurried back across the Black Range where they knew each peak, meadow, and hidden spring. Here, many had first found their Power and knew the story of each place, all of which echoed with the voices of those who had gone before. But even in their best hiding places, Lozen's ceremony showed that their enemies moved all about them. They kept changing camps and the lookouts posted on the high places saw the dust trails of their enemies on every side. So they decided to split up and make their way to the south. They could not raid near the Black Mountains for the soldiers were too close, but they had to get more food and ammunition. Victorio, whose dreams had grown dark, left his wife and youngest son Istee in a hiding place in the Black Range, unwilling to risk their lives on the dash down into Mexico. He hoped to bring back supplies and knew that as they raided south they would draw the soldiers away from their families in the Black Range.

Victorio and Lozen led the People south in several groups, spreading out like fingers on a hand to gather up the ammunition their American-made guns would require while they were in Mexico. Victorio and Lozen separated and went with different groups, to spread the protection of their Power. They fought briefly with soldiers chasing them in Cook's Canyon, killing five before continuing south. Near Lake Palomas, the soldiers caught up to a group of warriors led by Victorio, killing ten—including Washington.

The news hit Lozen like a blow when her group rejoined Victorio, for she had no children of her own and so had put her heart into the children of her brother. Now he had lost three children to the White Eyes, leaving only Istee, who was hiding with his mother in the Black Range. The only comfort was that Washington had died a warrior, a free man who had served his People and earned the respect of his relatives. So she cut off her hair in grief for the one whose name she could never again speak and prayed anew she might find the strength her path demanded. Heavy with grief, Lozen and Victorio crossed the Rio Grande and plunged down into Mexico, set on their course like an arrow that has left the bow.

▼

They moved down deep into Mexico, but even there the soldiers were never far away. Furthermore, they had a hard time finding enough ammunition for their American-made rifles. Victorio had increasing difficulty keeping the remaining Mescalero warriors with him, since they talked often of their home, even though the Mescalero there were living like prisoners in their own camps.

After hiding for weeks in Mexico, Victorio took a force of perhaps sixty warriors and went back into Texas, partly to get more ammunition and partly to satisfy the Mescalero warriors who fought with him: They had raided there in the past and knew that country well. They encountered a small force of soldiers near Eagle Mountain and trapped them there in a weak position. But before Victorio's warriors could finish them, more soldiers came and forced Victorio to retreat back across the Rio Grande, leaving behind seven dead. Lozen noted the way in which the Americans and the Mexicans worked against the Chihenne and wondered whether they had begun to cooperate. She could hardly bear to think about what that must mean, since the Chihenne's ability to move back and forth across the border had been the main reason they had survived the past two years.

Victorio continued to pray and to seek an understanding with his Power, so he could hold the warriors together. He longed for his wife and son in the Black Mountains and spoke of his yearning to Nana, who was as a father to him. Nana said at least Victorio still had Lozen, who was a sister, war leader, medicine woman, and the dearest family to him.

I'm glad Lozen is with us now, said Nana. *We need her help in locating the enemy. Attack may come from any source and we are far from the high mountains.*[5]

I think constantly of my wife and my little son. I left them in a safe place, for there was not time nor opportunity to go back for them, said Victorio.

Nana replied, *Why not go back for them?*

My duty is to my People. My family must share the dangers just as others do, said Victorio, sorrowing but knowing a leader had only the authority of his example.

My brother is a chief first, a father and husband second.

Enjuh! That is my intention, said Victorio.

▼

After resting for a time in Mexico, Victorio and Lozen led perhaps 125 warriors back across the Rio Grande into Texas in the Season of Large Leaves.[6] They took some supplies and ammunition from several settlements, but the soldiers picked up their trail. As the Chihenne warriors fled, they ran into an ambush set for them by another force of soldiers at Rattlesnake Springs on the south-western slopes of Sierra Diablo.

Initially, Victorio retreated, but then he realized only a few soldiers held the spring—which provided the only good water for a long distance. So he moved his warriors back into position, trapping the soldiers near the spring. He sent out riders to check for the soldiers' reinforcements and one rider returned to report a wagon train with only a few soldiers as guard coming along the road not far away. Victorio left enough warriors at the spring to trap the soldiers, then took most of his force to attack the wagon train, hoping to get ammunition the wagon train probably carried. But when the warriors sprang their ambush, soldiers who had been riding inside the wagons threw back the covers and began shooting. One warrior was killed and several others wounded before Victorio broke off the attack. Seeing he now had no hope of keeping the soldiers at Rattlesnake Springs trapped, he moved south, back into Mexico.

Once again, Lozen wondered why her Power had not warned her about the soldiers hidden in the wagons. She had been full of grief and darkness these past few months and perhaps this had offended her Power. Perhaps her Power had heard her nagging whispers of doubt, like the murmuring of forbidden lovers in the darkness.

Others had begun to doubt both Victorio and Lozen, saying their Power had deserted them. Old conflicts among them broke into the open again when they neared the border. The Mescalero chief Caballeso got up one morning and began saddling his horse, saying he was going back to the Mescalero Reservation and anyone who wished might follow him there.

Normally, no leader would force a warrior to follow. Each warrior chose his own path, following the leaders who had the most Power and luck. But watching Caballeso getting ready to go, Victorio knew most of the Mescalero would leave with him—which would cost Victorio nearly half of his fighting force. So Victorio moved forward into the sudden silence that had gathered around the Mescalero chief, who was in the center of all their eyes like a dancer in the firelight. Victorio said Caballeso could not leave. So the two faced one another, each testing the other with their eyes—knowing it had come to a fight. They fought because warriors would only follow a brave man—so neither could flinch from the fight and continue to command the respect of his followers. They circled one another warily as though bound together with a tether, the intensity of the watching warriors hemming them in like a corral of thorns. But Victorio's Power seemed to return, if only momentarily. Caballeso was the younger man, but Victorio kept the fight short—luring Caballeso into a lunge by stepping back and seeming to stumble. When Caballeso overextended his trust, Victorio stepped in alongside him and buried his knife between Caballeso's ribs. The rest of the Mescalero saw this and gained back a little confidence in Victorio. No one else challenged him, although Lozen knew Caballeso's relatives would look for their opportunity. Victorio turned away with the arrogant confidence of a true leader, knowing the warriors responded to such displays of strength. But Lozen wondered how long the Mescalero would remain and who would move first to seek Caballeso's revenge.

▼

A little while later, Eclode, the Mescalero woman who was near her time, came to Victorio and pleaded with him to let her go home to have her baby. After taking council together, Lozen and Victorio decided Lozen should go with Eclode back to the Mescalero Reservation, knowing it would help win back the loyalty of the Mescalero warriors and hoping she might bring back more warriors and more ammunition.

So Lozen took leave of her brother and of her People. She turned her face back toward her enemies and her duty, as though facing into a wind of stinging ice.

And all the rest of her life, in her darkest moments, she wondered why her Power had let her leave with no whisper of warning.

CHAPTER X

▼▼▼

Alone Among the Enemy

On the Rio Grande,
September 1880

After Lozen had delivered the baby, hung the afterbirth in the tree, and watched the scouts pass once more by the place where she and Eclode had turned off the trail, she took careful stock of their supplies and cast her mind forward along the path they must travel. Lozen had her rifle, a cartridge belt, a knife, a blanket, and enough food for three days. They needed more food, water, and horses before they could pass through the long stretches of waterless country between the Rio Grande and the Mescalero Reservation. So first Lozen moved Eclode and her baby to a better camp under an overhanging rock, well away from any trails. They did not camp beside water, as the White Eyes liked to do, because such a place could never be safe.[1]

The next day Lozen returned to the river and hid near a cattle path leading down to the water, as they needed meat they could dry for their journey. After several hours, some longhorn cattle came down to drink, wild creatures that could lay open a man's belly with a sweeping slash of their long, sharp horns. She could not risk a rifle shot that could bring soldiers, so she drew her knife and advanced on the bull. He wheeled about to face her, but she darted in under his horns, slashed open his throat and jumped out again before the creature knew what had happened. Then she stood aside as he bled to death. She cut off as many long strips of meat as she could carry, the stomach to make a water pouch, and several long strips of hide. Lozen hurried back to Eclode and the baby and together they spread the meat out to dry. Lozen then prepared the stomach as a water pouch and made a bridle from the strips of hide, knowing they could not begin their journey until she had obtained a horse. Next, they made a cradle for the baby out of willow shoots bent into a frame, fashioning a shade from the blanket they carried to protect the baby from the sun. Finally, they hung the cradle with the few charms they had with them. Then, resolved to find horses, Lozen gave Eclode careful directions about the route to the reservation in case she did not come back. She left all of her equipment with Eclode, even her rifle—taking with her only her knife and the rawhide bridle.

Lozen returned to the river where tracks showed some Mexican women came regularly to wash their clothing. She thought about taking some of the jugs the women left at the river, but she decided the clay jars were too heavy to serve her purpose. So she waited by the river for the women to return to see if they had anything useful. She had been hiding there most of the day when a detachment of Mexican soldiers rode into sight on the opposite bank, going to the river to water their horses. Lozen watched them carefully, her outline broken by bunches of grass she had tied to herself, remaining as perfectly motionless as a lizard blending with a rock. The soldiers watered their horses and then rode half a mile downstream—going so carelessly and with so much loud talking among themselves that she knew they were not hunting her and did not suspect any of the People were close by.

She moved down the river and watched them until darkness had fully gathered before swimming across the river and moving stealthily to their camp. She studied them carefully from hiding, seeking the pattern in their movements. They wrapped themselves in their serapes and sprawled down around the fire. They hobbled their horses nearby and set a guard to walk back and forth between the horses and the fire. Lozen watched the guard pass back and forth in front of the fire for a long while, measuring the length of his passage. Then she shifted her attention to the horses, studying them to see which was the leader, which were nervous, and which were calm. She prayed silently, murmuring to her Power, which had long ago given her influence over horses and an understanding of their ways. She settled on a powerful horse, one of the most restless—knowing she could soothe him, but fearing he would make noise if she concentrated on a different horse.

When her knowledge of the horses and the movements of the guard had become as natural as breath, she stole in toward the horses just as the guard turned and started back toward the fire. She moved to the horse she had selected, talking softly to him as her Power had taught her, so his ears came forward and he tossed his head, but did not neigh—only whickered a little. She gently tied the bridle of leather strips around his lower jaw, then reached down with an almost soothing motion and cut his hobbles. Nonetheless, the horse snorted and jumped back as she cut the hobbles, so she knew she had only a moment before the guard turned back to the sound.

In a single, graceful movement she grabbed a handful of mane and leaped lightly onto the stallion's back, as she had practiced doing since she was a little girl. The horse jumped sideways, but she slid into position on his back, then pulled his head around with the bridle around his jaw and kicked him so he jumped into a run. She heard the sound of gunshots behind her immediately, the whine of the bullets passing close by her head. But the guard had been half-blinded by looking into the fire and since she rode a black horse into the darkness, he had no target. She ran the horse until she was out of range of the rifles, then turned into the river.

Lozen returned quickly to where she had left Eclode and the baby. The cradle board was finished, so the girl put her baby into the bedding of soft grass and climbed up onto the horse. Lozen led the horse the rest of the night away from their hiding place, so they would have a good start if the soldiers picked up her trail in the morning. She did not think they would, as the soldiers had no Indian trackers and would be reluctant to follow her into the United States. She walked as quickly as she could, pushing along at a fast walk and breaking into a lope for long stretches. A seasoned warrior could cover fifty miles in one day on foot, moving at a speed just less than the trot of a horse. Just before dawn, Lozen found another place to rest—this one beneath an overhang in a washing a convenient distance from a spring. She left Eclode there and approached the spring carefully, moving along a ridge that would give her a glimpse of the area around the water before she risked approaching it directly.

As she had expected, soldiers had camped nearby. Unable to catch Victorio by chasing him, many of the soldiers now guarded the water holes all along the border. On the way back to the hiding place, she saw a deer, but she could not risk a shot. Sometimes, it was better to have a bow than even the best rifle—but she could not carry so many different weapons.

They waited three days near the water hole, hoping the soldiers would leave. They resoled their moccasins with hide from the longhorn Lozen had killed and ate most of their remaining store of dried beef. They worked on the cradle, singing songs over the baby, putting ceremonial care into the charms they fashioned to dangle from the crosspiece where the baby would watch them. Despite the uncertainties, the threat of discovery, and the dwindling of their food, Lozen enjoyed the time playing with the baby—as though she had a family after all.

Finally, Lozen decided they should return to the river for water and to steal another horse and more supplies from the soldiers' camp. Lozen and Eclode could bypass this water hole and push north, but if soldiers guarded every water hole they would soon run out of water. They traveled at night to the river. Lozen swam over first, with the baby in the cradle board. Then she hung the cradle board in a tree and returned for Eclode, who rode on the horse while Lozen clung to the horse's tail, thanking the horse for help in the crossing. They went west along the river for several hours and then crossed again. Lozen had learned to always assume she was hunted after the long years of living like a deer among many wolves. They were tethered to the river by their need for water and the threat of the guards on all of the springs. If she had been alone, she would have simply headed north, depending on her ability to go without water for days and to slip into the enemy's camp and take water when necessary. But she could not risk that with Eclode and the child, so she moved along the river, alert to an opportunity to get the supplies she needed. She hoped to find a line camp where cowboys lived so she could take a horse and other supplies without so great a threat of pursuit.

▼

It took several weeks of living on roots, cactus fruits, and the birds she could kill with a flung stone before Lozen discovered the camp of three vaqueros tending to a scattered herd of cattle. They had fashioned a corral in a small canyon with an opening so narrow only one horse could pass through at a time. Nearby was a small adobe shed with a thatched roof, where they slept wrapped in their serapes. They kept their own horses in the small corral so they would have mounts to work with each morning. They had no dogs, Lozen noted hopefully. Each night, she slipped away from where Eclode and the baby were hidden and went to watch the vaqueros, seeking their weakness as though watching an enemy in a knife fight. She memorized every detail of the terrain and every reliable habit of the vaqueros and waited for the dark of the moon.

On the evening she had selected, she helped Eclode and the baby get ready to travel. She showed Eclode a certain narrow arroyo and told her to be waiting there at noon the following day. Then Lozen stole up on the camp of the vaqueros, waiting until everything was quiet and dark before she slipped into the corral. She spent the rest of the night in the corral with the horses, soothing them. She picked the strongest horse and charmed him to her. When she saw the first traces of dawn, she mounted the horse and lay across his back, soothing him and waiting. As the light strengthened and the vaquero came to move the corral's brush gate aside, she burst past him. He jumped back and in an instant she was past him and galloping. She reached the place where Eclode was waiting without difficulty and they rode hard all day to distance themselves from pursuit.

Lozen was nearly ready now to undertake the long journey across the desert to the Mescalero Reservation. Once again leaving the girl and the horses at a safe distance, she approached another water hole. This too was guarded, but most of the soldiers remained in their camp, with only one man patrolling. Maybe they had been there a long time and had grown careless, thinking no one would come. Nonetheless, she would have passed by the water hole except the guard carried a large canteen. So she stalked him and when he was far enough away from the others, she slipped up behind him and killed him with her knife. She took his canteen, saddle, gun, bullets, blanket, and shirt, and then went back to where Eclode and her baby were still hiding.

With the canteen, they could risk setting out across the desert for the Mescalero Reservation, as they could now go a long time between water holes. They traveled carefully for weeks, moving mostly at night and skirting the guarded water holes. The signs of the soldiers were evident everywhere and often they saw columns of soldiers passing at a distance, marked by a distinctive thin line of dust. So Lozen traveled slowly, taking few risks.

They slipped onto the reservation as quietly as a mountain lion walking across rocks. Finding the camp of Eclode's mother, they were greeted with such joy and surprise that Lozen concluded Eclode's family had given her up as dead a long time past. Lozen rested little awhile with the Mescalero, playing with the baby, which stirred a smothered yearning in her.

Nonetheless, she had just resolved to return as quickly as possible to the Chihenne when the news came and her life changed. Power turned against her.

CHAPTER XI

▼▼▼

Death and Revenge

October 1880

Victorio was dead.

Someone said the Mexicans had found the Chihenne at Tres Castillos, far into Mexico. Everyone had been killed except a small group off looking for ammunition and the rear guard, which had not yet come into camp when the Mexicans attacked.

Lozen did not believe the news. Why would Victorio have gone to Tres Castillos, a small lake ringed by three insignificant peaks in the middle of a great plain? Victorio did not know the place well and he would have to pass through a large expanse of open and dangerous territory to reach it. Even if he had, she could not believe the Mexicans could trap him. Only the Indian scouts working for the Americans had ever surprised the Chihenne. How could the Mexicans alone strike a fatal blow, even if they were fighting with their Indian allies? Surely this was just another rumor on its black, eager wings—raucous as a raven.

Nonetheless, she set out immediately to find the Chihenne, praying she would find her brother alive and they would laugh together at this latest news of his death—for the Americans and the Mexicans had bragged many times of killing him. She searched for weeks, visiting the places along both sides of the border Victorio liked to camp. She had a riding horse and a pack-horse, so she could carry enough supplies and water to move freely without risking an attack on settlements. In some places, she found signs of her People, even some messages in the placement of certain pebbles and twigs alongside the trail. By these signs she knew a raiding party of Chihenne was moving about, going back and forth over the border. Finding the trail, she held to it— her hopes rising like quail from cover.

Then, one day, she looked up and saw Nana riding slowly to meet her. She sat motionless on her horse for a long time as he approached, telling herself Victorio was off raiding, or the bands scattered, although she knew from Nana's manner that the rumors were all true.

She camped that night with all that remained of her People— fewer than twenty warriors and a handful of women and children.

She heard from them the terrible story of the death of the Chihenne, who had paid this terrible price for yearning after their own homes. After she had left them, the Chihenne moved south into Mexico. To their dismay, the American soldiers and the scouts continued to chase them across the border. Moreover, they encountered many signs the Mexicans were gathering an army, so they seemed caught between two stones. Knowing the soldiers would look for them in the mountains, Victorio led them out onto a great plain toward Tres Castillos.

Victorio had called the headmen together to consider what they should do. He said to them,[1] *For a short time we may be comparatively safe here. The cavalry will look for us in the moun-tains, not on this plain. We need rest badly. We need food. Always, of course, our great need is ammunition. The warriors are away on a raid; some of them are hunting. Tonight three of them came in with thirty head of cattle. The rest will not return until they bring supplies. The cattle can be butchered tomorrow and the meat cut for drying. In two days of this sunshine, meat cut thin should be ready to pack. On the plain to the northwest, this side of Tres Castillos, there is a small lake and good grass. Between the lake and the ridges we can camp and prepare for the long and difficult journey west across the wide plains to the Blue Mountains. Once we reach the foothills of the range we will find ample food and many horses. There I have supplies of blankets, clothing, and ammunition, cached for just such an emergency as this. Before starting there we must prepare enough food for the ride. We may have to travel fast. What do you suggest?*

They waited, respectful in their silence.

Nana? Victorio asked.

It is for my chief to decide, Nana replied.

I need the wise counsel of my father, said Victorio.

I have fought with three great chiefs of my people, Mangas Coloradas, Cochise, and Victorio. The problems confronting you are more difficult than either of the others had to meet. Your wisdom has never failed us. Command and we obey.

My father knows well that I do nothing for credit, said Victorio. *I seek only the preservation of my People. Without your wise planning we would have been destroyed long ago. Never have we been in desperate need of ammunition that my father has not supplied it. Again, we are almost without it. Speak, I say.*

Said Nana, *Will you permit me to take a few warriors and make a raid for it?*

But Victorio countered saying, *It will entail great risk. Nearly all the men are away, and there are few left to protect the women and children. It is I who should take that risk.*

Nana considered Victorio's words, then with the courtesy and indirection necessary in a discussion among proud equals, he asked, *Which needs protection more, the warriors or the women?*

My father is wise, returned Victorio, seeing Nana's point and the delicacy with which he managed to disagree. *We shall both remain with our People, one to serve in the advance guard, the other the rear. Select a warrior for leading the raid for ammunition. He must be wise enough not to take unnecessary risk, but daring enough not to return empty-handed. Choose.*

Blanco, said Nana without hesitation.

Blanco, said each of the other leaders in turn.

Then Blanco it is, said Victorio. *He holds our lives in his hand. Select your men, Blanco, and notify them tonight to be ready to leave before dawn.*

So Victorio took charge of the advanced guard and Nana took a party of warriors and remained some miles in the rear of the slowly moving column of women and children.

Lozen listened with her face held expressionless as befits a warrior, but one thought inflicted a wound like a knife driven into bone. If she had been with them, Victorio would have asked her to conduct her ceremony—turning to the four directions in the watching circle of warriors. Perhaps as she faced Tres Castillos, she would have sensed their doom and turned them aside. But she was not with them. She had been turned to another path, for reasons only Ussen could explain, and the long, dark silence of the might-have-beens gathered now around her like the chindi spirits of the dead at the place of their killing.

So the advanced guard led by Victorio, followed by the women and the children, all rode unsuspecting into the trap set for them. Earlier, they had stolen a horse herd belonging to Joaquin Terrazas, a powerful man in Chihuahua. They had heard rumors he was raising an army, a group of soldiers going to each village in the region for more recruits. His army also recruited many Indians—especially the Tarahumara, longtime enemies of the People. But Victorio thought Terrazas's army was hunting them in the mountains.[2]

The Chihenne reached Tres Castillos just at sunset, the shallow lake glittering in the last light of the day. They unsaddled their weary horses—setting them loose to regain their strength by grazing on the good grass around the base of Tres Castillos. Suddenly, the Mexicans began firing on them.

People scattered, but many ran into the guns of the Mexicans. Victorio rallied his few warriors, but Nana and the rear guard were still miles away and other warriors were with either Blanco searching for ammunition or Kaytennae on a hunting party. The warriors fought back as best they could, although they had little ammunition. People were running everywhere, with the Mexicans chasing after them—killing even women and children where they found them. The soldiers closed in on Victorio and his warriors as they moved up to the southernmost peak of Tres Castillos. Darkness fell and the Mexicans surrounded them on all sides, so they could not escape during the night. The warriors rushed the Mexicans, but were thrown back. Then they lit a signal fire, to which Nana replied. But Terrazas sent a strong force to scatter the warriors drawn to Nana's signal fire, so they could bring no help to Victorio. The end came shortly after first light. Victorio and his closest warriors made a last stand and when they were out of ammunition they killed themselves with their own knives.[3] The last two warriors, who had barricaded themselves in a cave, held out for another two hours, disdaining demands for their surrender.

Not many escaped except the warriors who had been with Nana and Kaytennae and Blanco. All told, the Mexicans killed seventy-eight people, sixty-two of them warriors. They also took sixty-eight prisoners, plus two young Mexican boys the Chihenne had taken captive to be raised as warriors; 120 horses; thirty-eight mules; and a dozen burros. They made bonfires and burned many of the bodies. Then the Mexicans separated fifteen boys close to a warrior's age. Knowing what was coming, one of the boys encouraged the others saying, *Let us remember we are the People and show them how men can die.* Then the Mexicans killed the boys, shooting them one by one as their mothers and sisters listened.[4]

The shattered remnants of the Chihenne gathered after the battle, Nana going with his force of seventeen warriors to the rendezvous point. Only a few managed to slip away from the battle and crawl through the soldiers in the darkness and escape—including young Kaywaykla and his mother, Gouyan. Nana followed one of the columns of soldiers, hoping to free the prisoners who would be sold as slaves in Mexico. But they could only free one girl. So they rode away, weeping for all they had lost. Only Nana seemed to care whether he lived or died and spent weeks after the massacre gathering up stragglers and accumulating supplies, determined to mount a revenge raid.

▼

Lozen listened to all of this, holding tight to her face as her heart cracked in her chest. The thing that had hunted her all her life had finally found her, broken her open, and licked the marrow out of her bones—leaving her, unaccountably, alive. She could not contain the grief and the anger, but she had no place to put it. It was a lake of loss without an end, like the ocean she had seen once far down in Mexico where parrots flocked in the trees. Why had Ussen left her alive and taken everything else? Of what use now was courage or Power or strength—with the People dead? How could she go on, day after day, never more speaking her brother's name?

If not for Nana, Lozen might have lacked the will to ever wake up again or might have gone looking for some enemy who could send her to the Happy Place to catch up with her brother, who had hurried on ahead, not waiting.

Only Nana still seemed unbroken.

Victorio died as he lived, free and unconquerable,[5] said Nana with such certainty they could feel his strength seeping into them as water into dry sand. *We knew well the fate of Mangas Coloradas and of Cochise,* said Nana. *They too would have preferred death in battle; they would have envied Victorio. So, we are not to mourn for him. He has been spared the ignominy of imprisonment and slavery and for that I will give thanks to Ussen. His courage is to be the inspiration of those left to carry on our race and fortunately there are enough women and children that our People might increase. It is for us to rally and carry on the struggle.*

Then Kaytennae spoke, bitter and heartbroken, saying it was his fault because he had come back too late with ammunition.

Nana comforted him, saying, *It is not too late as long as one of the People lives. Now it is for the living to see that our tribe is not exterminated. We must live. We must carry on the fight.*

Lozen listened to him, numb with grief and guilt. But she knew Nana was right. Human beings were small creatures in the hands of great Powers. They could not turn aside their fate or even understand its necessity any more than an ant can comprehend a horse as it crawls through its mane. They could only fight and hope for a good death. Victorio had done everything in his power to find a safe place for his People, but he had found death instead. But then, death awaits everyone. You can put it off for a while, but the debt of life always demands repayment. Once, she had hoped to unlock Ussen's riddle in her dreams. Now she could only endure—finding solace only in revenge. And who could say? Perhaps some contentment would one day seep back into her dead heart.[6]

So Lozen and the remaining Chihenne prepared again to do the only thing that they knew: to fight and die as warriors.

▼

That night Nana gathered them to tell the old stories about Child of Water and how he killed the monsters and made the world safe for the People. Each time, Child of Water set out with prayer and a few weapons and his courage. Each time, he faced monsters that seemed unbeatable. Each time, he trusted his Power and listened to the advice of others who might help him. And each time, he overcame impossible difficulties.

Nana reminded them of how Child of Water had prayed to Ussen so the great arrows of the giant would miss him and his own small arrows would pierce the giant's heart. Or the time Child of Water had wrapped himself in the hide of the deer so Giant Eagle would take him up into his nest where Child of Water could kill the Eagle with his club. Or the time Lizard helped Child of Water kill the Giant Antelope that destroyed with its eyes. The old stories smoothed her mind and eased her grief and she understood why Nana told the stories. He sought to teach and counsel them, never offering direct criticism, only repeating things the ancient ones had said. So she listened, letting the stories soothe her.

After finishing the stories of Child of Water, Nana said, *Every difficulty prepares you for the next test. It is not good for people to have an easy life. They become weak and inefficient when they cease to struggle. Some need a series of defeats before developing the strength and courage to win a victory.*[7]

▼

The Chihenne took refuge in Juh's camps in the high Sierra Madre, living as the First People had done on deer and the gifts of White Painted Woman. Slowly, Nana rebuilt his strength—collecting warriors, praying, gathering supplies. He took the warriors on expeditions, relying on Lozen's Power to keep them out of the path of their enemies. They even went into New Mexico to visit Ojo Caliente, a homecoming that mingled joy and sorrow. Lozen felt the old places embrace her, as though they had been waiting for the People's return. She said each place-name as they drew near. She felt the wisdom sitting in those places, patient and ancient. She could hear the voices of the ancient ones who had named each place. She felt the stories pressing against her, like the voice of the storyteller through the long winter nights. She saw also that the land was empty, with only a few scattered ranches—a few huddled settlements. It made no sense: Why had the White Eyes taken this land from the Chihenne if they did not need it themselves? The Chihenne had killed many White Eyes fighting for their land—a price the whites had paid even though they did not really want Ojo Caliente, for now it stood as empty as a wickiup after a death. But who could know why the White Eyes did as they did?

They stayed a few days at Ojo Caliente, bathing in the sacred springs, rubbing their skin with fine sand and then soaking in the steaming waters for hours while sentries stood in high places watching for the approach of their enemies. Then they returned to Mexico to gather warriors and supplies before setting out to fulfill their obligation of revenge.

▼

They began raiding—not the careful raids to obtain supplies, but revenge raids to kill as many Mexicans as possible. They haunted the area around Carrizal, since many of the soldiers who had fought came from that town. They ambushed a detachment of nine soldiers, killing every man. One of the soldiers had a saddle that had belonged to Victorio, so they cut his body into little pieces and scattered it about so that even in the next life he would be in bits and pieces. That felt good, but it was like striking a blow in a dream when the sound does not come back to your ears. So they continued, never remaining more than a night in one place and killing anyone they encountered. Lozen did not count the dead as the White Eyes loved to do, but she knew the total soon far exceeded all those the Mexicans had killed at Tres Castillos.[8]

Lozen's Power came slowly back to her as they raided and she cleared her mind and released the anger and the grief through the killing of the Mexicans. Nana led them without flinching and without outward signs of grief, as sure and calm as water in a great river. So when he said they should turn north and raid in the United States, no one hesitated. They were all in the grip of Nana's Power and confident in Lozen's Power, so they did not fear even the thousands of soldiers and the scouts who rode with them. They crossed the Rio Grande with perhaps fifty warriors and moved toward the Mescalero Reservation where another twenty-five joined them.[9] After that, they moved back and forth through the country as they pleased for two months in the Season of Many Leaves,[10] covering three thousand miles. They slept in their saddles. They rode their horses to death, cut out a few strips of meat, then stole fresh mounts from the next ranch or from the next unwary cavalry detachment set out to find them.

Thousands of soldiers chased them, but they may as well have tried to catch the wind in their hands. Seven times the warriors turned to fight—each time standing their ground and inflicting serious damage before they slipped away without the loss of a single warrior. They moved across the land like a summer storm, killing many White Eyes, taking hundreds of horses, and laughing each night at the efforts of all the soldiers to stop them.

They seemed invincible, caught up in the hands of Nana's Power like children carried across a stream. At first, Lozen wondered in her grief why the Power that helped them now had abandoned Victorio at Tres Castillos. But gradually in the danger and the prayer and the hardships of the raid, she let go of her questions and her anger at Power. She even finally let go of the helpless wish she might have gone on to the Happy Place with her brother instead of being left behind with so little hope.

When they had enough ammunition and horses and blood, Nana turned them again into Mexico. Many of the Mescalero returned then to their reservation, leaving only the remnants of the Chihenne and some warriors of other shattered bands. Nana led them far to the south, where not even the Mexicans would expect them. They pushed down into a jungle, with brilliantly colored birds in the tangle of trees and vines and strange flowers blooming in the wet, oppressive heat.

Finally they held council to determine what to do. They had been fighting and fleeing for nearly a year since the death of Victorio and the others. They had satisfied their immediate need for revenge, but they had only a few women and children with them and they were living always in strange places. Some of the warriors had a long time back sent their families to live on the reservation in safety—some families were at the Mescalero and some were on the White Mountain Apache Reservation. These warriors yearned now to see their wives and their children. Other warriors had no wives and children, but they wanted to go back to the reservation where they could have families. The White Eyes did not know them by name and they were so few now that they could go quietly back to the reservation without notice. Perhaps the scouts would know them, but Nana said he did not think the scouts would betray them to the soldiers now that Victorio was dead.

So they talked a long time about what to do, as the longing for their families grew. Lozen thought Nana could probably fight forever and could never live contentedly in the cage of the reservation, nor did she have much interest in the reservation—for she drifted along like a puff of dandelion on the wind, running and fighting. But both Nana and Lozen saw the shift in the thinking of the warriors and so it was decided by the quiet growth of consensus they should go back to the reservation and see how things stood.

They went back calmly, not along a bloody path as they had before. They slipped onto the reservation, making their camp a little apart, except for the warriors who went off to find their families.

Lozen felt that her grief had burned down finally to ashes.

Perhaps they might put down their rifles and live peacefully now.

Perhaps the White Eyes had taken enough from them and would let them live in the one place they had left.

Perhaps she would turn off the path that had brought her only this pain and loss and hopeless struggle and live as a woman.

Now she would try to do as the White Eyes had always said she must and live in the place they had told her to live, fighting no more.

Why should they not let her do that now, with everything gone?

CHAPTER XII

▼▼▼

Death of a Prophet

Spring 1881

Nana, Kaytennae, and Lozen led the handful of remaining warriors and their few wives and children back to the San Carlos Reservation, selecting an isolated campsite as far as possible from the scrutiny of the agent and well away from the bands who had helped hunt Victorio. Some said they should go and live in the Black Mountains or someplace close to Ojo Caliente, but Nana said the White Eyes would never let them remain there; look what they had done to Victorio who had wanted nothing else. Not even the White Eyes would be inconsistent enough to let them stay there now. Instead, they should settle at San Carlos where they could rest, accumulate food and supplies, and reunite the families of the warriors. Perhaps they could recruit other warriors if they must leave again. Or perhaps they could live peacefully once they settled in a place that not even the greedy White Eyes coveted.

So they remained at San Carlos carefully and quietly, finding that even Geronimo and Juh had settled there. Nana and Lozen went to their camp and talked to them and Lozen decided they were like Nana—waiting and watching but unbroken.

San Carlos was as bad a place as ever, although they had a better spot than the last time they lived there. Everyone knew that the agent, Tiffany, was stealing most of their supplies, for he sent whole wagons loaded with goods off the reservation. He fixed the scales so a steer so scrawny you could count every rib gained three hundred pounds upon delivery. When the White Mountain headmen complained to Tiffany, he locked eleven up in jail for many months—and everyone waited the whole time to see if he would hang them. The army officers did nothing, only came running with their guns whenever Tiffany called them. General Crook, whom the People called Grey Fox, was a good fighter and an honorable enemy, but he had gone away to fight the Sioux. So there was no strong man and no one they could trust to keep a promise.

▼

Then the agent ordered all of the White Mountain bands to move from their beautiful, well-watered land near Fort Apache down onto the disease-ridden flats around the San Carlos agency. No one knew why they had to move. Some said the White Eyes were angry because other bands continued to do a little raiding in the area. Some said the White Eyes just wanted to save some money by concentrating the bands. Others said the White Eyes wanted the good land in the mountains.

Lozen heard this with some mingling of disbelief and satisfaction. The White Mountain chiefs had been the head dogs in the pack that had run down the Chihenne. Sometimes, Lozen could almost understand their motive. The White Mountain chiefs had resolved to do anything necessary to hang on to their own lands, whose hills remembered them, whose places shaped them, and whose Power sustained them. So they had welcomed the White Eyes and refused to fight, even when provoked. They had even urged their warriors to work for the army to hunt down the Tontos and chase the Chiricahua and harry the Chihenne. But after all that, the White Eyes had not taken away their land and sent them to live at San Carlos like all the rest. The army let just one White Mountain band keep living near the fort, so they would still have enough warriors to act as scouts. This started feuds among the White Mountain bands. In that feuding, the chiefs Diablo and Eskiole were killed by their own people. Lozen gathered in all of this news, shaking her head. She knew the White Mountain People were now finally getting what they deserved, like a man who stomps on a snakeskin and laughs. But she found herself wondering how they had all come to this, killing one another and losing the places that had made them the People.

Then she began to hear about dances held by a chief of the White Mountain People, a medicine man named Nocadelklinny, also known as the Prophet because he said he had visions of times yet to come. At first, she did not pay much attention. After all, the Prophet had been a scout for General Crook when he hunted down the Tontos, who had been forced to move to San Carlos where they dwindled from disease and hopelessness like everyone else. People said Nocadelklinny had gone to Washington, met with the Great Father, and received a great peace medal that he wore as a symbol of his authority. So at first, Lozen did not think such a man had anything to say that might interest her.

But the stories about the dances kept coming back to her, so her curiosity rose like the head of an antelope from the grass. People said Nocadelklinny had great Power and that the dead chiefs had appeared to him in a vision and promised they would return and drive the White Eyes from their land. Lozen felt a surge of fear and hope when she heard this, remembering her brother with such force she scarcely had room in her chest for breath.

The Prophet's Ghost Dances went on for days, with the dancers in a trance of Power so they could dance through the day and the darkness and back again into the day. People from many bands came, dancing as though they were from the same band. After a time, people said the Ghost Dances had healed the wounds dividing the White Mountain bands and had begun even to unite the other warring bands that had been thrown all together in the dark sack of San Carlos.

The Chihenne remained apart for some time as the stories about the Ghost Dances came back to them, for they had more reason than most to hate the White Mountain bands and the scouts. None believed in Nocadelklinny's Power, but they could see that a great excitement ran back and forth through the scattered camps of the People, like a frightened sentry. Nana said Nocadelklinny was telling warriors they need not fight the White Eyes, for Ussen would drive them out before the corn ripened. So Nana said the Prophet was simply a creature of the White Eyes, stalking the fighting spirit of the warriors like a hunter in an antelope skin. The Ghost Dances and the Prophet's dangerous talk about dead warriors coming back from the Happy Place were all tangled up with the Jesus Way of the White Eyes. The Prophet was only leading people on, collecting gifts and wearing away their warrior's spirit, like water running across sandstone. But at last Nana said they should go to one of the dances to see what was happening with their own eyes. Juh, Geronimo, and Lozen agreed to go, perhaps out of curiosity.

Watching the Ghost Dances warily, Lozen found herself unexpectedly moved.[1] The Prophet had an air of great Power, a certainty, serenity, and calm that came from wisdom—his mind was quiet, free of pride and fear. Lozen was struck also by the spirit running through the dancers. She had never seen warriors from so many bands gathered in one place, dancing side by side without paying attention to clans or bands or feuds. They danced in great circles, one inside the other, with the Prophet in the center. The

Chihenne and Juh and Geronimo stood aside, impressed at the unity of the warriors, but afraid the Prophet had such influence already that the warriors might give up fighting and wait passively for the deliverance he promised.

Near dawn, the Prophet left the circle of dancers and came to where Nana waited, watching. Nana and the Prophet talked for a moment, then Juh, Nana, and the Prophet walked away from the others up into the shoulders of the hills where a cold, gray fog had gathered. A dim glow of dawn appeared and Lozen thought perhaps they were going to pray together to the dawn. So she sat down facing east and offered up her gratitude to Ussen for the light, remembering as she prayed how the birds had played the moccasin game against the beasts and the monsters for the light.

Lozen waited a long while for the three to return. When they did come back, she was surprised to see a change in Nana and Juh. Lozen went to Nana, greeting him gravely and studying his face for a moment longer than was polite before dropping her gaze. She longed to know what had happened with the Prophet off in the fog, but she would not be rude by asking a direct question. The Chihenne gathered around him, along with the Chiricahua who had come with Juh and Geronimo, waiting for the leaders to speak.

Nana said the Prophet had asked them to join him in prayer and they had agreed warily, anxious to understand his appeal and see the trick in it. The Prophet led them up the hill and then fell to his knees and prayed for a long time, with Nana and Juh watching warily. After a time, it seemed the fog thickened and swirled around them in a peculiar way. Nana said he could feel Power gathering, seeping out of the ground. In the mist, he saw three figures rise out of the ground. Filled with fear and eagerness, he watched the figures take form. By the time they had risen to nearly their full height, with their legs below the knees still caught in the earth, Nana could recognize Cochise, Mangas Coloradas, and Victorio.

A murmur, astonished and fearful, passed through the listening warriors, like a breeze across a still pond. Lozen felt her heart fall, as from a high place. Everyone leaned forward, hungry as wolves for the next words. So Nana continued.

One of the three chiefs turned to the Prophet, saying, *Why have you disturbed us?*

The Prophet answered in fear and respect, *The White Eyes are everywhere in our lands. Tell us what we must do.*

Then the chiefs answered, *Live in peace with the White Eyes and let us be.*

Then they sank back down into the earth.

Everyone wondered at the story and Lozen felt a surge of loss and joy and yearning, wishing she could have seen her brother one more time and glad he had made it across to the Happy Place. Still, she wondered at what had been said, scarcely believing Victorio would urge them to live in this terrible place when he had given up his own life rather than lose the place that had made him. Perhaps it was as the Prophet had promised: They need only wait for Ussen to return to them what had been taken.

▼

After that, Nana spoke to everyone in favor of the Prophet, converted by his vision. Even Juh and Geronimo decided to stop recruiting warriors and to see what the Ghost Dances brought. Nana took the Chihenne to camp near Cibecue, where the Prophet usually camped and held the Ghost Dances.

One day during the dance, a force of scouts who worked for the agent arrived in the camp, well armed and nervous. They said they had orders to take the Prophet back to Fort Apache, because Agent Tiffany did not want him to hold any more dances. When the warriors heard this, they began calling to their relatives and soon an angry crowd of warriors surrounded the scouts. The scouts grew fearful, seeing that many of their friends and relatives were gathered in the crowd around them. The warriors took away the scouts' guns and sent them running back to the fort, scurrying like Coyote.

Later, a runner came saying a large force of soldiers and scouts from Fort Apache were coming up Cibecue Creek toward the camp of the Prophet. Everyone gathered excitedly, trying to decide what to do. Only the Prophet seemed calm, sitting in front of his wickiup with his wife and son. He calmed the warriors, saying neither the soldiers nor the scouts could hurt him. The Prophet said his medicine had made him bulletproof, which was something people said Geronimo could also do. So they all resolved to wait for the soldiers, trusting in the Prophet's medicine.

But Sanchez, who had fought alongside Victorio and had been a captive among the Mexicans, jumped on his horse and rode boldly out to meet the soldiers. He went up to them, brave and arrogant. Lozen thought perhaps Sanchez wanted the soldiers to shoot at him so the Prophet would not wait foolishly for arrest. But the soldiers did not shoot at Sanchez, so he rode boldly down their ranks, counting them and making note of their weapons.

Some of the scouts rode ahead, coming along bravely although they knew many people would like to kill them for leading the soldiers here. One scout named Mose, a respected White Mountain man, told the Prophet the soldiers just wanted to take him to the fort to ask some questions about the dances because he had refused to come when summoned. Mose was sure that once the nantan discovered the Prophet had urged all of the warriors to stop fighting the nantan would let him go.

So the warriors gathered around the Prophet's camp, but they did nothing to hinder the approach of the soldiers. When he arrived, the nantan talked to the Prophet, who was calm and unafraid. The Prophet smiled and said he would come to the fort in a few days when he finished the dance. But the nantan replied roughly and without respect that the Prophet would have to come with the soldiers right away. Even then, the Prophet smiled and said he would come along with them as soon as he finished his lunch and as soon as his son brought his horse. Lozen admired how the Prophet handled the matter. He seemed in control of things although he was small, frail, and surrounded by soldiers bristling with guns like the quills of a porcupine.

The nantan agreed to let the Prophet finish his lunch and then took most of his soldiers a few miles back down the creek, picking a place near the river with ground that could be defended if necessary. He left behind some soldiers and scouts under the command of an officer who had come only recently and knew so little about everything that everyone called him The Green One.[2] The Green One quickly grew impatient and one soldier grabbed the Prophet by the arm to force him to leave. The watching warriors might have fought the soldiers right then, but the steadiness of the Prophet's manner calmed them. He said he would go with the soldiers without trying to escape and he wanted no fighting on his behalf. So the soldiers and scouts rode with the Prophet back downstream to the main camp of the soldiers.

More warriors gathered at every moment and Lozen rode along with Sanchez, following the soldiers, always keeping the Prophet in sight and admiring the way he rode so unafraid, as though he were out riding for pleasure.

They took the Prophet into the soldiers' camp, which had been made on good ground in a clear space with the scouts camped to one side. Sanchez, Lozen, and several other warriors rode to the edge of the soldiers' camp so the nantan would see the warriors were nearby and would not hang the Prophet—or cut off his head and boil it in a pot. One of the officers walked crisply toward them along with another soldier, shouting at the warriors in the language of the People to go away.

Suddenly, a shot rang out. Lozen, who was watching the approaching nantan, did not see who started the shooting. Maybe it was Sanchez, who was very angry. But she thought it more likely the soldiers started the shooting, since many were young, green, and frightened. In any case, the air filled with bullets that buzzed past her head like bees from a shattered hive. The officer and his soldier fell immediately and in an instant everything was confusion. The scouts mostly ran away so they would not be trapped between the soldiers and their own People. Lozen thought some of the scouts also started shooting at the soldiers, but she wasn't sure.[3] Her attention was focused on an army mule loaded with ammunition boxes, for the mule had broken away from the soldiers in all the shooting. Now her Power, which had rested uneasily while she was living peacefully on the reservation, came and stood beside her so she knew immediately what she should do.

She lay down across her horse's neck so it would seem her horse was riderless and running in a panic. Then she kicked her horse into a run toward the mule, passing safely through the pelting of bullets. She barely slowed as she reached the mule, leaning far over to the mule's lead rope. She turned her horse, hoping the mule would not try to break away. But her Power was with her, even her Horse Power, so the mule turned easily and broke into a run that jostled the boxes of ammunition as they galloped back toward the shelter of the trees along the creek.

The soldiers tried to kill the Prophet as soon as the fighting started, but the Prophet wore a medicine shirt he had prepared with the help of ceremonies his Power had taught him. His Power told him that as long as he wore that shirt and acted in a right way no bullet could kill him. His wife, who was with him in the soldier camp, begged him to run away, but the Prophet said there was no use in running. A soldier shot him and he fell as though dead. But after a while, he got up again and began crawling away. So another soldier ran over to shoot him again. The Prophet's wife threw herself over his body and begged for his life, but the soldier shot him anyway. He lay on the ground a little longer, then woke up and began crawling away again. The Prophet's son rode bravely in through the soldiers to reach his father, but they shot him dead off his horse. Then a soldier put his gun against the Prophet's head and fired, but that could not kill him either because of his medicine. So finally a soldier split his head open with an ax, which was a blow the Prophet's Power could not protect him against. Seeing her husband and her son both dead, the Prophet's wife ran to one of the soldier's horses to pull the rifle from its saddle holster, so the soldiers killed her as well.

The warriors continued shooting at the trapped soldiers as long as the light held, killing only seven of them, but making off with more than fifty horses and mules—together with three thousand rounds of ammunition. With the Prophet dead, the various bands of warriors had no central leader and each fought separately. Some sent word to other bands, hoping to bring help. Others slipped away, knowing more soldiers would come. Many kept shooting to delay the escape of the soldiers. Finally, though, the soldiers slipped away during the night and the warriors let them go—partly because there was never much use in killing soldiers that grew back like spring grass. The warriors had to content themselves with digging up the dead soldiers left behind and demonstrating their anger and contempt on their corpses. Some warriors went to attack Fort Apache, shooting into the fort from a long distance and even running up to a few of the buildings to try to start a fire. But there was not much sense in fighting a fort either, as it would only cost the lives of good warriors without accomplishing anything. Mostly, people went back to their camps and waited to see what the soldiers would do.

▼

Soldiers poured into the reservation in the weeks that followed, searching for the scouts who had run away and for the leaders of the fight at Cibecue. Geronimo and Juh went in to talk to the agent at San Carlos, who said everything would be all right. He said the soldiers mostly blamed the scouts who had turned against them and some of the White Mountain leaders—but that the Chihenne and Chiricahua bands had done nothing wrong and had nothing to fear. But the soldiers continued going back and forth across the reservation, pushing rumors ahead of their coming until most of the scouts who had run away turned themselves in. The army had a trial and hung three of them—respected White Mountain men. Many White Eyes came to see the hanging, as though it were a social dance.

Juh, Geronimo, Naiche, and many of the Chiricahua also left the reservation—taking all the horses they needed and killing everyone they encountered as they fled south toward the Sierra Madre.

The remnants of the Chihenne decided it was only a matter of time until the soldiers came for them as well, and so they slipped away from the reservation and headed south for Mexico.[4] The Chihenne passed quietly through Arizona, making for the sanctuary of the Sierra Madre on the trail of rumors Geronimo had joined Juh and the Nednhi and Chiricahua in their last, best hiding places.

Once, they saw the long smudge of dust that represented a mule train coming toward them, very different from the long, thin line of dust raised by a column of soldiers. A wagon train makes a great billow. This dust cloud was between the two—so Nana decided they should set an ambush. The line of mules with their drivers walked stolidly into the ambush and the warriors killed the drivers easily. The load on the mules was heavy and compact and everyone assumed Nana's Power had led them to a pack train loaded with ammunition, the most valuable thing they could find. They quickly drove the mules on, changing direction so they would be harder to follow. When they reached a safe place, they opened the packs. Nana opened the first pack and dug down in, until a look of disgust came over his seamed face. He pulled a heavy bar of silver from the pack and threw it to the ground in disgust.

Silver, Nana snorted contemptuously.

No ammunition, said Sanchez, keenly disappointed.

Nana snorted, *After all this waste of time and life and bullets! This worthless stuff.*

We have the mules and the ammunition in the belts of the dead men, said Sanchez. He hefted one of the bars, as long as a man's arm and very heavy. Then he added, *If we could get this to Casas Grandes, we could trade it to the Mexicans for things of value to us. It is too heavy to move unless we trudge beside the mules. We might be attacked and forced to leave it. But if each man took two or three bars to trade for bullets . . .*

But Nana answered in a voice heavy with disgust, *Instead of ammunition, he would get mescal and be killed.*

Sanchez dropped the bar, knowing it was true. He asked, *Then why not bury it? We might come back for it some time.*[5]

So they buried the bars of silver. That night, Nana talked of other places where there was gold and silver, great veins of it, or caches left by White Eyes who had never returned. But Nana had no interest in such things, knowing Ussen had forbidden these worthless metals—too soft to be used even as bullets.

They went quietly into the Sierra Madre to a Nednhi camping spot. Nana sent out runners to find Juh and to unite the bands. The Nednhi came just at sundown, with Juh leading on a sturdy warhorse. Although Nana himself was six feet tall and muscled like an ironwood root, Juh towered over him—a great slab of a man, like a piece of granite too big to move. His braided hair fell to his knees and his features were broad, angled, and fierce.

Nana and Juh greeted each other warmly. They were much alike, both war leaders of great Power, wisdom, and confidence. With Juh was his wife, Ishton, who was also Geronimo's sister. Lozen and Ishton greeted each other, because they had known each other for a long time and because they had much in common. Ishton was a strong and insightful woman, with great wisdom and insight. Everyone knew Juh relied on her, even in planning his strategy and deciding when to move and where to camp. She did not ride with the warriors, like Lozen, but she was a good shot, a strong woman and respected by the warriors. She also created a strong bond between Juh and Geronimo. Lozen had heard Ishton had nearly died in childbirth, but Geronimo had prayed for four days as she labored. In the praying, his Power had promised him Ishton's life and also that he would be bulletproof and die an old man. So Lozen and Ishton talked together, sharing news of relatives and friends. They began preparations for a feast, relishing the chance to dance, sing, tell stories, and pretend they were still as they had been. Then He Who Steals Love, a Mexican captive whom Nana had raised, came running to say another group of warriors was approaching, their faces heavily painted.

Why the war paint? Nana asked Juh. The Chihenne also painted their faces, usually a single red stripe from which they had taken their name, but not when riding quietly into one of their own camps.

Geronimo, replied Juh, smiling. *He likes to scare the Mexicans. He hates them with an intensity hardly believable. He rides prepared for battle. Let's play a joke on him.*

So they quickly put out their small fires and everyone hid along the walls of the winding canyon. Geronimo rode at the head of a band of warriors, taking no precautions. He was a squat, powerful man with an insolent air of power, reflected by deep, black, dangerous eyes and a grim mouth like a knife slash across his face. Often in times past Lozen had resented him, for Geronimo's anger and hatred had driven him to stir up trouble. But now she could sense his Power and admire his strength, seeing they had lost everything except the courage to seek a warrior's death. Along with Geronimo was Naiche, a tall, slender man who rode with grace and skill. Naiche, the son of Cochise, was liked by everyone, because he was a kind, courageous man who loved to sing, make things with his graceful hands, joke, laugh, and tell stories. His face was light and handsome and unpainted. His warriors and all of the women loved him, but he had no Power and so relied heavily on Geronimo in war.

When Geronimo dismounted, Nana rose from his hiding place. *Welcome to my trap,* laughed Nana.

I knew all the time you were here, replied Geronimo, masking his surprise masterfully.

You did not, said Nana. *And you the sly fox of the Apache!*

So with much joking and laughter, which Geronimo at first took with bad grace, they relit the fires and continued their preparations for a feast. They gathered in a circle and the drummers and the singers faced to the east and began playing and singing while the warriors retired to the brush to prepare themselves to dance their accomplishments. The women gathered around the circle of light from the fire, calling out the warriors by name and making the same shrill trilling White Painted Woman had made. Juh came in first, with his gorgeously beaded moccasins and the skullcap of a Nednhi medicine man. His men came along after him, each painted and dressed as their Power had directed. They danced four times around the fire as the singers called out their names and the women trilled their applause.

Then Juh moved to the singer's position alongside the drummers and began to sing in a strong, soft, hypnotic voice, completely free of the stutter that made him reluctant to speak in council. With brilliant rhythmic improvisation, he recounted the exploits of his warriors, weaving together the themes and repeated choruses in a strong voice. Then a cry went up around the circle for Nana and the old warrior danced out into the firelight, wearing no finery save the great decoration of his dignity and grace. Then cries came for Geronimo, fiercely painted and insolent as a mountain lion. After him came Perico, Geronimo's half-brother, then Eyelash and Yanozha, also half-brothers to Geronimo. Dancing into the firelight also came Fun, also a half-brother to Geronimo. Fun was an exuberant, fearless, headlong fighter who moved always to the place of greatest danger—laughing and joking as though he were a boy running a horse for the first time. Also with the Nednhi was Gordo, a Chihenne leader whose band had been nearly all killed, who rolled a cowhide shield out into the firelight and ran behind it, bent over so skillfully you could not see him behind the rolling shield. Chato was also with Geronimo, a fierce fighter and an ambitious man who had moved from band to band seeking honor and leadership.

Then Nana moved to the position of honor, since he was the host of the feast. He led the cries for Naiche and Mangus, the son of Mangas Coloradas who had leadership of a small Mimbres band and who was respected, although he had little of the Power of his father. Then Nana called out in his clear strong voice that one other great warrior had yet to be honored. Everyone turned to him, listening carefully, waiting.

She whom we had mourned as dead has returned to her People, said Nana. *Though she is a woman, there is no warrior more worthy than the sister of Victorio. Come my daughter.*[6]

Glad cries of acclaim swept around the circle, the women and the men equally proud, knowing how much she had lost and how much they relied on her. Lozen walked carefully into the circle of light, her head bowed, her eyes downcast. Cheers broke out again, bursting from every throat like quail exploding from the brush. Lozen could not speak. She could not look up. Tears glistened, unbidden, on her cheeks. She felt a flush of embarrassment—pride, grief, joy, and loss all tumbled together. She bowed her head and turned quickly to leave the center of this attention, but Nana stopped her, his voice low and tender. He said this was her due and they respected her no less because she was a woman. Then he asked her quietly if she could make medicine and tell them if there were any enemies near.

So Lozen stood in the center of the circle of their eyes and their hopes and their pride. She extended her arms, her palms up and slightly cupped, lifted up her face, and closed her eyes. For a moment, she wondered whether her voice would betray her, as her tears had done. But when she raised her voice, it was strong and clear. Turning slowly in the hushed circle of her People, Lozen sang:

> *Over all in this world*
> *Ussen has Power.*
> *Sometimes he shares it*
> *With those of this earth.*
> *This Power he has given me*
> *For the benefit of my People.*
> *This Power is good.*
> *It is good, as he is good.*
> *This Power I may use*
> *For the good of my People.*

Her palms felt cool in the night air, although she could feel still the flush in her cheeks. She opened her eyes, which glittered still with her unspilled tears, and looked at the waiting circle of warriors, the proud faces of the women, and the expectant faces of the children.

No enemy is near, she said quietly.

For that we thank Ussen, said Nana.

CHAPTER XIII

▼▼

The Great Gamble

Early 1882

Looking back a long while later, Lozen wondered why they had not remained quietly in the Sierra Madre, living on the food the women gathered, the deer the men could kill, and occasional raids among the Mexicans. She knew many of the women prayed for that, hoping they could hold on to the little bit they had left. As always, she was caught between the world of the women and the wars of the men so she drifted back and forth in her thinking—neither frog nor tadpole, but caught in between. Sometimes she wished she could be one or the other, instead of neither one. Still, she knew women better understood the cost of fighting than did men, who had felt the glory of it when their names were called out in the firelight. She understood, also, the need to fight—the need for pride. But she knew they were like the remnant of a war party trapped in a box canyon, left only a choice of deaths.

Once, Juh had a terrible dream. He saw a cave open in the face of a cliff and watched as an endless stream of soldiers rode out, as though created by the earth and sent out like ants. Juh said the vision proved they were doomed—that the soldiers could come against them without number so every victory of the People could only delay the end. Juh told his warriors he had nothing for them save hardship and danger and a good death. Lozen sensed also the truth of Juh's vision, for she understood death and loss. So even in the good times in the hidden places in the Sierra Madre, Lozen lived in the deep shadow of Juh's vision.

Small parties went out raiding, although they took care not to molest the Mexican settlements around Casas Grandes, with whom Juh had established a peace so he could trade for supplies. They went back to the arroyo where they had buried the silver, thinking they could take a few bars into Casas Grandes to trade for ammunition. But although they dug a long while where they had left it, they could not find it again. Nana watched the warriors digging. Lozen thought he looked pleased they had lost the silver, which was forbidden to them by Ussen.

Each band began to suffer losses, like water seeping from a canteen. One warrior, investigating an apparently empty camp, was shot and captured and dragged alive through cactus until it killed him. Other warriors were killed when they went into Casas Grandes and got drunk. Lozen noted the losses with growing concern, knowing they could not replace these experienced fighting men. Soon they would not have enough warriors to mount raids or defend their refuge in the Sierra Madre.

So her thoughts turned to Loco and to the other Chihenne in his band who had remained on the reservation. She heard Geronimo talking about the need for more warriors and Chato talked angrily about warriors who had lost their manhood on the reservation. So when the bands next gathered in the Sierra Madre, Geronimo called for a council to talk about what they should do. Many came, including Nana, Geronimo, Naiche, Juh, Fun, Lozen, and other leading warriors.[1] After they had eaten, Nana rolled wild tobacco in oak leaves and blew smoke in the four directions— making medicine so their talk would be good.

Then Geronimo began by saying, *Summer is near, already at San Carlos people are dying of hunger, heat, and insects. When winter comes, how many of Loco's people will live?*

Nana only shook his head.

So Geronimo continued: *They are our brothers. They are your brothers and mine. I was born at the headwaters of the Gila, as was Loco. Loco has nearly four hundred people with him. Of these, seventy-five are warriors. How many will die during the heat?*

Many, replied Nana.

They will suffer for food. They will suffer from bad water and the bites of the insects with the long beaks. They will die of that terrible sickness that causes people to shake like leaves in the wind and to burn one minute and freeze the next. The soldiers had tried to live in that place and could not. They put Loco's people there not to live but to die.

True, said Nana.

As he said it, Lozen remembered the terrible time she lived with Victorio on the Gila River in the summer when so many had died. That summer had set Victorio on his path, because he could not watch helplessly as his People died. She recalled it now with a mingling of anger and fear and a longing to see her brother's face one more time, or even to speak his name.

Geronimo continued, *Loco belongs with his People. He is Chihenne and he has by far the greater part of those who are still alive with him. Why should he not fight with you?*

He has neither arms nor ammunition, replied Nana.

I have caches that he may use, said Geronimo.

They all fell silent, letting the idea grow. Then Chato broke the silence with a sneer, saying, *Loco is a woman!*

Lozen looked at him, holding her face impassive. What did Chato know of the strength needed to be a woman?

Nana replied sternly, *Loco is a man and a warrior. Loco has always spoken for peace, because he thought it was the best way to protect his People. But he has killed a grizzly bear with only his knife and is both feared and respected.*

Enjuh, chorused the other warriors.

But Chato would not be silenced. *Loco sits idle drawing rations from the White Eyes while we do the fighting,* he said.

Nana spoke slowly, as though to a child, *Each Apache decides for himself whether or not he fights. We are a free people. We do not force men to fight as the Mexicans do. Forced military service produces slaves, not warriors.*

Enjuh, chorused the council.

Nana then looked to Geronimo, who was leader of the band in which Chato fought and so was responsible for him. Speaking to Geronimo and ignoring Chato, Nana continued. *As chief, Loco was obligated to accept the decision of his band. He, himself, was convinced that further resistance was useless, even as was the great Cochise. Loco has given his word not to leave the reservation. He will not break that promise,* said Nana.

He could be forced to leave, said Geronimo. *If he refuses, there will be the loss of many lives, for he has given his word.*

Always your People! Chato sneered.

Always my People, agreed Nana softly.

You, Broken Foot, do not fight, said Chato, using in anger the name no one used to Nana's face. *You win by ambush and strategy.*

There could be no higher praise, said Nana.

Geronimo grunted his approval and Lozen smiled, seeing how easily Nana turned aside Chato's thrusts. A leader who was reckless with the lives of his warriors would soon find no one willing to raid with him. There was no honor in a useless death, only shame for the leader and grief for the families.

Nana continued, *Loco will not leave San Carlos unless forced to do so.*

That can be done, Geronimo replied. *But it may cost both him and us lives. But it will cost more if he remains during the summer.*

Loco is intelligent, except for trusting the word of the White Eyes. He is not stupid. He too is acting for the interest of his People.

Geronimo then turned and addressed himself directly to Chato. *You are ambitious Chato. If you wish to become a chief, learn first to think of your People, second, respect for your superiors.*

Rebuked and angry as a coiled rattler, Chato strode from the council.

His chatter is of no importance, said Nana. *But the loss of a good fighting man is. And Chato is a fighter.*

He will fight with us so long as it is to his advantage, said Geronimo. *I marvel at your patience with him. I respect your position. Loco is your warrior since you took command of the Warm Springs. It is necessary that a competent man protect the helpless in your absence. All acknowledge your courage and ability. Will you take charge of those who remain here while we ride to San Carlos?*

Gladly, replied Nana.

Have you suggestions? asked Geronimo respectfully.

A feint at an ammunition raid while the main body of warriors rides to San Carlos, said Nana. *Distract the attention of the cavalry from the main purpose. Take Lozen and no other woman, for you will be burdened with noncombatants on the return trip. Your success depends on swiftness and surprise.*[2]

▼

They quickly began preparations for the great raid to free the Chihenne under Geronimo's leadership.[3] They gathered all of the ammunition and good guns and food so they could move quickly to the reservation, without stopping to hunt or raid. Lozen watched Geronimo carefully, seeing his strength and cleverness. He seemed like a character from the Coyote stories he loved to tell with such a flourish. Geronimo's strengths and flaws all seemed outsized. Some loved and revered him, others feared and distrusted him—but no one could ignore him. His arrogance and cruelty and strife had called down terrible things, as when his raiding had prompted the White Eyes to take Ojo Caliente away from the Chihenne. But she admired the way he continued without flinching. Lozen felt drawn to him, to the simplicity of his anger—although they had no true hope of victory or even escape.

They moved quietly along the Sierra Madre and back into Arizona. Geronimo did his best to prevent the warriors from taking any horses or killing anyone, for fear it would spread the alarm. He sent runners ahead to get things ready, but he did not want to give the soldiers any warning. Lozen rode with the leaders and Geronimo consulted her Power, as Victorio had done. Just inside Arizona, two warriors captured a small herd of horses and decided to take the horses back down into the Sierra Madre. Geronimo did not like the loss of the two men, as he had only about sixty warriors to bring away hundreds of people, many of them women and children who had been living on the reservation so long they would have a hard time keeping up. However, each warrior remained free to make his own decisions. Of course, had he known what trouble would come from the departure of the two warriors he might have ridden after them and cut their throats. But his Power did not warn him and they were set on their fatal path.

They approached the reservation without incident, until they came upon a sheep camp on the south side of Ash Flat.[4] They surrounded the camp, which was kept by Bes-Das, a Mexican who had once been a captive in Geronimo's band. Geronimo had traded him to George Sanders, a white rancher, so now Bes-Das was the rancher's chief herder. There were ten Mexican sheepherders together with their wives and four White Mountain men, including a well-regarded warrior named Bylas with his wife and children.

The Mexicans were terrified to find themselves surrounded by so many warriors, especially when they discovered that Geronimo led them. The warriors began killing sheep and Geronimo shot a pony and forced the Mexicans' women to prepare a meal for the war party. Bylas and his White Mountain men looked on, knowing they had some friends among the war party, but knowing also that many Chiricahua hated White Mountain men who had scouted for the army. Geronimo toyed with his prisoners, like a jaguar kitten with a crippled bird. He even made Bes-Das give him his fancy, embroidered shirt. Geronimo then ordered all of the Mexicans tied up, and with some of the warriors he went among the prisoners, dashing their brains out with clubs. When Geronimo discovered Bes-Das's nine-year-old son hiding in the long skirts of Bylas's wife, he drew back to kill the boy. But to everyone's surprise, Naiche put himself between Geronimo and the boy, saying they had killed enough people already. Everyone waited to see if Geronimo would strike Naiche, for the lust for killing had taken Geronimo by the throat. But he mastered himself, seeing the boy was not worth a fight with Naiche. So they left the boy with the wives of the White Mountain men and two warriors to guard them. Geronimo took the White Mountain warriors along so they could not spread the alarm.

They rode to the reservation in the darkness, stopping at a hidden place not far from Loco's camp. Geronimo sent runners to the reservation to warn people who had agreed to help to be ready at first light. Geronimo bragged that he had established a network of men to kill the forty warriors who served as the police for the White Eyes. Lozen doubted this was true, but she knew that with Geronimo almost anything was possible. Geronimo sang four songs that went on for much of the night, so Loco's people would sleep deeply.

When the morning light was just strong enough to see a pebble tossed into the air, they set out for Loco's camp. Geronimo told several men to find places the telegraph wires passed through trees so they could cut the wires and tie the ends together, making it hard for the soldiers to discover the breaks. The main body of warriors splashed across the river along which the Chihenne had camped, riding out of the trees just as people emerged from their wickiups. Geronimo rode up and down the riverbank, telling the warriors to shoot anyone who resisted. Loco protested that his warriors had few weapons, but Geronimo said Loco had no choice but to come and therefore would not be breaking his word to the White Eyes.

Loco's people hastily gathered up whatever they could carry, their few horses, and their few weapons and followed the Chiricahua out of camp. Lozen rode up and down the line of frightened people, reassuring them Nana was waiting in the Sierra Madre where they would be safe. She worried to see so many women and children, knowing many of the children had never been hunted. But she felt also a rising of hope, knowing they would be a free people again instead of a doomed remnant. By the time they were under way, they had perhaps one hundred warriors and three hundred or four hundred women and children. It seemed impossible they could move so many people safely through the net of soldiers thrown out to catch them, but Geronimo had great Power and Lozen felt her own Power moving in her, like a mountain lion behind a screen of bushes.

They hurried on all the faster when the rear guard came up, saying they had killed the nantan in charge of the reservation police force who had come into the camp to investigate the disturbance. Loco seemed grieved, saying the nantan was a good man and a friend to the People. But Lozen noted the Chihenne came along more willingly after that, knowing the killings made it too late to go back. They hurried on to good hiding places in the Gila Mountains and sent out warriors to capture horses and cattle. Everyone began making saddles from bundles of reeds, so when the raiding parties brought back horses they could put the slowest people on horseback. The warriors killed many White Eyes as they raided for horses and food so no one could spread news of their passing.

In the midst of these preparations, one of the Chihenne girls came into her time. The leaders considered what they must do and Lozen said they must stop long enough to have some ceremony for her.[5] Geronimo, who was himself a medicine man who revered the old ways, agreed that a ceremony would strengthen the spirit of the People and give White Painted Woman and the Gan an opportunity to give them guidance in this hour of desperate need. So they squeezed the four days of the ceremony into one day and for that time White Painted Woman sat among them and walked in the footprints of pollen drawn on the buckskin.

They moved on quickly, but the pause had given soldiers time to catch up. The rear guard ambushed a force of scouts and soldiers, killing four. They might have killed the rest, but reinforcements came up quickly. The much larger force of soldiers attacked the warriors, killing several men and pushing them back until they came up with the women and the children. But Geronimo's war Power was strong and the warriors rallied and drove off the soldiers, knowing they must trade their lives for more time so the women and children could flee.

They made a long night journey to the sacred Stein's Peak and camped near a spring there. Just at sunrise, scouts who had found them in the night began shooting. The warriors grabbed their weapons and the women and children fled in every direction. Kaytennae discovered another ambush of soldiers coming toward them from the east and called two Navajo men—little more than boys—to help him turn back the soldiers. Kaytennae, who was the best marksman among all the warriors and who had Power to dodge bullets, charged the soldiers with the two boys. The soldiers fell back, expecting a swarm of warriors. They shot one of the boys, but Kaytennae grabbed a cavalry horse and rode back to the wounded Navajo, who grabbed the tail of the horse and so was pulled back to the safety of the rocks around the camp. Lozen, Geronimo, Chato, Naiche, and the other leaders rallied the warriors and held off the soldiers until the women and children had escaped. Then the warriors scattered, leaving the soldiers with the empty bag of their campsite.

They fled southwest toward Mexico, but they halted at the edge of the flat San Simeon Valley. They could not cross such a place in the day, as the dust of their passing would draw every detachment of soldiers for a hundred miles, and they would be slaughtered on the plain. So they waited for darkness, then pushed on as quickly as possible—with forty miles to cover before daylight. Geronimo asked Lozen for her ceremony so they would not ride into their waiting enemies. Then she rode with him through the long night, as he watched the stars wheeling across the heavens. Just past the middle of the night, it seemed obvious they would not make it. They had too few horses and too many women and children. Certainly, the warriors could take the horses or break into the ground-eating trot of the raiding trail and get across, but they would have to leave many people. Then Geronimo turned aside and sat down to pray. Lozen watched him curiously, seeing the Power in him. He prayed a long while, then remounted and rode to catch up with the rest. They pressed on and it seemed to Lozen the night lingered. The miles unfurled from their feet and the light she expected to see in the east did not come. So they made it safely across and it seemed Geronimo's prayer had delayed the daylight for two or three hours. So Lozen's hope stirred again.[6]

They rested in the Chiricahua Mountains, not far from Fort Bowie where Cochise and Mangas Coloradas had fought the soldiers trying to reach the spring. Then they pushed down through the relative safety of the mountains, moving as unpredictably as possible and relying on Lozen's ceremony to thread a path through their enemies. They crossed finally into Mexico with a sense of great relief, hoping the American soldiers would not pursue them. They made another long journey across the Janos Plains, this time laughing and joking and singing, the mounted warriors racing one another. The sense of muted doom that had hovered over Lozen since Juh had explained his vision began to lift. Perhaps they could make a new life as a free people in the safety of the Sierra Madre after all. Perhaps all their loss and suffering had been merely prelude to this. Perhaps Nana was right and they could not hope to come to terms with Power and have their own land until suffering had purified them. Perhaps Power would not help them until they had trusted in Power beyond all reason, as Geronimo had done in praying to the dawn.

They camped near a fine spring at the base of the Sierra Emmedio to rest from their long flight. They camped between the base of a great uplift and a rocky ridge, which overlooked a jumble of rocks around a small hill. There they rested for two days, gathering the great, spiked agave hearts for the mescal roasting pits. Each night they danced and sang and gave thanks. The girls blushed and laughed and looked down, dancing in a circle within a circle as they had always done. The young men gave gifts and let their hearts loose as young men had always done, dancing the great round of life. The boys and the young men played jokes on one another and strutted as they had always done. The singers teased them in their songs as they had always done:

> *Oh Mescalero maiden, don't be afraid;*
> *They are already gossiping about us,*
> *But don't be afraid,*
> *They who speak so chew rocks.*
> *Don't be afraid.*

So it seemed to Lozen in the firelight, watching the young people and the children born on the reservation free now for the first time in their lives, that perhaps they had come through the fire and earned their life after all. They had paid the great price and shown their courage—as the apprentice warrior who lets the sage burn into his arm without flinching.

At least, so it seemed in the light of the fire in the glow of the tizwin by the rhythm of the drums. But soon enough Lozen would find that Ussen had not finished tempering them after all.

▼

At dawn, a man and two women went to check the mescal cooking in the deep, rock-lined pits. Scouts who had climbed onto the ridge behind the camp during the night shot at them, killing the two women and wounding the grandson of Loco. They also fired down into the camp from the uplift behind it, killing six warriors before they could find cover. The band fled to the rocky hill, which offered good cover but no escape route that did not come under the guns of the scouts on the high ground.

After a time, they saw the dust of approaching soldiers and so knew that the one hundred scouts and soldiers on the high ground had only to hold them for the rest of the day until the four hundred soldiers could arrive and finish them off. Loco went to a forward position and shouted to the scouts who had them trapped, pleading with them to leave the soldiers and join their own people. But they only shot at him, wounding him slightly. Lozen crouched among the rocks, waiting for a target, determined not to waste her ammunition. She berated herself silently, because her Power had not warned her. She had prayed to the dawn, she had held her thoughts calm and reverent, she had offered her gratitude to the sun and the stars and the wind. But her Power had not whispered to her and had instead let their enemies trap them. So she waited for her target and saved her ammunition and wondered whether her brother might have felt this same way at Tres Castillos where his death had finally found him.[7]

Four warriors, seeing the women and children could not move from under the guns of the scouts on the ridge above, slipped away from the hill, stole like shadows across the open ground, and climbed the ridge behind the scouts as the sun began to sink. They opened fire on the scouts from behind, forcing them to withdraw from the exposed ridge. The women and children then fled from the hill where they had been trapped, with the warriors serving as a stubborn rear guard. Fortunately, the scouts and the soldiers did not chase them, but withdrew to join the approaching soldiers. The scouts were exhausted from their long chase and nearly out of ammunition, but they captured the entire horse herd and all of the camp supplies. The People fled on foot with what they had snatched up as they ran from their camp at dawn. They left fourteen dead on the plain and among the rocks where they had so recently danced and sung. They fled all through the night, desperate to cover ground before the larger body of soldiers could overtake them.

Geronimo, Lozen, and most of the warriors remained several miles in the rear of the women and children, prepared to fend off an attack. Naiche, Chato, Kaytennae, and a handful of other warriors went ahead. Everyone walked as quickly as they could and by daylight had covered nearly thirty miles. By dawn, the straggling column of weary people had spread out over a distance of two miles, with most of the warriors in the rear. The women at the head of the column smelled fresh coffee brewing and so hurried forward, thinking the advanced guard had made a camp and prepared food. But suddenly, they saw many Mexican soldiers riding toward them, shouting and shooting. In an instant, all of the women and children fled back toward the warriors in the rear guard. Only the fastest runners could stay ahead of the Mexicans, who rode in among the women and the children, slashing at them with their sabers and riding them down with their horses.

Only later did the People discover that the Mexicans had cap-

tured the two warriors who had taken the horses and turned back
for home. The captured men told the soldiers Geronimo and the
others would be coming back that way, so the Mexicans had prepared a trap. Moreover, no one knew what had happened to the
warriors who had acted as the advance guard and who should
have warned them of the ambush.[8] Some people later said they
had a fight with Geronimo and so went too far ahead and did not
return when they heard the shooting.

Lozen heard the shooting from among the main body of warriors far to the rear where they had placed themselves to fend off
the American soldiers, whom they expected to come along behind. As the gunshots and the cries of the people filtered back to
them, Geronimo and Lozen called on every warrior near them
and raced forward toward the fighting. Lozen ran as in a dream,
like the dreams of Tres Castillos that had haunted her. They
reached a shallow ravine that snaked across the line of advance
of the oncoming soldiers and many of the warriors jumped into
the ravine, which quickly filled up with women and children fleeing the Mexicans. The warriors began shooting, breaking the now
ragged Mexican charge. The women without guns began furi-
ously digging footholds in the side of the ravine, so the warriors
could stand up to shoot with only their heads showing. Lozen
found a foothold and took a position where a cluster of cactus
screened her head without blocking her own line of fire. The
calm of battle had fallen over her and she fired methodically. She
felt Power standing behind her, so it seemed she could not miss
her targets. She thought of Victorio as she killed the Mexicans,
feeling that in all the time since his death she had been truly
alive only when she was taking her revenge. Three times the
Mexicans charged the ravine, but accurate fire from the warriors
broke up each charge. Once they came so close one of the soldiers was shot from his horse and rolled into the ravine. Then the
Mexicans sent men to crawl into the ravine at one end, but

bends in the arroyo prevented them from getting a good shot at the warriors pressed up against the wall.

The Mexicans withdrew out of rifle shot, but the warriors could hear them saying, *Geronimo is in that ditch. Go in and get him!*

They took stock of their situation and saw they had not enough ammunition to hold off many more charges. Someone pointed out an ammunition bag on a horse that had been shot fifty feet in front of the arroyo. Loco crawled out of the ditch to try to reach the ammunition, but sniper fire from the Mexicans drove him back. They could see the soldiers massing for another charge and they feared they could not turn them back without more bullets.

Fun, seeing the dust stirred by the horses of the soldiers, cried out, *Somebody get the ammunition. I'll hold them off until he gets back. When they charge, run for the bag.*

The charge began in a great cloud of dust.

Help me up the bank, cried one woman.

So they pushed her up into the open in the face of the charge of the Mexicans. She ran quickly to the fallen horse and cut the bag away from the packsaddle. She could not lift the bag, so she dragged it. Bullets whistled all around her, but she did not hesitate. As the woman neared the arroyo, she stumbled and fell, but she did not loosen her grip on the bag. The bullets were thick around her now, so she extended her feet toward the ditch. Lozen rose up to stand in the open, feeling calm and protected in the deep shadow of her Power. She raised her rifle and fired back at the Mexicans, while other warriors crawled up from the ditch, grabbed the woman's legs, and dragged her to safety, still clinging to the precious bag of ammunition. The women tore open the bag and began loading the rifles of the warriors, passing each loaded weapon up to the men standing in the footholds. Still, it seemed the charge would sweep over them. Then Fun jumped up out of the ditch and ran toward the soldiers, dodging the bullets. His sudden appearance unnerved the soldiers, who were already faltering from the great increase in firing made possible by the bag of ammunition. So Fun broke the charge, laughing and screaming at them. The soldiers wheeled and fled back to cover.

Then Geronimo crawled out of the ditch and made his way along another arroyo toward the soldiers. He got close enough to listen to one of the officers haranguing his men, telling them Geronimo himself was in the ditch and this would be Geronimo's last day to live. Geronimo smiled his wolf's smile and rose up enough to bring his rifle to bear, shooting the officer just as he finished his pretty speech. Then Geronimo raced back through the bullets of his enemies to where the rest waited.

He had done a brave thing, but he had also seen how many soldiers had gathered now—perhaps 250. The warriors had killed eighteen in the day of fighting, but the soldiers still had the numbers to overwhelm them—especially since the warriors were nearly out of ammunition. Near dusk, the soldiers charged again and once more Fun jumped up out of the ditch to dodge back and forth through the bullets. His Power broke the charge again, although it cost the warriors most of their ammunition. Next the Mexicans set fire to the grass, when the wind had shifted so it would blow the smoke and fire down over the ditch. But everyone huddled against the walls of the ravine and covered their mouths and noses so the fire burned over the ravine without harm. But they were almost out of bullets now and few thought they could survive another charge.

As darkness gathered, Geronimo turned to the warriors, saying, *If we leave the women and children, we can escape.*[9]

What did you say? Fun demanded.

Come on! Geronimo replied. *Let's go.*

Fun raised his rifle. *Say that again and I'll shoot,* he said.

Geronimo gave him a long look, filled with anger, calculation, and sorrow. Lozen watched as from a distance, wondering whether the Chiricahua would run away now, leaving the Chihenne to their fate. She sensed that Fun held them in his hands, as Power stood behind him that day and turned aside the Mexicans' bullets. She had always admired Fun, so fearless, light-hearted, and impulsive. Fun had none of Geronimo's smoldering ambition and so in most things followed easily along behind his brother.[10] But now he stood aside from Geronimo and Lozen saw Fun could no more leave the women and children to face the soldiers than an oak could pull out its roots and find a better spot to grow. Geronimo saw this also, so he turned and climbed out of the arroyo. Some of the warriors followed him, but most were held in place by Fun's Power.

Now Fun spoke to the women and children, saying they should crawl out of the ditch in the darkness and make for the rendezvous point on which they had all agreed that morning. So the women and children prepared to go. He sent them quickly off through the darkness, saying he and Lozen and the other warriors would stay behind as long as they could to keep the soldiers from chasing them. In other sections of the arroyo, the warriors decided to go at the same time as the women—reasoning that if the Mexicans heard the noise of the women and children moving in the darkness they would charge in and kill the few warriors trying to cover their retreat. But if they all crawled out of the ditch together and the Mexicans heard some of the babies crying, then they might charge and catch them all out in the open. So in acts of sheer desperation, some of the women smothered their babies to prevent them from crying out and bringing death to everyone. Some of the people in the ditch with Fun and Lozen might have also killed their babies, but Fun would not consider it and everyone knew Lozen fought mostly to protect the women and the children—as her Power had told her to do. So Fun, Lozen, and the handful of other warriors decided to remain in the ditch waiting for the attack of the Mexicans as the women and children crawled away in the darkness.[11]

Lozen helped lift the babies carefully up to their mothers who crawled out of the ditch, soothing them so they would not cry. Then the warriors returned to their positions. They could hear the faint sounds of the women and children moving off in the darkness and the muffled cries of one or two babies. The Mexicans must have heard those sounds too, for now they charged again, calling out to their god for courage. Lozen, standing beside Fun, felt relief, almost joy. She had lived too long already and sometimes felt that all the time she had lived since her brother had died was a mistake because she had missed her proper death. But this would be a good death, fighting alongside Fun to cover the flight of the women and children. Victorio would have approved. So she faced the oncoming soldiers calmly, the fear long since gone, like grief that has used up all its tears.[12]

Lozen and Fun fired steadily, along with the other warriors. They could almost feel the charge of the Mexicans waver in the darkness. The horses thundered up to the very edge of the arroyo, then shied away. Some of their riders fell and the horses turned, so the charge did not carry into the ditch but was blunted with the last of the warriors' bullets. The Mexicans rallied and pushed forward again, but now the warriors knew the women and children had scattered, so the warriors also fled into the darkness. Some ran, others hid to let the soldiers sweep past, and others died bravely when they were overtaken. Lozen melted into the darkness, faint as a moon shadow, until she was far enough from the ditch to stand up and run, following the contours of the landscape and making for the rendezvous point. She took care to confuse her tracks in the darkness so her trail would be hard to follow.

By morning, most of the survivors had gathered on a mountain overlooking the battle scene. Geronimo was there, with the warriors who had left with him. Fun also came safely to the mountain. The endless night was a terrible mingling of grief and joy. Each person who stumbled out of the darkness was greeted with relief by whichever of their relatives had arrived before them. But with the morning, many families were already slipping into mourning for those who did not come quietly out of the darkness. In the end, the Mexicans killed seventy-eight and captured thirty-three, almost all of them women and children. All told, they had lost more than one-third of those who had started out from San Carlos. Loco also made it to the hillside, despite the wound in his leg he had suffered in the first battle with the Americans. His deep grief turned to joy, however, when one of the warriors brought his infant grandson safely to him. The warrior had stumbled over the baby lying on the ground in the darkness. Loco stood on the mountain, holding the baby, weeping. Even so, despite all the loss, Loco later told Nana they would have suffered even more deaths if they had stayed another summer at San Carlos.[13]

They could see the Mexicans moving over the battlefield below and were relieved the soldiers did not seem interested in following their trail. They could see a cluster of prisoners and grieved to know they would all be sold as slaves. After a time, they saw a large force of American soldiers approaching from the north, led by the same hated scouts who had hit their camp before. Lozen hoped the Mexicans and the Americans would fight, as the Americans were now deep in the wrong country. But perhaps the Mexicans and the Americans would hunt them together.

Instead, the nantans met and soon the Americans headed back north. This was a great relief, for she did not think the People could survive an agreement between the Mexicans and Americans, mostly because it would allow the scouts to seek them on both sides of the border. They did not truly fear the Mexicans, who could not remain a long time on a trail nor win a battle unless they had surprise and overwhelming numbers. The possibility the Mexicans and Americans would work together had plagued her ever since the great surprise of the American attack on their camp below the border. Fortunately, although the Mexicans and the Americans did not fight, they did not join forces.[14]

▼

Mournfully, the People took stock of their losses. They still had assembled the greatest force of free people seen in many years, with seventy-four of the one hundred fighting men who had started out. But they could not take any joy in their survival, with so many lost. Some of the warriors were too badly wounded to keep up and so remained near a spring in the mountains until they could heal enough to travel, including a White Mountain man named Tsoe and a relative of Geronimo named Kayihtah. They rejoined their People in the Sierra Madre after a month and were to play an important role in things later.

The People traveled carefully through the mountains, relieved the Mexicans had given up the pursuit—perhaps because they did not have scouts to follow the trail. They arrived finally at one of Juh's campsites thirty miles from Casas Grandes, on a plateau between two deep canyons reached only along an easily defended trail.

Lozen's heart lifted a little when they came finally to this safe place and she saw how many of the People had gathered here in the Sierra Madre—Chokonen, Nednhi, Chihenne, and others. Lozen hoped they might live peacefully there, safe from their enemies, remembering the old ways—safe from the poisons of the reservation that killed both spirit and body. As she had so many times before, she wondered if perhaps Nana was right and Ussen had merely tempered them, as a warrior hardens a wooden spear point in the fire. Perhaps they had suffered enough that they might now have some happiness and the sound of babies laughing. Perhaps. But in any case—she could only continue, holding her mind prayerfully, for she could not see ahead as some could.

And that was just as well. For if she had seen ahead, how could even her strong heart have borne it?

CHAPTER XIV

▼▼▼

The Last Free People

Summer 1882

At first, the People had great happiness in their refuge. Perhaps six hundred people had gathered now in the Sierra Madre, a third of them warriors or boys old enough to be trained as warriors.[1] They visited happily with their relatives and with members of the clans that united the different bands. Some found friends and family members they had not seen in years and many children who had grown up on the reservation had their first taste of the free life. The mountains had all the foods they needed: wild onions, sumac berries, raspberries, strawberries, wild grapes, chokecherry, mulberry, potato, and wood sorrel. In the canyons, they could find cactus, beans, and prickly pear. They harvested the yucca fruit in the winter, gathered the heart of the agave for mescal, harvested the sacred pollen from the tule, and sought out the beehives for honey. They grew corn or traded for corn so they could brew tizwin, a sweet, mild drink made for social and ceremonial occasions.

Happy in one another's company, many people held tizwin parties where everyone sat around talking and joking, refusing to let anyone of a bad disposition or a sour mood enter in. They teased one another and played practical jokes. They told the old stories and passed along the new gossip. They played the moccasin game, re-creating the first contest between the birds and the beasts as they played for daylight. The games went on for hours, sometimes days, with the teams using gambling Power amid much laughter, betting everything that came to hand on correctly guessing where the opposing team had hidden the bone. The men set up hoop-and-pole courts and played that sacred game for hours—keeping the women strictly away. For their part, the women played the many variations on the stave game, with a small stone and sticks of different colors arranged as a playing board. They played other games that involved pitching rocks into holes dug into the ground thirty paces apart—scoring four points for tossing the stone into the hole or one point for any stone closer to the hole than an opponent's. They also selected teams to play different ball games—ususally with a buckskin ball tightly stuffed with grass. In one game based on dodging a thrown ball, they drew three circles on the ground and then tried to get everyone from their team to run from one circle to another without being thrown out by the other side. Those games could go on all afternoon, with each team scoring a point each time a player could move through the whole sequence of circles without being hit.

Lozen especially loved to play shinny—for she was one of the fastest runners in the band. In shinny they marked out a playing field about half a mile long with goalposts at either end. Two teams would gather in the middle, each armed with a curved stick. They would throw a wood- or buckskin-covered ball into the air and then each team would try to drive the ball down to their goal—using anything but their hands. It was a rough no-holds-barred game in which the team with the best runners always won in the end. Lozen joined in happily, glad to simply play after so much death and fighting. Sometimes she joined in the games dominated by the men, although she did not play hoop-and-pole, which was only for the men. And she did not often play the pure strength games of the men—like the wrestling matches whose object was simply to throw the other fellow off his feet. Or the tugs-of-war, sometimes with the strongest man tying a rope to his waist and then letting three or four fellows try to pull him off his feet, as the spectators made their bets. They also often raced, on foot and horseback.

Even so, the bands began to drift apart. The People did not follow leaders as the White Eyes did. No man had authority over another warrior. No man was elected to leadership. Each leader acquired influence because of his character, courage, and reputation for Power. Often, the sons of respected leaders became leaders, but only if they were capable and respected. Usually, they could count on the unswerving loyalty of only those family groups with whom they had close ties. These related groups might frequently follow another leading man in most things—but they each jealously guarded their independence. Always, leadership depended on personal character, backed by family and clan relationships. Often, people considered a man's Power in deciding in what areas to follow his advice. So even a widely respected war leader like Geronimo could not thereby become a chief, with influence in settling disputes and ordering the affairs of the camp. He could only declare his intention to go raiding and see who would dance out into the circle to join him. The warriors who always went with him were mostly his relatives, usually the children of his sisters and brothers. The head of each family made his own decisions about where to camp and whom to follow. So men like Nana, Loco, Chihuahua, Juh, Geronimo, and Victorio each had their personal followings and certain leaders often worked together. Other rising leaders—like Chato and Kaytennae—had small followings of warriors and often allied themselves with the more influential men. All of this made for a fluid, constantly shifting net of influence and leadership even among the closely related bands of the Chihenne.

The divisions grew even deeper when the different Chiricahua bands were mixed together—Chihenne, Nednhi, and Chokonen. So the independence of the warriors and the leaders was sometimes a great strength and sometimes a great weakness. A single warrior could survive on his own and the family groups could move easily so they did not exhaust the food supply in one place. But this also made it hard to hold any force of warriors together. So the bands quickly began to fracture along the old lines and scatter throughout the mountains.

Moreover, the war leaders grew restless. Perhaps they could have survived on the game they killed and the food the women gathered. Although they would run quickly out of ammunition, they could have used bows in the old way. But they had grown used to all the things they could take from the Mexicans and trade in Casas Grandes. No father could host a respectable Sunrise Ceremony without the food, horses, and cattle obtained on a raid. No warrior could impress the family of a girl he wanted to marry without bringing back horses taken from the Mexicans. And no band could be sure of getting through the winter without a stockpile of supplies taken from the Mexicans. Besides, war leaders like Geronimo loved to raid—thirsting for it like a man with a swollen tongue. Geronimo had an insatiable hatred for Mexicans. Killing them did not diminish it, but fed it like sticks thrown into the fire.

Lozen understood this in Geronimo. She had not so much hatred or such pleasure in the killing herself, but raiding made her feel she was using the gifts of Power to help her People. Sometimes she led raids, for she was respected by Geronimo—partly because she was now among the leading Chihenne and pivotal in connecting the Chihenne to the other Chiricahua bands.

Fun also distinguished himself in raiding and Lozen rode often with him. Once, Mexicans fell upon a group of women and children who were tending the mescal baking pits. They killed and scalped the older boys and took the women and children captive. Fun set out alone to follow their trail, tracking them back to the village from which the Mexicans started. He went into the village and found the house in which the women were held prisoner. He snuck into the house itself and talked to the women, learning that the Mexicans would all assemble for a ceremony in the church in four days. Fun then slipped away and brought back Juh, Geronimo, Lozen, and the rest of the Chiricahua warriors. When the villagers were all assembled in the church, the warriors barred the doors and Fun climbed up to the roof and dropped a chili bomb down into the church, setting it on fire. As the Mexicans inside died, the warriors watched grimly. Then they looted the town, freed the prisoners, and went on their way.

But despite the many successful raids, disunity in the bands continued to grow. To make matters worse, the arrogance of the warriors and their old weakness for the strong liquor of the Mexicans spurred disaster. The raiders often took the cattle, horses, and goods they acquired through raids to Casas Grandes to trade. The people in the town welcomed the warriors in friendly fashion and for days traded for their goods and welcomed them into the cantinas. Nana and Lozen would not often go into the towns of the Mexicans nor drink their liquor, but Geronimo and Juh sometimes did. Once, the villagers of Casas Grandes waited until the warriors were all drunk and then attacked their camp just outside town, killing perhaps twenty warriors and capturing thirty-five women and children to sell as slaves. Geronimo managed to escape, but his wife was taken prisoner and sold as a slave so he never saw her again. Two of Chato's children were also taken.

A short time after this great loss, the Mexicans surprised Juh's camp in the Sierra Madre, killing Ishton, Geronimo's sister and Juh's wife, who had contributed so much to Juh's Power and influence. Moreover, Juh's daughter was shot in the knee and crippled.

This attack stirred Juh to new activity, and he waged a renewed war on the Mexicans. He fought one battle against a large force of Mexicans who ventured into the Sierra Madre. He let them come nearly to the top of a steep trail, then directed his warriors to roll boulders down on them—killing most of the Mexicans without losing a single warrior. In the meantime, Geronimo and Lozen and others covered long distances on their raids, striking throughout Sonora and killing many Mexicans with little loss to themselves.

In the Season When the Earth is Reddish Brown,[2] Juh, Geronimo, and Nana joined forces for an attack on Galeana, a town twenty miles south of Casas Grandes. They heard that a Mexican cavalry force stationed there was commanded by Juan Mata Ortiz, who had been the second in command of the soldiers that killed Victorio at Tres Castillos. The combined force of warriors scouted the ground and found a good place for an ambush. The leaders sent three warriors to steal a horse herd from just outside the town, lingering long enough for the soldiers to see them and fleeing slowly enough for the soldiers to overtake them.

The twenty-two Mexicans rode directly into the ambush, as though Nana's Power were pushing them to it. The warriors emerged from good cover on either side of the Mexicans as they rode into a ravine. Geronimo had hoped the Mexicans would panic and scatter so they could be picked off easily one at a time. But they held their discipline and Juan Mata Ortiz led them to the top of a rocky hill nearby, where they dismounted and made their horses lie down so they could use the animals for breastworks.

Geronimo, Nana, Juh, Lozen, and the other leaders decided to let a young warrior named Slender Legs take charge of the battle.

He was a fearless warrior and a great runner, so people expected great things of him. He was still young and headlong—for in these days of constant fighting warriors moved quickly into prominent positions. Perhaps Geronimo pushed to give the battle to Slender Legs because he remembered when Mangas Coloradas had given him the leadership of the battle of revenge for the killing of Geronimo's mother and wife and children. Geronimo, Kaytennae, Lozen, and other good marksmen took up a position where they could shoot at the soldiers. Meantime, most of the warriors wriggled up to the base of the hill—each one with a rock about the size of his head. They began crawling up the hill, protected by the rock each warrior pushed in front.

The Mexicans, seeing the snare closing on them, shot at the warriors behind their rocks—although in the process they exposed themselves to Lozen, Geronimo, and Kaytennae. The warriors came on carefully, so by the time they came close enough to charge the last short distance, the Mexicans had used up most of their ammunition. The warriors carried the top of the hill and killed the Mexicans quickly in hand-to-hand fighting. Only one of the soldiers ran down the hill and escaped. Some of the warriors rose to chase him, but Geronimo said to let the Mexican go so he would bring more soldiers for them to kill.

When the warriors finished killing the soldiers, Slender Legs jumped up on the horse of Ortiz, proud of his victory. Everyone cheered and hooted and laughed as the horse pranced among the bodies of the Mexicans, admiring the casual skill with which Slender Legs controlled the horse—skittish with the smell of blood. Of course, if Geronimo had been on top of the hill he would have first made sure every Mexican was dead and stripped their bodies of anything useful. But Slender Legs was a young man, full of life and enthusiasm and proud of his victory in front of Juh and Geronimo and Lozen and others he feared and respected. And because everyone was looking at Slender Legs showing off on the horse of the hated Ortiz, they did not pay enough attention to the bodies of the Mexicans. So no one saw that one of the Mexicans was not yet dead until he fired his gun, knocking Slender Legs off his horse in the moment of his triumph. The warriors fell upon the wounded Mexican and hacked him to pieces. But it was too late. Slender Legs lay on the ground dying already. He died without complaint—chagrined at his carelessness. Of course, the death of Slender Legs had spoiled the victory, so they did not have a victory dance.

After this, the People and the Mexicans went back to continuous war. Geronimo took a large party including Lozen on an extended raid through Sonora. They plundered whole towns and killed many people. In one town, the Mexicans hid on their rooftops as the warriors rode past the village—and the warriors jeered the villagers. The people on the roofs were mostly women and children, so the warriors did not bother climbing up there to pull them down and kill them. Besides, the relations between the People and the Mexicans were complicated—full of hatred and revenge, but also intermarriage and dependence. Often the warriors told one another they had best leave some Mexicans alive, so there would be someone to raise horses and cattle. On the journey back to the refuge in the Sierra Madre, they captured a pack train loaded with whiskey. The warriors all got drunk that night, leaving only a few apprentices to stand guard.

▼

In the meantime, Chato led a raiding party back into the United States to replenish their ammunition, as most of the warriors had American-made guns and needed American bullets.[3] Chato hated the White Eyes, who had killed his father and his brother, so he took his revenge as he went along. In one week, they killed twenty-six White Eyes—everyone he came across—so that no one who saw them remained alive. The raiders covered four hundred miles in six days, sometimes riding seventy-five miles in a single day. No soldiers could keep up with them, for a warrior could ride his horse to death and still outwalk the soldiers on horseback trying to follow. Moreover, when warriors used up their horses they could steal more mounts at the next ranch, while the soldiers had to make their horses last.

The raiders suffered only one loss at the hands of the White Eyes—a well-liked warrior named Beneactiney, the son-in-law of Chihuahua, a rising Chiricahua chief. The death filled Beneactiney's good friend and relative Tsoe with despair. So Tsoe decided to go back to the reservation at San Carlos. Tsoe was a White Mountain man who had married a Chiricahua woman and so came to live with the Chiricahua, but his wife had been killed and now he longed for peace—even at the cost of his freedom. So Tsoe left the raiding party and headed back toward San Carlos. Chato let him go because Tsoe had been Chato's friend also and because every warrior must make his own choices. Chato did not know it at the time, but letting Tsoe go would prove a fatal mistake. Later, Lozen wondered whether everything would have been different if Chato had talked Tsoe into staying or had killed him when he tried to leave. But who can say? Perhaps all trails lead to the same place and differ only in the distance traveled before arriving.

▼

Back in the Sierra Madre, the raiding parties brought one hundred cattle to the refuge, and the People began to prepare a victory dance. But when Lozen performed her ceremony, she felt the approach of enemies.[4] Riders rode back the way they had come and saw the dust of a large force of Mexican cavalry following them into the sanctuary. The warriors positioned themselves above the narrow trail leading up to the plateau on which they were camped, readying boulders to roll down onto the trail. They let the Mexicans pass the place of ambush and come nearly to the top, and then opened fire. The soldiers retreated in confusion down the narrow trail, going back into the ambush. The warriors rolled the rocks down on them. Some said the Mexicans were the same ones who had ambushed the Chihenne in Loco's band when they first fled into Mexico, which gave Lozen much satisfaction.[5]

After this battle, they rested for a time in camp. Chato's raiding party returned and everyone gathered for great victory dances and songs. The Gan Mountain Spirit dancers whirled and leaped, cajoling the spirits for their blessings. The Grey One raced through camp, clowning for the delighted audience. He drew certain girls out to dance with certain boys. They had enough food and enough bullets and had demonstrated they could raid freely in Mexico and even go into the United States for ammunition.

Nonetheless, Lozen felt a growing unease. She noted that Juh's following had dwindled, never having recovered from the attack by the Mexicans that had killed Ishton. Only half a dozen warriors camped now with Juh and he seemed shrunken in spirit. Perhaps his vision was too difficult for the others, for he offered no hope of victory, only the promise of a warrior's death. Nana remained revered, but he had grown so old he could not easily lead raiding parties. The decline in the influence of Juh and Nana muffled two strong voices in favor of resistance.

Lozen also worried about the news that Grey Fox, known to the whites as General Crook, had returned to command the soldiers in the United States. Loco said Grey Fox was a strong enemy, but an honorable man. Lozen heard this talk running through the camp, especially among members of Loco's band. Some said Grey Fox had already sent away the agents who had been stealing the rations and replaced them with army officers who treated people with justice. They said he would not cheat the People on the reservation and not lock people up for no reason, for Grey Fox had always treated fairly people willing to live peacefully. For those who weren't, Loco and the others said Grey Fox was a dangerous enemy who would guard every water hole and keep his soldiers moving constantly. Worse yet, Grey Fox used scouts to do most of his fighting and Lozen feared the scouts far more than any soldiers. Warriors could always evade soldiers, melting into the rocks when pursued and fighting only when they had an advantage. But the scouts could follow their trail, knew their hiding places, and were much harder to ambush. The People could fight the soldiers indefinitely—but scouts would eventually wear them down.

In addition, the attack by the Mexican soldiers in one of their most secure refuges was worrisome. Although they had shattered the Mexicans with no loss to themselves, what the Mexicans had attempted once with 150 men they could try again with 400.

All of these things had strengthened the peace faction among the leadership. Loco talked openly about returning to the reservation. Chihuahua, who was a rising leader, also sometimes supported the idea. Chihuahua had been a scout for the soldiers when they were hunting Victorio, although Lozen and Kaytennae now sometimes joked with him about it. Once Kaytennae had trapped Chihuahua and his warriors at a water hole and driven off their horses, leaving them to walk back to the soldiers in embarrassment. In return, Chihuahua's scouts had once trapped Kaytennae and driven off his horse and made him hide in the bushes for a long while, although they knew he was there. They all laughed about it now, telling the stories back and forth on one another. But Lozen did not forget that Chihuahua had worked for the soldiers and helped them harry Victorio to his death. She thought he might soon join Loco in urging a return to the reservation. Chato had now attached himself to Chihuahua's band and remained ambitious, arrogant, and unpredictable. He had gained stature among the warriors, but Lozen did not trust him.

Geronimo still remained strong in leading raids and talked

about living a long time as a free people in a place their enemies dared not attack. Although Naiche was a lighthearted man who liked to joke, gamble, and flirt, he was influenced by Geronimo's Power and fighting spirit. Kaytennae also had become a strong voice for fighting and for living free, having moved respectfully into the space left by the Nana's dwindling influence. Lozen was also respected and revered, especially among the women. She tried to strengthen the resolve of the women, knowing their memory of the relative safety of the reservation was perhaps the greatest threat to remaining in the Sierra Madre.

After the warriors were well rested from their raids, Geronimo held a war dance to gather volunteers for a new raid on Casas Grandes. He wanted to capture some Mexican women and children to trade for their own women and children who had been captured some months earlier, including one of his wives. He assembled a force of about thirty-six warriors and set out for Casas Grandes.

In the meantime, Lozen camped with Nana and Kaytennae, enjoying the bounty of the Season of Many Leaves.[6] She could almost believe they might live like this for many years, teaching their children the old stories and the old ways in a place so high and hard it remained safely out of reach of the American soldiers and the scouts. She tried to put aside her fears, calm her mind, and learn patience from the rocks, the wind, and the trees.

But looking back, she realized that even her worst fears had been only foolish hopes.

CHAPTER XV

▼▼▼

Trapped by the Grey Fox

May 1883

The news came like a thunderbolt.

Scouts had attacked Chato's camp just at dawn, killing nine people and capturing five children, together with all of Chato's supplies. The scouts waited in the camp and after a time were joined by soldiers, led by Grey Fox who had several hundred scouts and about fifty soldiers, together with several hundred pack-mules. Some of the older, more cautious leaders had warned that the White Eyes might strike back if Geronimo and Juh and others continued to raid in the United States. They had even warned that someday the Mexicans and the Americans might work to-gether against them—but no one had expected the Americans to come so boldly into the heart of the Sierra Madre. Later, they learned that Tsoe, Chato's friend who had returned to San Carlos after the death of Beneactiney, had led Grey Fox straight to Chato's camp.[1]

Grey Fox released several of the prisoners he had taken to carry the message to the other bands that he had come to take them back to the reservation and would treat them well and forget about past incidents. Grey Fox said the Mexicans and Americans had joined forces now, so they would hunt down anyone who stayed.

Immediately, people began going into his camp and surrendering—mostly Chihenne from Loco's band and Chiricahua from Chihuahua's band. Grey Fox gave one of the prisoners Chihuahua's favorite horse, which he had captured, and released her so she could convince Chihuahua to surrender himself and his band. This was what made Grey Fox so dangerous: He knew how to weaken the will to fight. Soon, one hundred people had surrendered to Grey Fox and were living in his camp, eating his supplies, and mingling in a friendly way with the White Mountain scouts.

Nana, Lozen, Kaytennae, and the thirty-eight warriors who were camped in their group did not know what to do. They did not want to surrender, but they were bleeding people and warriors into the camp of Grey Fox as from a wound. Moreover, Geronimo and his warriors—who would be the strongest voices against surrender—were still off looking for Mexican prisoners in Casas Grandes.

Later, they learned that Geronimo's Power told him of the attack as soon as it happened. He was on his way back from Casas Grandes with the wives of Mexican soldiers he had captured. One night while sitting by the fire, Geronimo suddenly exclaimed that the soldiers had seized their camp. The warriors hurried back to the Sierra Madre, arriving four days after the attack on Chato's camp.[2]

Nana, Lozen, and Kaytennae remained apart, waiting to see whether Geronimo could dissuade the other Chiricahua from surrendering. They talked a long time about whether they could survive in the Sierra Madre with only their own warriors. They knew Juh would not surrender, but he had camped a long way off and had only a few warriors. His two sons had been taken prisoner by the Mexicans and tortured to death and he seemed a shadow of himself now, with only an echo of his Power and no more luck.

Then they heard Geronimo had arrived to find that most of the bands had already surrendered. When Grey Fox learned Geronimo had returned, he did a brave thing by taking his shotgun and going off into the bushes away from the protection of the scouts and the soldiers as though he wanted to hunt.[3] Geronimo's warriors surrounded him and began talking. Grey Fox seemed a man of Power and not at all afraid of the warriors. He told them he was giving them one last chance to surrender and then he and the Mexicans would hunt down anyone left out. He spoke with great confidence, as though he did not much care what Geronimo did. The negotiations continued for several days.

Grey Fox used a fierce man named Mickey Free to translate for him. Lozen remembered Mickey Free, for he was the half-breed son of a Mexican and a Chiricahua woman whose kidnapping many years ago had started the war between Cochise and the Americans in Apache Pass. Mickey Free had been raised by the Coyotero band that had taken him, but he was like a coyote—skulking and solitary and loyal to no one. He had become a man-hunter and a scout for the army and was also useful to them as a translator because he could speak the language of the People, as well as Spanish and English. He was a great tracker and a sly, fierce, deadly fighter. But no one trusted him. Now, the leaders found themselves at his mercy, for he could twist their words any way he wanted when he translated for Grey Fox.

Geronimo tried everything he could think of to strengthen the warriors, who rattled toward surrender like pebbles down a hill. He tried to make Grey Fox say something he could use, but Grey Fox stalked him with words. Geronimo warned the others that Grey Fox might hang them when they returned to the reservation. He reminded them that Grey Fox was always asking about the white boy who had been taken captive on Chato's raid, but that boy had been killed by a man whose mother had been shot by the scouts. Then Geronimo tried to convince the others to invite the White Mountain scouts to a social dance with the Chiricahua women, saying the warriors and the women with hidden knives could fall on the scouts and kill most of them by surprise. Without the scouts, the soldiers would be nearly helpless and the warriors could kill them on the trails leading out of the Sierra Madre. But Djilikine, a White Eye who had been captured as a child and raised by a White Mountain band before marrying a Nednhi girl, spoke against that plan for he had relatives among the scouts. Djilikine was a respected warrior and Geronimo's father-in-law, so his opposition strangled the plan. Besides, even when Geronimo and others invited the scouts to a dance their nantan would not let them go.

Nana, Kaytennae, and Lozen finally went to Grey Fox with their warriors about ten days after the attack on Chato's camp. By that time, about 220 Chihenne and Chiricahua people had come in to camp near Grey Fox. Then one of the scouts brought news that a large force of Mexican soldiers was coming toward the Sierra Madre, having gathered up the cattle Geronimo had abandoned when his Power warned him his People had been attacked. So it seemed Grey Fox had not lied when he said the Mexicans would help him. Geronimo and Nana conferred, each preferring death to captivity, but neither seeing a way to sway enough warriors to their position now that Loco, Chihuahua, and even Chato now advocated a return to the reservation. Moreover, they were nearly out of ammunition and had not enough supplies to see them through the coming winter. So at length they decided to go with Grey Fox and see if his promises would hold or crack and fall into pieces like the broken pottery of all the promises made to them before. Most of the women now longed for a peaceful life on the reservation, but if disease stalked their children and hunger their camps perhaps they would once again have the heart to leave. If nothing else, they could get through the winter on the rations from the agent.

So Geronimo conferred with Naiche and agreed to surrender, as did Nana, Kaytennae, and Lozen. However, Geronimo asked for a little more time to gather up other families scattered through the Sierra Madre. He also wanted to get up more cattle and horses from the Mexicans so they would have their own herds on the reservation. Grey Fox agreed to the delay reluctantly, although he tried to make it seem it did not matter to him what Geronimo did. Grey Fox was anxious now to return to the United States, perhaps because he was feeding so many people. Lozen and Kaytennae decided to go with Geronimo.[4] All told, 325 people, 52 of them warriors, went with Grey Fox and his scouts. Other Chiricahua leaders, including Mangas, Geronimo, Chato, and Chihuahua, stayed behind with more than one hundred people to gather up other bands, promising to come to the reservation in the next cycle of the moon.

Geronimo, Lozen, and others continued to raid for another eight months in Mexico, still hoping they might free family members held by the Mexicans as they gathered up horses and cattle to take back to the reservation. No longer burdened by the women and the children and the old people who had gone back to the reservation with Grey Fox, they moved easily and stayed out of the way of the blundering patrols of the Mexicans. All the time, they wondered whether they could bear to give up their freedom and wear metal tags around their necks like branded cattle. But they did not know how long they could remain out or whether they had the heart for it now that many had family members living back on the reservation. Bad news also came with the arrival of Daklugie, Juh's son. He said Juh had fallen suddenly from his horse into a river while riding away from Casas Grandes. His son had held his head above water, but Juh had already drowned. His son buried him beside the river. The news grieved Lozen, for Juh had been a leader of great Power whom the People could not afford to lose.

They kept in touch with events on the reservation, as warriors passed back and forth. Most of the news was good. Grey Fox treated the People who came in with him well, letting them settle over a wide area. Army officers had charge over the reservation, instead of the agents who stole all of the supplies. So the remaining warriors began to think more seriously about going back to the reservation, hoping Grey Fox would keep his promises and they could live peacefully.

They gathered up perhaps 350 cows and horses and headed north in the Season of the Ghost Dance.[5] Geronimo sent Lozen and a Chiricahua woman named Dahteste ahead to see whether soldiers were waiting to attack them when they crossed the border. Geronimo sent Lozen because the soldiers dismissed her as a woman—a squaw, the ugly word the White Eyes used for women, which was a reference to their private parts. The White Eyes would not bother to kill a mere woman and never suspected that the woman who came so quietly into their camp had fought longer and harder than any man of the Chiricahua. Geronimo also sent word to Chato and Chihuahua who were still in Mexico, saying he was preparing to return to the reservation. Lozen found a young nantan named Britton Davis with a patrol at the border and learned Grey Fox had sent him to escort surrendering groups of warriors back to the reservation. This seemed wise, as the area was full of White Eyes itching to kill the People. So Lozen returned to tell Geronimo where to meet Davis.

Geronimo then crossed the border, anxious to get north before the Mexicans could find the plain path of the hundreds of cattle his warriors drove ahead of them. Once he crossed the border, Geronimo slowed the herd and headed for a place with water and good grass so the cattle could put back on the weight they had walked off in getting out of Mexico. But Davis immediately began to give Geronimo trouble about the cattle herd, saying they must push on to the reservation quickly. Geronimo refused, saying they must rest the livestock. Then two other White Eyes came and argued with Davis, looking often toward Geronimo. The warriors watched warily. Some said the White Eyes wanted to take the cattle for themselves and hang Geronimo and the other leaders. That night, Davis called Geronimo to his tent to say they must leave quickly and quietly, because the two White Eyes wanted to take away the cattle herd.[6] Geronimo grew angry, thinking he should kill the White Eyes and return to Mexico, as it was already clear the promises of Grey Fox were drawn in the sand. But Davis convinced him they could play a great trick on the White Eyes by getting them drunk on good whiskey and then sneaking out during the night with all of the cattle. They did this, moving so quietly the White Eyes never stopped snoring. The warriors laughed and joked about it, delighted to have played so good a joke on the White Eyes.

But when Geronimo got his cattle to the reservation, Grey Fox took them away. Crook said the cattle belonged to the Mexicans. However, he promised the government would supply the People with horses and cattle so they could start their own herds. Then Grey Fox refused to let the Chiricahua settle on Eagle Creek as he had agreed to do during talks in the Sierra Madre.[7] Instead, Grey Fox let the Chiricahua settle on Turkey Creek, which was a day's journey from Fort Apache. It proved almost as good a place as Eagle Creek, with plenty of game and a good stream surrounded by trees in the middle of a great plain that abounded with antelope and other game. Turkey Creek was well away from the White Mountain bands whose warriors had been scouts against the Chiricahua and who feared and distrusted Geronimo and the other war leaders. Geronimo was among the last of the leaders to come in, and he found Naiche and Mangas had already arrived. Chato, also, had come in and to everyone's surprise joined the scouts, together with his friend Tsoe. Most of the Chiricahua now considered Tsoe—who was a White Mountain man—a traitor and the dog of the White Eyes. But Tsoe had spent a long time talking to Chato—who had been his good friend—until he convinced Chato that the surest path to influence lay in winning the confidence of Grey Fox and Davis. Chato saw it was useless to go on fighting against such hopeless odds and reasoned that he could best protect his family by helping the soldiers keep the peace.

Grey Fox put Davis in charge of the bands at Turkey Creek. Nana, Kaytennae, Lozen, and other Chihenne settled nearby. In all, 423 Chihenne and Chiricahua settled near Turkey Creek, including perhaps 83 warriors. Most of the leaders quickly came to respect Davis, a stout, energetic officer who treated the People with respect and courtesy and no trace of the hostility, condescension, and disdain that marked the attitudes of most of the White Eyes. He laughed easily and appreciated the jokes and humor of the warriors. He worked hard to get harnesses and wagons so they could use their horses for plowing and farming. But when the warriors tried to put the harnesses on their tough little war ponies, they found the straps were so big it was like putting a saddle on a dog. Moreover, the horses were not trained to walk along in the slow, plodding way necessary to pull a plow. So when the warriors harnessed their ponies to the plows to break up the soil, the ponies took off running with the warriors clinging helplessly to the handles of the plows. Everyone watching howled with laughter, Davis as loudly as any. Davis also did his best to keep his word and treat every person fairly and many people said he was the best White Eye ever put in charge over the People.

They were also glad to be camping a long way from the White Mountain bands, because much bad blood lay between them. Sometimes, they still clashed. One time Kaytennae was leading a hunting party when they encountered a White Mountain man named Kaysegohneh, who was traveling with his family. Seeing the flash of the signaling mirror Kaytennae and one other man wore around their necks, Kaysegohneh started shooting at them to give his wife, mother, and children time to run and hide. Kaytennae did not fire back, as he did not want trouble with the White Mountain bands. But the other warrior who wore the signaling mirror shot and killed Kaysegohneh. Then Kaysegohneh's mother ran at the warriors, berating them for killing her son. She had seen the flash of the mirror around the neck of the man who shot her son and when she reached the warriors she accused Kaytennae of the killing. Kaytennae said nothing, as any defense he could offer would put the blame on the other warrior.

She yelled at him, *You killed my only son with that gun. You killed him for no cause whatever and made his wife a widow and his children orphans. Now they have no one to protect them and no one to hunt for them. Your rifle is loaded. Shoot me! Shoot his poor wife! Shoot his children! A quick death is more merciful than starvation.*[8]

The other warrior should have spoken up and taken responsibility, but he said nothing. When they returned to camp, the warrior disappeared. Some days later he encountered Gouyan, the wife of Kaytennae.

He spoke to her very humbly, saying, *My sister, there is something that bothers me so much that I cannot sleep.* He said he was so ashamed of something he had done that he must go away.

She urged him not to leave his wife and his children, saying, *I am but a woman, but I know that other women need the protection and care of a husband. Without you, your wife, mother, and children may go hungry. For one time, listen to a woman who, although she is weak and foolish, is trying to help both you and your family.*

But the warrior would not stay, saying, *I wish I might, but something stronger than I drives me. I came to ask if you will try to help my poor mother and wife and my little helpless children, for you have a kind heart. But I must go. At night animals prowl about but do not attack me. Sometimes I think I have been witched. Some-*

times a bear stays near my camp and I hope that he will kill me, but he does not. Perhaps he keeps guard over my family. It is well known that bears protect those in need of care.

That should keep you here, said Gouyan.

If I go, the bear may protect my family, he replied.

So that man went away. Perhaps he was witched or perhaps he was just so ashamed he could not remain with the other warriors. Kaytennae arranged for his family to receive food and supplies, not telling them these things came from him. Sometimes, people would find that man's tracks around the camp, but no one saw him again until much later when he appeared suddenly at the campfire of a raiding party in Sonora. He was clothed in skins from which the hair had not been removed and he still wore the mirror around his neck, although he no longer had anyone to signal.

The warriors urged him to stay with them, but he said, *I cannot stay. There is something that drives me and will not let me have peace. I am doomed to be an outcast for the rest of my life. I was not banished by my tribe, but by this thing that nags me. I am the victim of my own mind. I have no companions, no friends, no family, nothing but bears. Always there are one or more with me. They bring me food. If I move, they follow. If I sleep, they guard me. I no longer fear them, but I dread them as I do the bad thoughts that torment me both sleeping and waking. For me there is no hope, nothing.*

Then he went away into the darkness, for fear he would bring trouble to the warriors if he stayed.

Still, despite the problems between the Chiricahua and the White Mountain bands, they might have lived peacefully except for the trouble among themselves and the mistakes Davis made about whom to trust. Davis did not understand the divisions among the different bands. Geronimo remained wary and camped away from Davis's tent, having little trust in any White Eye. Kaytennae, who had never been on the reservation, camped on a hill where he could keep an eye on Davis and remained wary and suspicious. But Chato, Tsoe, and Mickey Free all made them-selves very friendly to Davis and so gained his trust. They were always warning Davis against other leaders like Kaytennae and Geronimo in order to gain power and influence. Even when others went to talk to Davis, he would use Mickey Free as the translator, so no one knew if their words were translated correctly. Geronimo and Nana told warriors to keep an eye on Davis, Mickey Free, and Chato. They soon reported Davis had a network of informants who came secretly to his tent at night to tell him who was talking about leaving the reservation, who was still making tizwin, and who was stirring up anger. Geronimo told his own son, Chapo, to sign up as a scout and keep track of what Chato and the others were doing, but Davis gradually grew more suspicious of Geron-imo, Kaytennae, and others and more and more dependent on Chato and Mickey Free.[9]

Moreover, Davis soon began to meddle in their private affairs. He forbade drinking and the making of tizwin, which was impor-tant to many ceremonies and social functions. He also said no man could hit his wife and forbade the punishment of women who had been unfaithful. The leaders objected to these things, saying Davis was barely old enough to be a warrior and should not tell chiefs what to do.

Although he seemed honorable and well intentioned, Davis did not understand many important things. The People placed a high value on the control of sexual drives and on trust between a man and a woman. They did not hold people in marriage as the White Eyes did, so a woman could break off a marriage by simply putting her husband's things in a pile outside her wickiup. She did not even have to return the wedding gifts. Many women did this if their husbands hit them, lay down with other women, became lazy, or did not bring back enough meat from the hunt. Since a woman lived with her husband in the camp of her parents to whom her husband owed his efforts and loyalty, women had an important and respected place. As a result, few men ever hit their wives or children.

However, the People also placed a high value on faithfulness. A woman who lay down with men before she was married inspired much talk and disapproval. And a married woman who lay down with other men brought shame and ridicule on her husband. People said she should just put her husband's things outside the wickiup if he no longer satisfied her, rather than shame him. If a woman was unfaithful, the man had an obligation to punish her. Sometimes men killed such women and their lovers, although that would usually set in motion a bloody feud between families. More often, a man who had been humiliated by the affairs of his wife would cut off her nose and divorce her, so people would understand the cause of his leaving. In the old, free days, this did not happen often, but the threat was important in maintaining social order and right thinking.

But things were different on the reservation, where people could not move away and warriors sat around all day without anything to do except drink the strong liquor of the White Eyes. Many warriors grew sullen, restless, and drunk, so they began more often to beat their wives. Moreover, people were always crowded together instead of moving freely with their own bands, which made for more trouble. So on the reservation these kinds of fights between husbands and wives increased. But Davis said Grey Fox had commanded no man might hit his wife and no one could cut off the nose of a woman who had been unfaithful.

The resentment this caused broke open when Davis arrested and jailed a warrior who had beaten his wife after she lay down with another man. Many of the warrior's relatives had urged him to kill her or cut off her nose, but he only gave her a beating. Of course, when Davis questioned him, he offered no defense because the shame of admitting what his wife had done would have been much worse than going to jail.

The leaders resented Davis's punishment of that man. Moreover, some people said that the White Eyes were eating human beings. They found the White Eyes had cans of man meat, with pictures of a man right on the front. Some soldier gave a boy a can of the man meat and he opened it up—eating the meat and bringing the can home to his mother because the women liked to cut up the cans to make jangles for their dancing dresses. She saw the picture of the man on the front of the can and took it to Nana who said the picture showed what kind of food was in the can—so he threw the can away and called in a shaman who held a four-day ceremony to purify the boy.[10] Lozen could scarcely believe such a thing, but with the White Eyes you could never be certain.

▼

Even the leaders who had favored returning to the reservation grew alarmed at the way Chato had turned Davis against them. When Chihuahua learned Chato was going secretly to Davis's tent and saying Kaytennae and Geronimo planned an uprising, Chihuahua stormed into Davis's tent himself. When Davis called Mickey Free to translate, Chihuahua said he would only speak through another translator and when another translator arrived, Chihuahua spoke strongly.

I have served as a scout longer than Chato. I have served faithfully and told no lie. All that I have reported has been true; and there is proof of my faithfulness. I have told no lies. I have not sneaked to your tent at night. But I am not a spy and will not work for anyone who employs one.

How do you know what Chato has told me? Davis asked.

I heard. I do not speak much English, but I understand. He told you that Geronimo and Kaytennae are plotting an outbreak. He told you that I am planning to kill you and go with them. Had I wished to do that, I could have done so long ago.

Then Chihuahua threw all of his scout equipment down in a heap and continued, *Take this stuff and give it to your spies.*

You can't quit, said Davis. *You just reenlisted. You have a long time yet to serve.*

I am quit, repeated Chihuahua.

Then he went indignantly back to his camp to await arrest. But the other chiefs gathered around him and Geronimo said they knew Chato was a spy who was filling Davis to the brim with lies.

And you permitted this? Chihuahua demanded.

It was one sure way to learn of Chato's treachery. Nana knew. Kaytennae knew, said Geronimo.

Then why wasn't I told? Chihuahua asked.

My brother is honest and loyal, but he is hasty, said Geronimo.

When I see treachery, I speak, replied Chihuahua.

That quality all respect. This White Eye is young, In many ways he has done well. In time, he will learn to judge people and not be deceived by people like Chato.

And I have antagonized him unnecessarily?

Perhaps not. Chato will be so eager for promotion that the officer will think of what you have said. Once he gets suspicious, he will find proof.

Does Chapo know? Chihuahua asked, knowing that Geronimo's son was a scout and wondering whether Geronimo had trusted the boy with his suspicions.

I told him nothing, said Geronimo, whose plans were deep and layered. *Chapo lacks years. But he has long suspected that Chato was working against Kaytennae and has warned me.*

What can we do? asked Kaytennae.

Wait, replied Geronimo.

But worse was yet to come.[11]

▼

Davis summoned Kaytennae to his tent and Kaytennae came cautiously, backed by his warriors. Davis confronted him, speaking harshly and saying he knew Kaytennae planned to kill Davis. Kaytennae demanded the name of the man who had accused him, although they all suspected Chato and Tsoe. Later, they learned that Davis's spies had told him Kaytennae and others were drinking on a hill when Davis came along up a ravine hunting turkeys and had determined to kill him when he reached the top of the hill—but Davis had turned aside at the last moment. It was a lie. Kaytennae had no plans to leave the reservation or to kill Davis, but Chato and his allies thought they would gain power if they could turn Davis against Kaytennae.[12]

Lozen watched the confrontation and saw that Davis had pushed Kaytennae to the very edge of fighting and so prepared to fight herself. But at the last moment, Kaytennae gave Davis his gun, unwilling to start the killing to save himself. He knew if he killed Davis there would be no turning back and the women and children would suffer the greatest harm. So Davis arrested Kaytennae and sent him away, where some said he was chained to a rock in the middle of a lake so great no one could swim across it.[13]

▼

Then a good thing happened. One day, soldiers brought to the camp of the Chihenne several gaunt and ragged women in a wagon. People gathered around and were astonished to discover the three women were all Chihenne—Nana's wife, another woman, and Huera, a midwife and noted tizwin maker who had Lightning Power as a result of having been struck by lightning when she was a girl. They had all been with Victorio at Tres Castillos all those years ago. Everyone gathered around in astonished delight to hear their stories. The women had been taken far down to Mexico City where they had been sold to the owner of a great ranch to work as slaves. They had worked quietly for nearly two years, watching for their opportunity to escape. After Huera stole a knife and some blankets, they esaped and traveled alone by foot more than a thousand miles to the border, timing their departure with the ripening of the fruit of the nopal cactus so they would have something to eat all the way north. One night a mountain lion attacked Huera as she lay sleeping, but she awoke and fended him off, so when the lion bit her on the head he only got a mouthful of skin instead of biting through her skull. Nonetheless, the lion ripped her scalp loose from her head before she could kill him with her knife, which she clutched in her hand every night when she went to sleep. But Huera was a woman of great Power and had ceremonies for healing, childbirth, and making tizwin, so she recovered from the attack quickly. The women had come safely through to Ojo Caliente, where soldiers found them and sent them to Fort Apache to be reunited with the Chihenne. Lozen listened to their story with great admiration, proud the women accomplished such strong things.

Huera quickly resumed a position of influence, in part because she was a wife of Mangas, the son of Mangas Coloradas. Some said Mangas was not as happy as he might have been to have her back, as she was a strong woman with a sharp tongue. She was also one of the most respected and sought-after makers of tizwin, as her blend was sweet, strong, and lucky. When she learned Grey Fox had forbidden the making of tizwin, she began speaking against Davis, mocking the men for being like sheep harried by dogs. Some said she stirred up Mangas, a good fighter but kindly and mild. He knew many trails everyone else had forgotten and everyone remembered the days of his father with longing and loss. Although Mangas was not ambitious or aggressive, he seemed to speak up more and move closer to Geronimo's position after Huera returned.

The canyon between Davis and the other leaders continued to grow deeper, as the floodwaters of suspicion dug it out. Geronimo, Lozen, Nana, Naiche, Chihuahua, Mangas, and others agreed that Davis was a good man, but that Chato and Tsoe had thrown so much dust in his eyes he could no longer see things clearly. More and more, they stayed away from Davis's tent and met among themselves to consider what they should do. Then they learned of the departure of the agent who had charge over Davis—a nantan named Crawford who was stationed at Fort Apache and had command over the whole reservation. Many of the leaders trusted Crawford, who was an honorable man who treated people fairly, although he was a bad man to have on one's trail when he had command of the scouts. The chiefs wondered if he had been sent away so the agents who stole all the supplies and locked people up for no reason could take charge again.[14] Oftentimes, soldiers would go up to Geronimo or Naiche and draw their fingers across their throats, but no one knew whether they were mocking the warriors or trying to warn them. Finally, the leaders decided to confront Davis and so held a big tizwin drink and the next morning went to Davis's tent to demand a discussion.

The talk went badly. Loco started out in his halting, careful way, explaining they had kept their promise to live peacefully on the reservation but had made no promises about tizwin or how they conducted themselves with their families. But Chihuahua, who was still a little drunk from the night before, interrupted Loco saying they had all been drinking and Davis should either arrest them all or keep quiet about it. Davis began speaking sternly, as though to children, saying Grey Fox had forbidden their drinking and they must treat their wives with respect. Nana listened to this insulting talk for a time and then rose in anger.

Nana spun on Mickey Free and said, *Tell the Fat Boy that I had killed many men before he was out of baby grass.* Then Nana stalked out of the tent, followed by everyone except Loco, who tried to smooth things over.

They went back to their camps and waited, their apprehension growing by the hour. Lozen talked to Geronimo and they agreed to get ready to leave quickly. They had all been stashing supplies and gathering up ammunition for months, knowing only a fool would put all his trust in the promise of a White Eye. The day passed with no word from Grey Fox. Then another day passed as well, the hours oozing like blood from a wound. They talked frequently, speculating on what this long silence betokened. Huera said she'd heard Grey Fox had decided to turn Geronimo and other leaders over to the people in town. Many White Eyes had complained bitterly when Crook accepted the surrender of the Chiricahua in the Sierra Madre and brought them back to Arizona. Others said the Chiricahua were still slipping away from the reservation to steal horses and kill people. In truth, outlaws, Mexican bandits, and some bands that had still not surrendered committed many murders and thefts—many of which were blamed on Geronimo and the Chiricahua. The newspapers had been saying the army should hang Geronimo and the others immediately, Huera told them.

Many people thought Grey Fox must have gotten the message from Davis but put off responding until he had gathered up his soldiers to cut off any escape from the reservation. Once he had them trapped, he would arrest them and imprison them for drinking tizwin. Perhaps he would hang them as the newspapers wanted. So Geronimo began making preparations, conferring with Nana, Naiche, Chihuahua, Mangas, and Lozen. He secretly told Chapo and Perico to stay with the scouts and look for any chance to kill Davis, reasoning that once Davis was dead Mangas and Chihuahua would realize they could not turn back. Geronimo also told Chapo to kill Chato if he had the chance, for Chato had shown himself a traitor and Geronimo did not want him leading scouts on his trail.

On the third day after the confrontation with Davis, Geronimo went off alone to pray and consult his Power. When he came back, he seemed set in his course. He said Grey Fox was coming to hang him and the other leaders so he was leaving the reservation. Nana and the others agreed they could wait no longer, for Grey Fox must surely be gathering soldiers to arrest them all.[15] They all remembered the story about how Grey Fox had sent his scouts out to hunt down the Tonto chief Delshay and had paid a bounty when they dumped eight heads on his porch.

So they made preparations quickly and quietly, aware the spies among them would soon give away their intentions. Nana, Geronimo, Lozen, Mangas, and Chihuahua all resolved to go along, as did Istee, the last son of Victorio, and Daklugie, the last son of Juh. Mangas and Chihuahua hesitated, saying they wanted to wait until someone saw the soldiers coming—but Geronimo lied and told them Chapo and Perico at Fort Apache had already killed Davis and Chato. Mangas and Chihuahua saw that the first rocks of the avalanche had already started down the mountain, so they all left together—about thirty-five warriors, eight boys old enough to fight, and one hundred women and children. Loco and about three-quarters of those on the reservation remained, determined to take their chances with Grey Fox. They knew, too well, what chance they had if they left.

The warriors moved ahead and to the sides of the swiftly fleeing column of women and children, scooping up horses and killing any White Eye they encountered. Nana sent several warriors to find places to cut the telegraph wires. They had not gone very far when Chapo and Perico caught up, saying Davis had been very careful, giving them only a few bullets and no opportunity to kill him. When Mangas, Chihuahua, and Naiche heard Davis was not

already dead as Geronimo had told them, they grew so angry
Lozen thought one of them might kill Geronimo.[16] In the end,
they did not quite come to blows, but the group shattered like a
dropped pot. Chihuahua went north, hoping to circle back and
return to the reservation. Naiche took a few warriors and their
families and went his own way, also considering a return to the
reservation. Mangas took a small group, saying he would find some
place to live peacefully in Mexico. The rest, including Lozen,
stayed with Geronimo and Nana, determined to return to the
Sierra Madre. Lozen decided it was actually better they should
break up, so they would leave a fainter trail for the thousands of
soldiers and hundreds of scouts already chasing every rumor of
their passing.

Lozen felt a great sense of relief in having left the reservation,
where she had felt her spirit wilting like sage pulled up by the
roots. She enjoyed working with the other women on the reservation, watching the children and sleeping at night without starting at each noise. But she could not feel the stir of her Power
inside while living under the White Eyes. She feared Power would
fade out of her mind entirely if she remained on the reservation,
leaving her alone.

Of course, she always had the company of Nana, her relatives,
her clan members, and the warriors, but no one had ever filled
the space in her left by Victorio's death. Sometimes it seemed
most of the people she knew were dead already and that more
people remembered her in the Happy Place than in this world.
So she found comfort in the whisperings of her Power, which cast
her out as its shadow. Her Power seemed most alive and present
when she was with the warriors, moving ahead of their enemies,
risking everything.[17]

Besides, she remembered what Nana had said about Victorio:
that she need not mourn him because he had died as a warrior,

protecting his People—the death he deserved. Perhaps she could earn that death also, for Grey Fox would not rest until he had killed them all.

Geronimo knew this as well and now called this last group of fighters Indeh—the Dead.

CHAPTER XVI

▼▼

Indeh

May 17, 1885

The group led by Nana and Geronimo moved quickly through the mountains, running down into Mexico, relying on Lozen's Power and their intimate knowledge of the country to evade soldiers scrambling to intercept them from every direction. They killed at least seventeen people as they fled south and gathered any ammunition they could find. They fell upon a supply train, killing the drivers and looting the wagons. They attacked a military mule train loaded with ammunition in Skeleton Canyon near the Mexican border, killing three soldiers and capturing all the horses and supplies. They crossed into Mexico two weeks after leaving the reservation without having lost a man. However, they later learned soldiers had found both Chihuahua and Naiche as they moved back toward the reservation, forcing them to flee toward Mexico as well.

Geronimo's group pushed quickly south into Mexico into the shelter of a familiar mountain range and then set a watch on their back trail. Soon they saw a strong force of scouts under Crawford cross the border and the small hope they had nurtured faded to a grim determination. Lozen had expected the scouts to come after them into Mexico as Grey Fox had threatened, but she had prayed they would not. She noted bitterly that Chato led the scouts. They would have a hard time now, as Chato was a good fighter who knew every hiding place, water source, and trail.

So they played a deadly game with the scouts who chased them, like a boy dodging arrows. They learned that Chato's scouts found Chihuahua's band in the Bavispe Mountains near Oputo three weeks after they left the reservation, killing one woman and capturing fifteen women and children, including Chihuahua's daughter and son. The scouts hit another band a month later in the Haya Mountains, killing four warriors.

Geronimo stayed out of the way of the scouts for nearly two months, thanks in part to Lozen's ceremony. Mangas also joined them. But then seventy-eight scouts found their camp northeast of Nacori, killing one woman and one boy and capturing fifteen women and children, including Huera and three wives and five children of Geronimo.[1] The rest of the warriors and women and children scattered in the face of the attack, reassembling mournfully a day later. The losses were having an effect on everyone, as it seemed they could find no safe place. Lozen saw how the warriors with families grieved and decided her Power had blessed her after all in turning her from a woman's path, away from a family and a husband. Now with Victorio gone, she had less to lose than others, which made courage easier.

One day, Geronimo said he was going to return to the reservation with a raiding party to bring back his wives and children. Four other warriors who had lost family members said they would go with him. Lozen, Nana, and most of the others decided to wait for Geronimo in the Sierra Madre. So Geronimo set out, with his Power going before him like a wind. He came back with one of his wives, one of his daughters, and another woman. They also brought back some Mescalero women and their children as captives. Lozen did not like the idea of taking women of other bands against their will, but she understood the need. The warriors could live a long time alone in the mountains. They could kill their enemies, steal horses, and go on great raids. But what did it mean if they had no families? What good was a victory dance, without the women making the cry of applause? They were not fighting merely for horses, bullets, beef, and revenge. They were fighting so the People would not vanish from the earth. But if they had not wives or children or hope of keeping the round of life unbroken, then why should they fight on?

So they moved from place to place in Mexico for months, the bands reuniting and putting aside old angers because they were the last free people and could rely only on one another. They all needed Lozen's ceremony to find their enemies, Nana's Power to find ammunition, and Geronimo's Power to see ahead.

When the People ran low on good ammunition for their American guns, Ulzana, a brother of Chihuahua, went back into the United States with ten warriors. The war party avoided the many guarded water holes and rode fifty miles each day. In the Season When the Earth is Reddish Brown,[2] the raiders attacked several camps on the San Carlos Reservation, killing five warriors and boys, eleven women, and four children, and capturing six other women and children. They did this to punish the bands of the scouts hunting them and to bring back more women and children to replenish the bands hiding now in Mexico. The next day they killed two herders and took horses belonging to Benito's band, who had remained on the reservation with Loco and whose band had provided scouts. Chato's scouts chased the raiders and killed one, but then they lost the trail. The raiders covered twelve hundred miles, killed thirty-eight people, and stole 250 horses and cows before returning safely to Mexico.

Even so, the snare seemed to tighten. After that raid, Crawford and his scouts came back down into Mexico to harry the Chiricahua. The scouts surrounded one camp, but the warriors heard the sound of the scouts' horses and slipped away, leaving all of their own horses and supplies behind. Each loss bled a little more strength from them. Only a few of the warriors still had their families with them and all yearned for wives, children, brothers, sisters, and parents still living on the reservation. Even the strongest warriors felt the longing growing and the hope fading, seeing they could not survive without ammunition and that any raid into the United States provoked months of pursuit by the scouts. Geronimo held many of them to him by his Power.

Even so, some people wondered whether Geronimo's Power was not hungry for lives. Geronimo's Power protected him, but those who stood beside him often fell—even his wives and his children. Sometimes it seemed Geronimo could fight on forever, like a scorpion still stinging after you have cut off its head. But others tired, seeing no hope of winning, just as Juh's vision had predicted. Moreover, Mexican soldiers and enemy Indian bands were now all scouring the countryside for them and the government had promised a reward that had drawn many bounty hunters.

▼

Nana, Lozen, Geronimo, Naiche, Chihuahua, and Mangas talked among themselves, debating whether the White Eyes might still accept a surrender. Some advocated surrender as the only way to survive. Seeing this, Geronimo suggested that by offering to negotiate they might stall the soldiers for time and give the warriors a rest. Nana said even if the warriors decided to fight on, they should perhaps send the women and the children back to the reservation, as there seemed little hope now and Grey Fox had always treated the women and children with compassion. Eventually they decided Lozen and Dahteste should go talk to Crawford, who was chasing them again with the scouts. After Ulzana's raid, Crawford would not let go of their trail, hanging on like a Gila monster with his jaw locked shut.

Lozen left the warriors on a hillside behind good cover where they could look down on the camp of the scouts. Then she went to talk with Crawford, who told her they would not be harmed if they surrendered to him. She stayed for a time in his camp, counting his men and his guns and trying to get information from the scouts. Then one of the scouts rushed into camp saying some Mexicans and Tarahumara Indians led by a well-known scalp hunter were approaching. When the Mexicans arrived, they suddenly began shooting at the scouts, wounding several. Convinced the Mexicans had mistaken his scouts for Geronimo's band, Captain Crawford climbed on top of a big boulder and waved a white handkerchief, shouting he was an American army officer hunting Geronimo. The shooting stopped for a moment, but then the Mexicans fired again. A bullet hit Crawford and he fell backward, smashing his head on the rock close by where Lozen stood.

Up on the hillside, Geronimo watched the Mexicans and Americans fighting and laughed out loud.

The scouts returned fire, killing five Mexicans, including the commander. The second nantan among the scouts, a man named Lieutenant Marion Maus, managed to stop the fighting and withdraw the scouts out of range of the Mexicans. After the shooting stopped, Maus told Lozen nothing had changed: They should surrender to him and return to the reservation. Lozen nodded, giving nothing away, and promised to take his words back to Geronimo. Then she slipped away, returning to the warriors watching on the hillside.

▼

Geronimo and the nantan talked the next day, Maus sitting down with Geronimo and fourteen warriors.

Why have you come down here? Geronimo asked.

To destroy you and your band, said Maus boldly.

Geronimo smiled and shook Maus by the hand in the fashion of the White Eyes, saying now he could trust Maus to report accurately to Grey Fox whatever Geronimo said. Then Geronimo explained he had left the reservation because he heard Grey Fox had sent orders to have him hung and that many people were telling lies—especially Chato and Mickey Free and Tsoe.

But Maus waved away these grievances, saying the only important thing now was for Geronimo and the others to surrender and so save their own lives. They talked a while longer, then Geronimo said he would meet with Grey Fox in two moons in the Canyon de Los Embudos, just below the border. To show his good faith, he would send back members of his band now. This would include Nana, who was an old man and whose broken foot had grown worse in all of the riding, running, and hiding of the past nine months. The prisoners would also include one other warrior, one of Geronimo's wives, the wife and child of Naiche, the sister of Geronimo, who was also a wife of Nana, and one other woman. Maus was impressed Geronimo would give up members of his own family, but Lozen saw Geronimo mostly wanted to protect people who could no longer keep up with the warriors.

So they left Maus and moved back into the mountains, wary lest the Mexicans find them before they could meet with Grey Fox. Lozen felt a sorrow growing as they moved camp over and over again. She felt like someone awaiting her own hanging, so each sunset seemed beautiful beyond expression. She rose every day before the dawn and prayed, thanking the sun for its gifts and feeling the world stir and change around her. She did not understand what the People had done that they should lose everything. And she did not understand what she had done that she should be denied a warrior's death, but returned instead to the cage of the reservation.

They went to the Canyon de Los Embudos in the Season of Little Eagles.[3] They picked their camp with great care, building wickiups on a small hill made of lava rocks with deep ravines on both the front and back and a good escape route into the mountains. They camped about half a mile from Maus and the scouts and went into Grey Fox's camp only one or two at a time, keeping guards continually posted so Grey Fox could not send the scouts to capture them.

They were surprised and happy to see that Grey Fox had brought Kaytennae with him. Many had said Kaytennae had died chained to the rock in the middle of the great lake, but here he was wearing the red headband of the scouts. Lozen went eagerly to him, remembering all the times they had fought together and saved one another. But he seemed subdued, saying he had seen great and terrible things in his time among the White Eyes. He said they had cities with buildings higher than a pine tree, lined up like the chambers in a beehive. He said he had seen more White Eyes than he could count, more White Eyes than the buffalo that once covered the plains, more White Eyes than the geese that flew south overhead every winter. He said they had terrible machines and a demented desire to build things and own things—which they rarely shared with one another. He seemed broken in spirit, like Loco. He had come back to convince them not to fight anymore, saying they had seen only the tip of the tail of the power the White Eyes could muster. Not many people believed him, thinking he had dreamed it, or been witched. But Lozen was shaken by the change in him, remembering that Kaytennae had been afraid of nothing and was as straight, swift, and unswerving as an arrow. She understood then how clever an enemy Grey Fox was, to have broken Kaytennae and used him to weaken the others.

So once again Geronimo, Chihuahua, Naiche, and the other leaders faced Grey Fox. Lozen remained in the back, not talking, but keeping her rifle ready. The White Eyes had never paid much attention to her and she did not want them to pay attention to her now. The leaders hid her importance when talking to the White Eyes, partly to protect her and partly so she could continue to be their messenger and go into the soldiers' camps, counting their guns. So Lozen did not speak and Grey Fox did not bother with her because the White Eyes did not think women important. They made their women wear clothes that hobbled them and did not seek their advice or let them fight.

Geronimo tried to explain that he had left the reservation because Chato and Tsoe had poisoned Davis against them. But Grey Fox was gruff and unpleasant, saying Geronimo was a liar. Grey Fox said even if Geronimo did fear arrest and hanging, that was no reason to kill so many people. Grey Fox stalked Geronimo with words, the way wolves cut one elk out of the herd. He aimed for the bonds that connected Geronimo, Naiche, and Chihuahua. Grey Fox knew he could not convince Geronimo to surrender, but if he could separate Geronimo from the others they would fall into his hands—and then Geronimo would stand alone. Lozen saw this and both admired and feared it. Only an enemy who knew them could defeat them, by turning even their strength against them, like a feinting knife fighter.

It was skillfully done.

They talked for hours. Grey Fox said they must be imprisoned for a time—perhaps two years—as punishment for the killing since leaving the reservation. But he said they would be reunited with their families and after two years allowed to return to the reservation. The leaders moved aside to talk among themselves. Geronimo urged them to fight on, saying they could not trust Grey Fox. But the others were swayed and began to blame Geronimo for the troubles.

Lozen did not speak much. She did not want to surrender and live on the reservation, which seemed like slow death. But Nana was gone now and Kaytennae was broken. The only real fighters left seemed to be herself and the warriors in Geronimo's personal following. Lozen had little responsibility for this decision, since she had no family and no followers. She had decided already when she left the reservation she would fight on as long as anyone else would fight. But the others still missed their families, especially Chihuahua. Moreover, they felt Grey Fox had Power and would kill every one of them if they did not surrender. At the same time, Grey Fox was a man they might trust and they had not encountered many such White Eyes. Some said they should surrender to him because he had honor. Lozen listened quietly to the talk and sadly watched as the current turned against Geronimo, like wind that carries away a sand dune.

After two days of talking, Chihuahua gave way.

He went to Grey Fox and said, *I am anxious to behave. I surrender myself to you because I believe in you and you did not deceive us. You must be our God. You must be the one who makes the green pastures, who sends the rain, who commands the winds. You must be the one who sends the fresh fruits that appear on the trees every year. Everything you do is right. You send my family with me wherever you send me. I ask you to find out if they are willing to go or not,* he added, by which Lozen understood the longing that had moved Chihuahua to surrender.

Next Naiche spoke, a brave man who had never loved fighting as did Geronimo and who had tried all his life to live up to the memory of his father without succeeding. Naiche said, *When I was free, I gave orders, but now I surrender to you. Now that I have surrendered I am glad. I'll not have to hide behind rocks and mountains. I'll go across the open plain. There may be lots of men who have bad feelings against us. I will go wherever you may see fit to send us, where no bad talk will be spoken of us. I surrender to you and hope you will be kind to us.*

Finally, Geronimo spoke. He did not wish to surrender, but

he could not go against all of the others. *Two or three words are enough,* said Geronimo. *We are all comrades, all one family, all one band. What the others say I say also. Once I moved about like the wind. Now I surrender to you and that is all.*[4]

So they returned to their camp and prepared for the journey back to Fort Bowie. Lozen did not speak much, for everything had been said already. The wind had come up now and she was only a bit of milkweed seed in that wind.

That night, there came into camp a trader named Tribolet who had been selling whiskey and bullets and guns to the Chiricahua for years. He was a valuable man and Lozen could not decide whether he was a good man who thought of the People as human beings or just a greedy man willing to sell them guns to use against his own people. He brought with him whiskey and a warning. He said Grey Fox intended to take away their weapons when they crossed into the United States and then hang Geronimo and some others. He said the Americans were roused against the Chiricahua and would never let them go back to the reservation.

No one knew whether to believe these warnings. Some said Grey Fox would not lie in this way. Others remembered Mangas Coloradas and all the lies of the whites, layered like sandstone cliffs. Geronimo began drinking and the others along with him— except Lozen and a few who remembered how much drinking had cost the warriors at such times.

The next morning, Geronimo and the others were too drunk to break camp as Grey Fox demanded. So Grey Fox said he must go back and make arrangements for their surrender. He left Maus to bring them along. Lozen and the others thought hard about the implications of the departure of Grey Fox. On the one hand, it seemed to prove he was telling the truth when he said he did not much care whether they surrendered or made him bring all the soldiers and the scouts to kill them. On the other hand, some said maybe Grey Fox was going to get more soldiers to surround them so he could hang them.

They covered only a few miles that day before making camp again. The Chiricahua camped well away from the scouts and the soldiers, selecting a secure spot with a good escape route so they could not be surprised in the night. Tribolet came into their camp again, having stayed out of the way of the soldiers during the day. He brought more whiskey and repeated his warnings. Once gain, Geronimo and the others began to drink, talking and quarreling among themselves.

Toward morning, Geronimo decided he would not surrender himself for hanging, but would leave with whoever cared to ac- company him. When Naiche said he would go as well, Naiche's wife got up from the edge of the circle of firelight and ran back toward the camp of the scouts. Naiche called on his wife, Eclah- heh, to come back. She was a good woman, and strong hearted, but all of the women save Lozen longed to sleep the night without fear and to return to the reservation, where their children might survive. Only hardship and death or slavery waited for them on the warpath. So Naiche's wife did not stop. Then to everyone's surprise, Naiche shot her—hitting her in the leg. Great confusion broke out, as everyone thought the gunshot would bring the scouts running. Geronimo rushed to gather up his things.

Lozen stood a moment as the fear and the excitement swirled around her, like a rock in a stream. Then she turned to gather up her few things. She had made her decision already, back when her brother died. Had she not earned a warrior's death? Had she not done everything expected of her? Had she not given over her life to protecting the People, so long as they were free and proud and still the People? Had she killed so many enemies and lost so many loved ones only to become a prisoner now? Why should she go starve on the reservation, gnawing her pride like a piece of dry rawhide? Why should she go and wait for the never-ending cough, when she still had her weapons? So she gathered up her things and joined the twenty warriors, fourteen women, and six children who had decided to leave. She looked at their faces in the darkness and saw that eight were relatives of Geronimo or Naiche and included the strongest spirits in the band. Fun was there along with Naiche and Perico and Yahnozha. Chihuahua refused to go, saying he wanted to go back and see his wife and children on the reservation.

So they slipped away in the darkness and put as much distance as possible between themselves and the scouts, who would be on their trail as soon as the morning sun made tracking possible.[5]

Lozen rode near the front of their small group, her senses alert, her mind thrown out ahead seeking the vibrations of the enemy. She felt the familiar mingling of relief and loss as they turned again to the warpath. This time, surely, they could not turn back. They must ride this flood to the place where all the rivers go. She looked at the other warriors in the darkness and realized they were all Chiricahua. She was the last of the free Chihenne, having ridden beyond Victorio and Nana and Kaytennae and all the others. She wondered at it a little, surprised when she noted it.

In the beginning, she had ridden out onto the warpath to protect the People. But the People were broken, their hope thrown down. What had she to protect now by fighting, except perhaps the memory of what the People had been?

CHAPTER XVII

▼▼▼

The Final Surrender

March 1886

They rode now like a storm.

Every man's hand was turned against them, so they were reckless with their lives. They asked no quarter and gave none.[1] They called themselves Indeh—the Dead. They called the White Eyes Indah—the Living. There was freedom in this for they had nothing left to lose and so nothing left to fear.

Geronimo led them like the falcon in a dive, relying on Lozen's ceremony to keep them safe. They raided through Mexico, so that for many years after mothers used Geronimo's name to frighten their children into good behavior. Whenever they pleased, they went back into the United States, raiding up the Santa Cruz Valley past Tucson all the way to Fort Apache.

The White Eyes and the Mexicans chased them without pause. Lozen heard that Grey Fox had gone. They heard rumors the Great Father was so angry Geronimo and the others had slipped away again that he took command away from Grey Fox and gave it to a different nantan. This made Geronimo laugh a long while. But the soldiers kept coming. Strangely enough, they did not come with the scouts, but chased them in small detachments that kept after them for months.[2] Of course, without the scouts it was not hard to stay out of the way of the soldiers, but Lozen was impressed with how doggedly the soldiers came on—riding their horses to death and walking the bottoms off their boots. But it was easy to evade those soldiers, because they remained so dependent on their horses. If the warriors were too closely pursued, they rode into the mountain until the horses could go no further and then started climbing. Once the soldiers were afoot, they had no chance of catching the warriors. The chief danger they faced was bad luck, as there were so many soldiers looking for them it would be easy to run into their enemies by accident. However, Lozen's ceremony helped keep them safe, warning them when their enemies approached too closely. The weeks passed into months and while the Chiricahua killed more people than they could count and stole hundreds of horses and cattle, the soldiers never killed a single warrior. They lost one warrior who decided to go his own way and another who foolishly went into Casas Grandes to drink and was killed by the Mexicans.

Still, living like hunted creatures wore on them, for they were like a war party whose village has been destroyed. War was a fine and honorable thing and Lozen believed Ussen would be pleased they had killed so many enemies, and she, Geronimo, Naiche, Fun, and the other warriors showed such courage that Lozen was again proud to be of the People. But their lack of families ate into them, like a pine tree leaning out over a stream undercutting its roots. They could not hold proper ceremonies or dances or councils. They all yearned for the sound of children running through the camp and the boys practicing endlessly with their small arrows and the girls with their laughter and baskets filled with berries. The warriors had ridden beyond fear, but they were a broken hoop that can roll only a short distance before falling on its side with longing for its missing part. Of course, Geronimo held firm, tangling the spirits of the others with coils of rage and cunning. But Lozen could see the resolve bleeding slowly from the other men, who sometimes stood looking north where their families and relatives struggled to survive on the reservation without them.

When they ran low on supplies, Geronimo told Lozen and Dahteste to take money they had stolen from the Mexicans and the Americans to get supplies in Fronteras, about thirty miles south of the border. They went carefully into that town, relying on the Mexicans' belief that women were not even worth killing. The band had a wary relationship with Fronteras and a few other towns. They knew the people in Fronteras would kill them all if they could, but greed might protect them. Geronimo had suggested Lozen talk to the Mexican headman about making a peace, which might delay a Mexican attack and convince the Mexicans to trade for needed supplies. Of course, the Mexicans would hope they could use their old trick and invite the warriors into Fronteras for a fiesta to kill them when they were drunk. So Lozen went into Fronteras and talked to the Mexican headman, speaking carefully and looking modestly down at the ground as she counted every fighter and every gun. She saw soldiers were gathering from other towns to set a trap. Then she took three mules loaded with supplies the Mexicans gave her, including the mescal Geronimo insisted she should buy.

Lozen went carefully back to the camp in the Torres Mountains, which could be reached only by an easily defended trail and sat so high on the mountain they could see any enemy approaching from half a day's journey. The warriors greeted her warmly and listened to her news, but they seemed most eager for the mescal. Most of the warriors quickly found a bottle and began drinking. Geronimo talked to Lozen for a little while about what she had seen in Fronteras, flashing his wolf smile with his eyes glittering when she said the soldiers were gathering to trap them. But then Geronimo's interest in the mescal won out and he went to the packsaddles with the others. They drank heavily that night, smothering the longing and desperation with the potent liquor of the Mexicans. Often lethal fights broke out when a group of warriors got drunk—but this time no damage was done and they forgot they were Indeh for one night.

The next day lookouts reported two men approaching along Lozen's trail. The warriors gathered to watch the two men approach, as though looking down on two ants. Kanesah, who had the field glasses, said the two men were familiar Chricahua, Martine and Kayihtah. But Geronimo did not care that they were related to some of his warriors. He knew those two men and did not think they had come to join them in their exile. They came, instead, to kill them with words.

So Geronimo said, *It does not matter who they are, if they come closer they are to be shot.*[3]

But Yahnozha replied, *They are our brothers. Let us find out why they come. They are brave men to risk this.*

Geronimo only glared at him, saying he would not let the two men approach closer.

Then Yahnozha answered, saying. *We will not shoot. The first man who lifts a rifle I will kill you.*

Lozen watched the confrontation tighten between the two men, knowing they were each strangers to fear and capable of killing in an instant, the way one slaps a mosquito without thinking.

Then Fun spoke. *I will help you,* he said to Yahnozha, in his offhand way.

Lozen saw the effect of Fun's words on Geronimo: first irritation, then calculation, then acceptance. Perhaps Geronimo could face down Yahnozha, but not Fun as well. Many believed Fun was the bravest of them all and more willing to sacrifice himself than any other man among them. So Geronimo saw he had no choice but to let Martine and Kayihtah come into the camp.

Their relatives greeted Martine and Kayihtah warmly, but Geronimo eyed them warily. The two warriors said Grey Fox had gone and a man named General Miles was now the commander. Miles had sent Gatewood, whom the People called Long Nose, to give them a chance to surrender and go home to their families.

The troops are coming after you from all directions, said Kayihtah. *Their aim is to kill every one of you if it takes fifty years. Everything is against you. If you are awake at night and a rock rolls down the mountain or a stick breaks, you will be running. You even eat your meals running. You have no friends whatever in the world. But on the reservation I get plenty to eat. I go wherever I want, talk to good people. I go to bed whenever I want and get all my sleep. I have nobody to fear. I have my little patch of corn. I'm trying to do what the white people want me to do. And there's no reason your People shouldn't do it.*

Lozen saw the effect Kayihtah's words had on the other warriors. He had turned their thoughts to their families and friends on the reservation, so they imagined sleeping straight through without listening for the faint clinking of metal or the snapping of a stick that warned of a trap nearly ready to close. Geronimo saw it too and realized most of the others would want to hear what Long Nose had to say. So he told Kayihtah and Martine they should go back to Long Nose and say they would meet with him, but only with him.

The warriors came to the meeting place warily by ones and twos, so they could not be ambushed all together. Geronimo came last of all, approaching Long Nose in a friendly manner and remarking on how thin and sickly he looked. Long Nose was a tough, slender man who laughed easily and seemed to enjoy the jokes, good humor, and courage of the scouts he usually commanded. Those who had fought with him said he was a good man, brave and shrewd in battle. They also said he respected the People and did not treat them like camp dogs, like so many officers. People also said Long Nose was an honorable man, whose words

260 A Peter Aleshire

had strength. So Geronimo and Long Nose rolled a cigarette and passed it around, smoking in a friendly, ceremonial way. Lozen appreciated how Long Nose politely smoked and talked about little things, rather than barking out orders and demanding deference like most White Eyes. Once everyone had smoked and visited a little, Geronimo brought up the thing they had to settle.

All of us here have come to listen to the message of General Miles, said Geronimo.

Long Nose nodded and spoke directly and clearly. He had with him a White Eye named George Wratten who spoke the language of the People well and had married a Chiricahua woman. Speaking through Wratten, Long Nose said, *Surrender and you will be sent to join the rest of your People in Florida, there to await the decision of the President as to your final disposition. Accept these terms or fight it out to the bitter end.*

The silence stretched on a long time after this. Lozen studied the faces of the other warriors and saw there the weariness and longing. Geronimo passed his hand across his eyes and then extended his arm toward Long Nose. His strong, weathered fingers trembled.

We have been three days drunk on the mescal the women brought back from the Mexicans, said Geronimo by way of explanation. *The Mexicans expected to play their usual trick of getting us drunk and killing us, but we have had the fun; and now I feel a little shaky. You need not fear giving me a drink of whiskey, for our spree passed off without a single fight, as you can see by looking at the men sitting in this circle, all of whom you know. Now in Fronteras there is plenty of wine and mescal and the Mexicans and Americans are having a good time. We thought perhaps you had brought some with you.*

But Long Nose replied he had left Fronteras so quickly he had no mescal with him, nor any whiskey.

Then they talked a long while. Geronimo said he would stop

fighting, but only if they could all return to the reservation and live again at Turkey Creek on the farms they had started. But Long Nose replied he could only give them the message from General Miles and this was their last chance to surrender. The talking went on for hours, most of the time filled with Geronimo's attempt to explain the wrongs that had forced them to leave the reservation. Then the warriors talked among themselves, with Geronimo trying to strengthen the others against Gatewood's promises. Then they ate a little and returned to talk again with Long Nose.

Geronimo explained that once they had gone as they pleased over a great area and taken what they needed. But now they could see the White Eyes had taken nearly all of it and so were willing to give in and fight no more forever. All they wanted was a little land on the reservation where they could live peacefully with their families. Geronimo spoke strongly and in anger, the fire rising behind his eyes. Lozen saw Gatewood listening, glancing from face to face nervously.

Naiche saw that also and hastened to reassure Gatewood, saying no matter how the talk went they would not harm Long Nose, who had come in friendship and peace and could leave in the same manner.

Some of the tension went out of Long Nose then, for he had the promise of safety from the leader of the band, who had more influence even than Geronimo. So Long Nose told them the thing he had been holding back. He said all their families and friends had been sent already to Florida, Naiche's mother and wife along with them. They had been sent to live with Chihuahua's band, which had already surrendered to Grey Fox. They all felt the blow of this, like a wound in the stomach that is fatal but does not knock you down. They sagged under the weight of it and something broke in them, like a just-fired pot dashed with cold water.

The warriors drew aside once again to talk, but Lozen could

see that the news about their families had changed them, as the flood changes the streambed. Geronimo still had hope he could gain some advantage from surrender, perhaps a promise to return the People to the reservation after they had been punished. It all depended on Miles and whether he could be counted on to ride the horse of his promises.

So they returned again to talk to Long Nose, although it seemed he was growing weary of the talking, which had gone on all day. Geronimo sat down in a friendly and earnest way with Long Nose and questioned him carefully about Miles. How old was he? What color were his eyes and hair? Was his voice agreeable, or harsh? Did he say more than he meant, or less? Did he look in your eyes when he spoke, or down at the ground? Did he have many friends among his own people? Do the soldiers and officers like him? Do they believe what he says? Had he experience with other Indians? Was he cruel or kindhearted? Would he keep his promises? Lozen listened carefully to the answers along with each of the warriors, although she knew the White Eyes had never kept their promises—even the good ones. Long Nose praised Miles patiently in all his details, so even Geronimo was impressed. At length, Geronimo said Miles must be a good man, as the Great Father had sent him from Washington and he had sent Long Nose all this distance to them.

Then Long Nose suggested his party go back to the camp of Captain Lawton, which was about four miles distant, so the warriors could make medicine, pray, and make a decision. They agreed, impressed Long Nose respected the way in which they must decide.

Then Geronimo said to him, *We want your advice. Consider yourself one of us and not a white man. Remember all that has been said today and as one of the People advise us what to do under the circumstances.*

Long Nose responded quickly: *I would trust General Miles and take him at his word.*[4]

They all considered this for a time, not speaking. Then Geronimo asked whether Long Nose could go to the nearest fort and communicate with General Miles to see whether he might let them live on the reservation after all. But Long Nose replied General Miles had made up his mind and would not change it. So they bid Long Nose farewell and promised to send word to him the next morning.

After Long Nose and the others left camp, Geronimo told Chapo to go join Long Nose and sleep close to him that night to listen for anything that would tell them whether they could believe the message from General Miles. But Chapo came back a little later saying Long Nose had sent him back out of fear the scouts in Lawton's camp might attack Chapo, as there was bad blood between the scouts and Geronimo's band. Geronimo and the others saw the truth of this and respected Long Nose all the more. They had spent all of this war trying to find an honorable white man whom they could believe and Naiche said perhaps Long Nose was such a man and so they should trust him. They talked a long time that night, like a team trying in desperation to decide in which moccasin the bone had been hidden.

Perico, one of the bravest of them all, said, *I am going to surrender. My wife and children have been captured and I love them and want to be with them.*

The others agreed, one by one.

Geronimo stood a long while without speaking, and then said, *I don't know what to do. I have been depending heavily on you men. You have been great fighters in battle. If you are going to surrender, there is no use in my going without you. I will give up with you.*[5] At length, they all decided to go with Long Nose and meet with

Miles to see whether he was the sort of man Long Nose had described.

The next day the twenty-four warriors and the fourteen women and children in the band rode to Lawton's camp and agreed to go with Long Nose to talk to General Miles in Skeleton Canyon, just over the border. They would travel with the soldiers, who would warn off any Mexicans they encountered. But the warriors would camp apart along with Long Nose and his small party and keep their weapons so the soldiers could not kill them in treachery.

On the long journey to meet General Miles north of the border, they encountered perhaps two hundred Mexican soldiers. When they spotted the Mexicans who were undoubtedly hunting the Chiricahua, Geronimo, Lozen, and the others riding with Long Nose took flight. They stopped at a safe distance to see what the Mexicans intended. Lawton sent word back that the Mexican commander wanted to meet with Geronimo to be sure the band would surrender to the Americans and stop making trouble in Mexico. So Geronimo met with the Mexican commander. The little man was so arrogant Geronimo nearly shot him, but Long Nose stepped between them and smoothed things out. Finally, the Mexican commander agreed to send one or two men with Lawton to be sure Geronimo left Mexico to surrender.

Things went along better after that and Lozen began to feel a little more hopeful when she saw Long Nose was a good man, courteous, funny, and brave. They had more worries when they passed through Guadalupe Canyon, where they had killed some of Lawton's men in another fight. The soldiers seemed angry, casting many hard looks at the warriors. So Geronimo and Naiche kept their camp well apart, ready to fight or run. Geronimo suggested the band go into the mountains near Fort Bowie to wait for Miles, but Long Nose said it would be best if they went ahead to Skeleton Canyon as they had promised.

So they came at last to Skeleton Canyon and waited uneasily there for two days until General Miles arrived.[6] He was a tall, imposing man, who spoke pleasantly and directly, as Long Nose had said. Miles spoke in the careful and polite way of one warrior to another, with none of the harsh bluntness of Grey Fox. So they were reassured that Long Nose had spoken truthfully about him. They began talking, resolved to trust his promises. Miles said no harm would come to them if they surrendered. They would go to Fort Bowie and lay down their arms and then go to Florida, where they would see their relatives within five days. He showed them with stones on the ground how the Great Father in Washington wanted to bring the People together, including Chihuahua's band in Florida and the people who had been already taken from the reservation, plus Geronimo and Naiche's band. They would remain with their families in Florida for two years, on a reservation with good land, horses, cattle, plows, and tools. Then they could return to the San Carlos Reservation.[7]

They talked in a friendly way and it seemed Geronimo had won a victory after all, with the promise they might one day return to the reservation. Of course, once San Carlos had seemed like a terrible place, but Lozen found comfort in the thought she would again see Nana and Kaytennae. She felt a great weariness and loss, softened only by her determination to endure whatever came to her—as a warrior with a mortal wound who does not cry out in the dying. Her Power seemed a long way off, not speaking to her now. She did not even perform her ceremony anymore, as she had no need of it. She was surrounded by her enemies and needed no ceremony to see that.[8]

So Geronimo and Miles stood in the space between the soldiers and the warriors and placed a stone in the middle of the blanket on which they had been sitting.

Geronimo said, *Our treaty is made by this stone and it will last until the stone should crumble to dust.*[9]

They all bound one another with an oath, raised their hands to heaven, and swore to do no harm one to the other.

Then they rode with Miles to Fort Bowie. The night before they arrived at the fort, three men, three women, and one boy slipped away, but Geronimo did not leave, as he was bound by his promise. Nor did Lozen leave, for she was weary and far from her People.

When they reached the fort, Miles repeated his promises. He held out his hand to them, palm up, saying, *This represents the past; it is covered with ridges and hollows.* Then he rubbed one hand across the other, and added, *This represents the wiping out of the past, which will be considered smooth and forgotten. Leave your horses here, maybe they will be sent to you; you will have a separate reservation with your tribe, with horses and wagons, and no one will harm you.*

So they put down their arms, placed themselves in Miles's hands, and waited to learn their fate.

Of course, they had made a great mistake.

They had trusted the word of a White Eye.

▼

Once General Miles had Geronimo and the others in his hands, he called in all of the people who had been living peacefully on the San Carlos Reservation, saying he needed to make a count to be sure no one could accuse them of raiding. Instead, he put them all in corrals, took away their weapons, and made them prisoners. A few warriors, like Massai, tried to stir them up to fight—but their position was hopeless. Then the soldiers marched the 381 people to the railroad, including 103 children, most of whom had never been off the reservation. A great, belching, steaming, roaring train came to carry them away, appearing so fierce that some people prayed to it. The soldiers put them all on the train, packed together like cattle. With them were many of the scouts and their families.

When Lozen heard this news, she saw they could not even surrender to the White Eyes nor understand them nor survive in their shadow. A warrior understood war, revenge, and the value of killing ten of your enemies for every death suffered. A warrior understood the value of fear in an enemy and the importance of breaking the will of a foe. But this seemed an incomprehensible way of making war, stripped of honor or ceremony. The White Eyes had sent into exile even the warriors who had fought against their own People. Could it be the White Eyes did not understand that sending the People into exile was a way of killing them—not their bodies, but their spirits, which was worse? Did they not know that a people are fitted to a certain place, led to wisdom by a certain arrangement of rocks, a certain bend in a stream, a certain sound in the trees, and the stories of the naming of each place?

Perhaps not. Perhaps the White Eyes had been driven out of the places that knew them because of their greed or anger or hatred. Perhaps they had lost their ceremonies and Power had turned against them so no place was different from any other place for them now. So they had gone out into the world in despair and bitterness to cut all others away from their own places. Or perhaps the White Eyes understood these things very well indeed. Perhaps in their anger and Power they had resolved to kill the spirits of those who had fought them, the way a warrior intent on revenge sometimes will shoot arrows into a prisoner, avoiding the vital places to make the suffering last.

It did not matter, of course. It had never mattered. The riddle of the White Eyes had no solution. They had merely come upon the People, like a fire that filled up the whole sky with its smoke, impossible to fight or evade. Who could reason with a fire?

Lozen went without resistance down to the railroad tracks. The soldiers treated her carelessly and without respect, not even the respect of hatred they showed for Geronimo and Naiche. They thought she was just a woman and paid no attention to her. The warriors had agreed among themselves they would not tell the White Eyes that Lozen was one of the leading warriors among them who had fought in more battles than any of them. They did not know what the White Eyes would do if they understood this, so the warriors decided Lozen would be more protected if the soldiers paid no attention to her.[10]

When they were ready to leave, the soldiers pushed Martine and Kayihtah forward to go with them as prisoners as well. They learned even Chato and Loco had been made prisoners, after going to Washington to talk to the Great Father. Some of the warriors laughed at this, saying it was the only comfort left to them, for the treachery of the scouts had been betrayed by the even greater treachery of the White Eyes.

Lozen went into the dark, bad-smelling boxcar quietly, smoothing out her mind and remembering the places that had led her toward wisdom. Finally the train lurched, throwing them one against the other.

Lozen stayed by the small window as much as she could, watching all the places she had ever known slip past. At first, she counted each mountain. She had taken many long journeys in her life, guided by the movements of the sun and stars and counting the mountain ranges so she could find her way home. But after a long while in the train, she lost count of the mountains they passed, scarcely stopping. She watched until the country grew so strange she knew not a single mountain nor even the plants.

So she gave up hope of home and of the outline of the sacred mountain and of the places that had shaped her. And she wondered, as the train went on without remorse or mercy, whether any of those places would miss her and the People, as she missed them now already.

Lozen rode as a warrior unto death—never knowing what she had done, what the People had done, that these things should happen.

So she prayed, seeking only the strength to go on.

But no voice came back to her.

The only answer was the steel sound of the wheels on the tracks, taking her away from the places that knew her name.

EPILOGUE:

▼▼

An Undeserved Death

October 1886

Lozen vanishes from the historical record after her surrender with Geronimo. The military never recognized her importance or bothered to record her movements. Geronimo and most of the warriors were imprisoned for a time at Fort Pickens, Florida, while the women and children from their band were sent to Fort Marion, Florida, with the other Chiricahua and Chihenne prisoners. Presumably, Lozen would have been included in this group. Thus, General Miles's promise of a quick reunion with their relatives was quickly abandoned. The warriors soon became something of a tourist attraction and were amused and baffled by the jostling and staring of the onlookers. Meanwhile, the nearly four hundred people crowded together at Fort Marion soon became prey to disease in the tropical Florida climate.

The officers supervising the prisoners in both locations reported them to be cooperative, good-natured, and compliant. Most of the officers given command of the twin prison encampments soon began appealing for better conditions and treatment—a futile effort. Of the 394 people imprisoned at Fort Marion, 18 died within three months. At one point, authorities reported seventy-six cases of illness among the prisoners at one time, sixty of them with fevers. But rather than give the mostly women and children better living conditions, the ever-frugal government cut the rations. Moreover, the military forcibly removed many of the older children and sent them to a newly established school in Pennsylvania for an education that would teach them to adapt to a white man's world. Instead, the Carlisle School proved a death trap, and tuberculosis claimed forty-four of the children sent there.

As word of the condition of the Apache prisoners spread, various Indian rights organizations took up their cause. These groups, many of which drew their strength from religious and former abolitionist groups, enlisted General George Crook as one of their leading supporters. This triggered a fierce political struggle between General Crook and General Miles and enduring controversy about the terms under which the Apache had surrendered. General Crook had no sympathy for Geronimo and the other final resisters, whom he blamed for his own resignation and the catastrophe that had overtaken the Chiricahua. But he bitterly criticized the imprisonment of the scouts. A later census showed that sixty-five of the eighty-two adult male prisoners at Fort Marion had served as scouts. Moreover, most of the Chiricahua and Chihenne imprisoned at Fort Marion had not only been living peacefully on the reservation, but had repeatedly refused pleas by Geronimo and the other resisters to leave the reservation.

The controversy eventually convinced the army to move twenty family members of Geronimo's band from Fort Marion to Fort Pickens. At the same time, the army moved the other Chiricahua prisoners to Mt. Vernon Barracks in Alabama on the Mobile River some thirty miles north of Mobile. Lozen was probably in this group, although there's no official record.

The army kept news of the impending relocation secret up to the last minute, afraid lobbyists for the railroads might block the transfer because the railroads were doing a booming business bringing tourists to gawk at the prisoners at Fort Marion. Geronimo's group was finally also allowed to go join the rest in Alabama in May 1888.

Conditions improved at the thickly forested, swampy, 2,160-acre Mt. Vernon military reservation, but disease still ravaged the prisoners. Of the 353 prisoners confined there, two men, ten women, and nine children died in the first year—mostly from tuberculosis and pneumonia. The base surgeon reported an appalling death rate among the prisoners, noting that they had lived almost entirely free of such diseases in Arizona. All told, one-quarter of the prisoners died within the first four years of captivity.

After inspecting the conditions at Mt. Vernon, General Crook began campaigning to move the prisoners to Fort Sill in the Indian Territory, a place with a climate at least vaguely like the Southwest. However, Crook died in the midst of the debate and the momentum for moving the Chiricahua died with him. Disease, despair, and alcohol continued to take their toll among the prisoners. On a drunken binge in March 1892, Fun became enraged over his suspicions that his wife was sleeping with another man and shot and wounded her. As she lay unconscious on the ground, he feared he'd killed her. He then killed himself in despair.

Still trying to break up the tribe and save money, Congress considered parceling them out to other reservations. However, General Nelson Miles pushed to have them moved to Fort Sill, having opposed the same move when General Crook was alive. Congress approved the move of the 296 surviving prisoners to Oklahoma in 1893.

The army and the public remained frightened that these aging warriors would break out and pillage their way along the seven hundred miles back to New Mexico. Geronimo became the most famous Indian in America and even rode in President Theodore Roosevelt's inaugural parade. He later begged Roosevelt to let his people return to their homeland, but the President replied that too many people in Arizona and New Mexico still feared the Apache.

Geronimo's death in 1908 finally cleared the way for a governmental change of heart, greatly augmented by a desire to use the tribe's land in Oklahoma as an artillery range. The government in 1912 finally allowed the survivors to either settle on farms in Oklahoma or move to the Mescalero Indian Reservation in New Mexico. Of the 261 still alive after twenty-eight years of imprisonment, 78 decided to remain in Oklahoma. The remaining 183 moved back to New Mexico, including Naiche, Perico, Yahnozha, Chato, Kaytennae, Martine, and Charles Istee, the only surviving son of Victorio, who was therefore the closest Lozen had to a surviving descendant.

Lozen herself never saw her homeland again. Lozen died in Alabama, probably of tuberculosis, sometime during the stay at Mt. Vernon. James Kaywaykla said he learned Lozen had died at Mt. Vernon of "the coughing sickness" after his return from the Carlisle School. Her death was not officially noted by the military and she was buried at Mt. Vernon, although no record of the grave site survives.

So the woman Victorio described as "the shield of her people" died in a strange place surrounded by her enemies, where not even the coyote's call could be heard.

But she had served her People, remained true to her Power, and earned passage through the bears and monsters and enemies to the Happy Place, where her brother waited. She had done everything courage, Power, and duty had asked of her, not flinching as she walked the hard path on which her feet had been set.

NOTES

▼▼

INTRODUCTION

1. Ball, *In the Days of Victorio,* 124. This book contains the firsthand accounts of Apache who fought with Lozen and Victorio in the Apache wars and remains one of the most important primary source on these events from the Apache side.

2. Her Apache name was Lizah, according to Kaywaykla, but I am using the name most often used by historians.

3. Ball, *In the Days of Victorio,* 11.

PROLOGUE: ON THE RIO GRANDE

1. The names applied to various Apache bands remain a frequent source of confusion, especially the Chihenne. Most historians have referred to Victorio and Lozen's band as Warm Springs, or Mimbres Apache. Historian Eve Ball, who interviewed members of Victorio's band decades after the events in question, refers to them as Chihenne or Red Paint People. The term appears interchangeable with Warm Springs Apache and the band probably represented a subdivison of the Mimbres Apache—although historian Dan Thrapp uses Mimbres interchangeably with Warm Springs. I settled on Chihenne, since it is the name members of the band used in referring to themselves. The Chihenne were usually closely allied with various divisions of the Chiricahua Apache and some authorities consider the Chihenne or Mimbres bands to be an eastern division of the Chiricahua, which are mostly associated with Cochise's Chokonen, Juh's Nednhi, and Geronimo's Bedonkohe.

2. This version of Lozen's decision to accompany the Mescalero woman back to the reservation is based on the account of James Kaywaykla in Eve Ball's *In the Days of Victorio,* 115. Kaywaykla, who was a member of Victorio's band as a child, recounted the incident in some detail. I based some of the speculation as to her motivation for leaving the Chihenne to accompany a single Mescalero woman back to the reservation on accounts by Kaywaykla and others that Victorio was struggling to keep the Mescalero warriors, who composed perhaps half his fighting force, from deserting.

3. This account of the ceremonies and treatment for childbirth comes from Opler, *An Apache Lifeway*, 7. Kaywaykla, the authority for this incident, does not specifically say that Lozen was experienced in supervising childbirth, but she was a noted healer.

CHAPTER I: THE MID-1830S

1. White Ringed Mountain is south of Deming, New Mexico.

2. This version of the Chiricahua Apache creation myth was recorded by Morris Opler in *Myths and Tales of the Chiricahua Apache Indians,* 2. Presumably the Chihenne, who were closely related to the Chiricahua culturally, told a similar tale.

3. Opler recorded the origins myth with the tale of a great flood in the early 1900s, but the story of the flood may be a result of Christian influences rather than an element of the original creation myth.

4. Opler notes different Apache groups tell different stories about the relationship between Child of Water and Killer of Enemies. In some accounts, Killer of Enemies is a twin. In others, he is the older brother. In still others, he is White Painted Woman's brother and so Child of Water's uncle. Killer of Enemies is the principal cultural hero among the Navajo, Western Apache, Lipan Apache, and Jicarilla Apache, but among the Chiricahua and Mescalero he is either the uncle or brother and the sponsor of the whites, while Child of Water is the much more potent, courageous, and admirable cultural hero. For a more detailed explanation, see *Myths and Tales of the Chiricahua Apache Indians,* 3.

5. In some versions of the myth, White Painted Woman had borne many other children, which the giant ate. In other versions, Killer of Enemies was her brother or an older child who the giant had not eaten for reasons that were not explained.

6. Other variants of the tale told in different bands say Child of Water jumped up on a rainbow to avoid the giant's arrows, or that the arrows simply missed Child of Water. One variant says bolts of lightning destroyed the giant's arrows. Individual Apache storytellers introduced their own entertaining variants.

7. Little is known about the year or place of Lozen's birth. Chiricahua mythology suggests that the People originated near Ojo Caliente, which was clearly the emotional, mythical, and territorial homeland for Lozen's Chihenne band. Victorio, her brother, was born in about 1835, according to his biographer Dan Thrapp in *Victorio and the Mimbres Apaches,* although other sources place his birth as early as 1820. Thrapp also deals with the debate about whether Victorio was a Mexican child kidnapped and raised as an Apache. Several Mexican sources claim Victorio was Mexican by birth, but Thrapp points out various inconsistencies in those claims. I have in this account accepted the persuasive evidence that Victorio was a full-blooded Apache. I have also elected to use the Anglo names used most often by historians for both Victorio and Lozen, rather than their Apache names. Victorio's Apache name was variously rendered as Bidu-ya or Beduiat.

8. The parentage of both Lozen and Victorio remains obscure. *The Prescott Arizonan* in 1879 wrote that their father was a "hereditary chief of the Apaches, descended on his father's side from a long line of royal ancestors." (Reprinted in the *Arizona Sentinel of Yuma,* Nov. 1, 1879, cited in Thrapp, *Victorio and the Mimbres Apaches,* 11.) I have accepted that assertion, which appears consistent with Victorio's rise to leadership and the later deference to his leadership shown by Nana, who was already a much more experienced leader when he began following Victorio's lead. However, even if Victorio and Lozen were from an influential family, leadership positions among the Apache were earned anew by each individual.

9. This description of the cradle board and the ceremony that attended its construction comes from Opler, *An Apache Lifeway,* 12.

10. This account is based mostly on James Kaywaykla's description of Lozen in adulthood recorded by Eve Ball in *In the Days of Victorio.* He indicated she learned all of the things expected of women, but was also one of the most respected warriors in the band—being both faster and more dexterous than most of the men.

11. For the convenience of modern readers, I will throughout this account use the person- and place-names of the whites and Mexicans rather than the Apache names.

12. The April 22, 1837, massacre of Juan Jose Compa's band by Kentucky scalp hunter John James Johnson was later described to John Russell Bartlett, who headed the border survey commission that camped in the area in 1852. Victorio and Lozen were probably present and could have been ten or twelve years old. The death toll is speculative, but it was probably substantial. Johnson, seeking to collect the bounty on Apache scalps offered by the Mexican states of Sonora and Chihuahua, convinced the residents of Santa Rita to break their truce with the Apache. Sonora offered 50 pesos for the scalps of women and children and 100 for the scalp of a warrior starting in 1835. Chihuahua upped the bounty to 200 pesos for a warrior in 1849. In 1849, Chihuahua paid out 17,896 pesos—a measure of the toll taken. The Apache rarely took scalps, although they sometimes in retaliation cut away a piece of the scalp, leaving it on the body. Although the Chihenne and Mimbres bands remained at peace with the residents of Santa Rita, they raided regularly further south. The Apache for a long time made the mistake of comparing the Mexican political organization to their own, reasoning that they could remain at peace with one town, or "band," while raiding a nearby town.

13. Apache tradition suggests Mangas Coloradas's warriors exterminated virtually the entire population of Santa Rita, which seems unlikely given the normal Apache tactics of ambush and retreat. It seems more likely that the town was abandoned because continuing chaos, revolution, and corruption in central and northern Mexico made it impossible for the central government to continue to provide troops and supplies to the distant city. In any case, the town was abandoned and remained vacant for the next eighteen years. However, throughout this account I will accept the Apache version of events unless it is contradicted by strong documentary evidence.

CHAPTER II: COMING OF AGE

1. James Kaywaykla related this story to Eve Ball, saying that his grandmother, who was Nana's wife, told him the tale. The story sounds suspiciously romantic, the embellishment of the childhood of a leader whose stature had grown to almost mythical proportions by the time Kaywaykla told the story—especially with the detail concerning the twelve guards and the mysterious woman with whom Grey Ghost left. However, other records do suggest a Seneca chief may have passed through the region at about this time, seeking a new reservation for his People further from the encroachments of the whites. It is also possible that the story was added to Lozen's legend to protect her from criticism for not having married and for her defiance of convention in becoming a warrior.

2. These are all summaries of stories involving women that appear in Opler's *Myths and Tales of the Chiricahua Apache Indians.*

3. This description of the importance of Apache place-names is based on Keith Basso's *Wisdom Sits in Places,* based on his thirty years of cultural anthropology fieldwork among the Cibecue Apache in the 1900s. I have assumed here that these place-names would have been equally important and prevalent in Lozen's time and among the Chihenne Apache.

4. Basso, *Wisdom Sits in Places,* 24. This is one of the place-names and the story that goes with it offered by Basso's informant on the White Mountain Apache Reservation near Cibecue. I have moved the place-name and the story to Ojo Caliente and attributed it to Nana on the assumption that the Chihenne had a similar system of place-naming. Most of these stories have some moral about proper social behavior. Normally, the Apache walked at least a mile from their camp to go to the bathroom and Apache camps were clean and virtually disease-free before the reservation period.

5. These place-names all come from Basso's work among the Cibecue Apache.

6. Basso, *Wisdom Sits in Places,* 52.

7. Basso, *Wisdom Sits in Places,* 94.

8. This description of the Apache view of wisdom is based on Basso's examination of place-names among the Western Apache. Basso, *Wisdom Sits in Places,* 132.

9. This recounting of the origins of the Sunrise Ceremony comes from Kaywaykla's account of the story told by Nana in Ball, *In the Days of Victorio,* 40. Opler indicates that the ceremony originated directly with White Painted Woman and Child of Water before they ascended, 128.

10. The story of Gouyan comes from Stockel's *Women of the Apache Nation.*

11. This description of the Sunrise Ceremony comes from Opler, *An Apache Lifeway,* 85.

12. Opler notes that although most Apache and Navajo groups consider Killer of Enemies the primary cultural hero, the Chiricahua give the primary role to Child of Water in their legends. However, the presumably earlier preference for Killer of Enemies appears to be preserved in the Sunrise Ceremony songs. Opler, *An Apache Lifeway*, 95.

13. This description of the Coming of Age Ceremony and the wording of the songs is from Opler, *An Apache Lifeway*, 92–134.

14. Apache accounts agree that Lozen gained through prayer and fasting and visioning the spiritual Power she used to protect her People. Commonly, people seeking Power went alone for an extended period of solitary fasting and dreaming. No accounts specifically state Lozen isolated herself for this period of fasting and prayer, but it seems probable that she did so. I am here speculating that this seeking after spiritual Power came immediately after the Sunrise Ceremony. I am also speculating that such a sojourn would have lasted four days, the sacred number for the Apache.

15. Opler, *An Apache Lifeway*, 300. Opler's informant offered this as a ceremonial song by a shaman with Horse Power. I am here attributing it to Lozen because she was thought to have Horse Power. Kaywaykla indicates that she was the most skilled horse thief among the Apache, and her name in Apache means "dexterous horse thief."

16. Here I am accepting James Kaywaykla's statement that she fell in love with Grey Ghost and could never bring herself to love any other warrior.

17. Ball, *In the Days of Victorio*, 15.

CHAPTER III: THE COMING OF THE WHITE EYES

1. Brigadier General Stephen Watts Kearny reached the Mimbres River in October of 1846 and met with Mangas Coloradas on October 20 on the banks of Mangas Creek. The chief swore "everlasting friendship" to the whites, but scout Kit Carson advised Kearny not to trust any Apache. First Lieutenant William Helmsley Emory noted that the warriors were garbed in "fantastical" style with Mexican dress and saddles augmented by helmets with black feathers and accoutrements that made them resemble ancient Greek warriors. The United States pursued its war with Mexico without any help from the Apache, which concluded with the Treaty of Guadalupe Hidalgo in 1848. The treaty ceded California, Arizona, and New Mexico and obligated the United States Army to prevent Apache raids into northern Mexico from the newly ceded territory.

2. This describes the encounter between the Chihenne and the 1852 Boundary Commission under the direction of John Russell Bartlett, who came to Santa Rita on February 19 and remained for some months. Captain John Cremony left a vivid account of the encounter in *Life Among the Apaches*. Bartlett described Mangas Coloradas as a man of "strong common sense and discriminate judgement" who strove to maintain peace and who had an undeserved reputation among the settlers in the region as a ruthless savage (Thrapp, *Victorio and the Mimbres Apaches*, 25).

3. James Kaywaykla told historian Eve Ball in *In the Days of Victorio*, 152, that Nana had the Power to find ammunition and also legendary endurance. Opler, in *An Apache Lifeway*, 214, indicated that Goose Power was associated with extraordinary endurance, no doubt because of the continent-spanning flights of geese.

4. Kaywaykla described Victorio to Eve Ball as the "most perfect" human being he had ever seen. Ball, *In the Days of Victorio*, 83.

5. Thrapp, *Victorio and the Mimbres Apaches*. Thrapp describes the July 1852 conference between Acting Superintendent for Indian Affairs for New Mexico John Griener, Victorio, Mangas Coloradas, and other Mimbres chiefs. Griener quoted Mangas Coloradas in his dispatch to his superiors. The government was trying to find a way to curtail Apache attacks on the stream of prospectors passing through the territory en route to California as a result of the 1848 gold strikes. Many who were unsuccessful in California worked their way back east through Apache territory, hoping to strike it rich. The whites also hoped to claim the choice land along the Rio Grande north of El Paso that the Mimbrenos considered their own. This conference led to the provisional compact of April 7, 1853, which was eventually ratified by the Senate and signed by President Franklin Pierce on March 25, 1853. The treaty resulted in a marked decline in Apache attacks, although the government never abided by the treaty, neither delivering the rations nor curtailing white incursions into the reservation.

6. U.S. government policy and leadership was in disarray in this period, as one agent succeeded another and the Indian Bureau and the army began a long, tragic feud about who should control the reservation. The government hired a man named Fletcher to teach the Indians how to farm, but under his tutelage only about twenty-five acres came under cultivation. He then tried to sell the government farm back to the government. In the meantime, he apparently ran a whiskey-smuggling operation out of Mexico—giving the warriors an incentive to steal livestock they could trade for whiskey.

7. *Steck Papers*. August, 1854, cited in Thrapp, *Victorio and the Mimbres Apaches*, 41.

8. The treaty of 1855 with the Gila and Mimbres Apache ceded about twenty-four thousand square miles of territory in return for two reservations each with about two thousand square miles of land. However, only about fifteen square miles of the shrunken reservation could be farmed. Even so, rumors of mineral deposits on the reservation convinced the Senate not to ratify the treaty, which the Apache were already observing. The Senate also refused to allocate the money needed to provide the promised rations. Meanwhile, the well-intentioned Agent Michael Steck labored to convince officials to move the Mimbres to the more remote Gila Reservation to protect them from prospectors and settlers. In addition, he argued, moving the Mimbres would open choice land for development. In 1855, a reported seventy-five hundred Apache were living on the two reservations, a number that is almost certainly about 25 percent too high and may have been inflated so the agents and contractors could collect more money.

9. In April, 1856, Lieutenant Colonel Daniel Chandler led a force in pursuit of raiders who had stolen 250 sheep and thirty-one horses and mules. They hit the camp of the raiders, killing one and recovering the livestock. Returning through the Burro Mountains, they attacked one peaceful band of Mimbres without warning. Chandler then split his force and with sixty soldiers encountered Delgadito's camp. Chandler reported that the trail of the raiders led to Delgadito's camp and they therefore attacked. Steck vigorously protested the action, but Secretary of War Jefferson Davis accepted Chandler's explanation.

10. The so-called campaign of clowns mounted to retaliate for the murder of Navajo Agent Henry Dodge was a study in ineptitude, commanded by drunken and incompetent officers. The military columns blundered about and enjoyed most of their success through surprise attacks on impoverished encampments protected by a scattering of poorly armed warriors.

11. Steck in 1860 wrote, "These Indians complain very much about our permitting the people to settle in their country. They say they are occupying the best portions of it and fast running them out—and every word of their complaints is true. There are now at least forty settlers on the Mimbres (river and reservation), most of them with their families and not less than one thousand souls living at or near the copper mines. If some steps are not taken to set apart a portion of their country as a reserve they will have none worth having left." Thrapp, *Victorio and the Mimbres Apaches*, 65. Steck recommended removing the Mimbres to a fifteen-square-mile reservation on the Gila near present-day Gila, Cliff, and Buckhorn, New Mexico.

12. The December 4, 1860, incident was recounted by James Tevis, who said it started when an Apache band killed a mule that they thought belonged to him (he had previously indicated that they could take some of his livestock). The actual owner of the mule incited the miners to retaliate and Tevis reluctantly agreed to lead the punitive expedition.

CHAPTER IV: WAR

1. The blundering of Lieutenant Bascom in 1861 drove Cochise into a decade of all-out war with the Americans. Bascom's account insists his prisoners were executed only after Cochise had tortured and killed his hostages. Most accounts agree, however, that Cochise was betrayed and wrongfully accused and that he had maintained an almost unblemished peace with the Americans before this incident.

2. The Apache did not realize that their attacks coincided with the outbreak of the Civil War. Pressed for professional troops in the East, the Union withdrew most of its forces from the West, abandoning forts and terrified settlers.

3. Confederate Lieutenant Colonel John Baylor occupied the abandoned Fort Fillmore, New Mexico, on July 26, 1861, to establish the Confederate Territory of Arizona. He issued an infamous order to exterminate all Apache, even advising his field commanders to lure the Apache in under a flag of truce and then kill every warrior. He

ordered them to sell the women and children as slaves to underwrite the cost of his campaign of extermination. Confederate President Jefferson Davis eventually revoked the order and named Brigadier General Henry Sibley to the post in December 1861. However, Sibley pursued basically the same policies regarding the Apache until victories by Union volunteers from Colorado and the approach of the California Volunteers drove the Confederates out of Arizona and New Mexico and back into Texas.

4. The Battle of Apache Pass took place on July 14, 1862, when the 122 men commanded by Captain Thomas Roberts of the First California Infantry encountered the combined forces of Cochise and Mangas Coloradas. The detachment was the leading edge of an eighteen-hundred-man force under General James Henry Carleton sent to help drive the Confederates out of Arizona and New Mexico. Apache tradition holds that both Victorio and Geronimo were present, which suggests Lozen was also present. The first fire from the warriors killed one man and wounded another. The warriors withstood several hours of shelling before they withdrew. The army's summary reported ten Indians killed, but Apache reports indicated they suffered few, if any, deaths. However, Mangas Coloradas was wounded by Private John Teal who was part of a six-man detachment sent to bring reinforcements. It's possible Lozen rode with Mangas Coloradas to head off the soldiers, but none of the Apache accounts of the battle specifically mentions her.

5. I am speculating here that Lozen would have treated Mangas Coloradas. There are repeated references in Apache accounts regarding her skill in treating wounds, and Apache tradition suggests she and Victorio were at the battle. It seems reasonable to assume she would have remained with Mangas Coloradas for the journey to Janos and that she would have used her Power to treat him.

6. Carleton established Fort Bowie in Apache Pass in the summer of 1862 to control the spring and serve as a base of operations for campaigns against the Chiricahua and Mimbres. Carleton assumed military control of Arizona and New Mexico on September 18, 1862. He promptly ordered his subordinates to kill any Apache warriors they encountered, specifically advising them to not negotiate or accept surrenders. He ordered Colonel Joseph R. West to mount a campaign to destroy the Gila and Mimbres Apache, particularly the band of Mangas Coloradas.

7. Ace Daklugie, the son of Juh, recounted to historian Eve Ball the efforts of Victorio and Nana to dissuade Mangas Coloradas from going to meet with the whites. Ball, *Indeh*, 19.

8. Mangas Coloradas was killed on January 18, 1863, after he approached a group of whites under the leadership of mountain man Joseph Walker at Pinos Altos under a flag of truce. Conflicting accounts of the incident exist, but the most reliable comes from Daniel Connor, who was in Walker's party. According to Connor, Walker seized Mangas Coloradas to guarantee his party's safe passage across Chihenne territory. His party then encountered soldiers who took control of their prisoner. Colonel West, who had been ordered by Carleton to destroy Mangas Coloradas's band, in a conversation with the

guards implied he wanted Mangas Coloradas killed. Connor, walking sentry for Walker's group, later reported that he saw the guards heating their bayonets and holding them against the chief's feet. They shot him when he protested. The soldiers later cut off his head, boiled it, and sent the skull to the Smithsonian Institute where phrenologist Orson Squire Fowler examined it and declared to general astonishment that Mangas Coloradas had a greater cranial capacity than Daniel Webster. The skull was subsequently lost. Geronimo, in his autobiography, declared the murder and mutilation of Mangas Coloradas the greatest wrong ever done to the Apache.

9. James Kaywaykla, who was in Victorio's band as a child, told historian Eve Ball that he never saw anyone tortured, although he saw hundreds of people killed. He also reported that the warriors sometimes mutilated the bodies of their slain enemies after the murder and mutilation of Mangas Coloradas. Ball, *In the Days of Victorio*, 38.

10. Dr. Steck was reassigned as Superintendent of Indian Affairs on May 23, 1863, several months after New Mexico's admission as a territory. Steck took up his duties in July and immediately tried to initiate contact with Apache bands driven into hiding and retaliation by General Carleton's unremitting war of extermination. Steck waged a bitter bureaucratic struggle with the zealous and autocratic Carleton, who pursued his campaign to destroy the Apache with missionary zeal. Steck urged the establishment of a single reservation noting, "If every Indian was a Spartan they could not long bear up against the restless tide of emigration. Humanity then demands of us if we wish to save even a portion of this interesting people that they be relocated and to secure a home for them in the future that their reservations be secured to them by patent at as early a day as possible" (Thrapp, *Victorio and the Mimbres Apaches*, 86). Steck estimated that in three years civilians had lost five hundred thousand sheep, five thousand horses and cattle, and two hundred lives as a result of the war with the Apache.

11. Carleton was an unrelenting, righteous, energetic, almost obsessive forty-eight-year-old man with a penetrating eye, a mustache, and heavy sideburns who presented a picture of indomitable self-confidence. He was intelligent, driven, religious, determined, resourceful, and a brilliant organizer with an overweening ambition and an outsized ego. He entered the Southwest with the California Volunteers who drove the forces of Cochise and Mangas Coloradas out of Apache Pass. He set about to exterminate the Apache, determined to settle them all, along with the Navajo, at the barren concentration camp of Bosque Redondo on the Rio Grande. He proved incapable of compromise and eventually alienated almost everyone by his stubborn insistence that Bosque Redondo would solve the Indian problem in New Mexico.

12. Cremony, *Life Among the Apaches*, 201. Cremony provides a compelling, first-person account of this crucial, poorly documented early period of the white contact with the Apache, including descriptions of Mangas Coloradas and other important events such as the Battle of Apache Pass, Bosque Redondo, and campaigns against the Mescalero. He is prone to exaggeration and inaccuracy, but he provides a highly readable,

historically invaluable account of the period, filtered through the white assumption of cultural and spiritual superiority.

13. After that meeting, Steck launched a campaign to transfer authority over the Indians from the War Department to the Interior Department—an ongoing struggle that produced confusion and tragedy in the relationship with the Indians for the next thirty years. Carleton clung to his insistence that all the Apache be confined at Bosque Redondo. Steck wrote to his superiors saying, "There are no Indians in this department more faithful than the Mimbres band of Apaches when at peace" and that between 1854 and 1859 they had been "driven by the treachery of our own people into their present hostile condition." Thrapp, *Victorio and the Mimbres Apaches,* 89.

14. General Nelson Henry Davis was dispatched as an emissary when Carleton learned that Steck was trying to conclude a treaty with the Mimbres. Davis, in reporting on Victorio's refusal to surrender and accept confinement at Bosque Redondo, concluded: "Death to the Apaches and peace and prosperity to this land is my motto." Thrapp, *Victorio and the Mimbres Apaches,* 91.

15. About fifty bow-armed Apache stole thirty-one horses from the Fort Craig horse herd in 1866. The same or another group stole thirty-six horses and five mules from Camp Mimbres. It is likely that the raiders were Chihenne, since the area in the San Mateos was Victorio's favorite haunt. I am here speculating that Lozen would have played a leading role in that action, as her skill as a horse thief was well recognized and often commented upon.

16. This speculation concerning Lozen's thought process is based on Kaywaykla's descriptions of her. He indicated that she was Victorio's chief counselor, but shy about speaking in council. The song that she sang in locating the enemy emphasizes that her Powers were a gift of Ussen to be used only in service of the People.

17. Worn down by his battle with Carleton and the frustration of his inability to protect the Apache, Steck resigned as agent and went into private business. Control of Indian affairs seesawed after his departure. Governor Robert Mitchell, a Civil War veteran infamous for his threat to execute 350 soldiers in his Union cavalry regiment who resisted his commands, declared war on the Navajo and Gila Apache by executive order on August 2, 1869. He authorized the killing of any Indian found off the reservation, which included most of the Indians since they were in hiding. Federal officials annulled his order and in 1869 military agents replaced the civilian agents, many notorious for corruption.

18. First Lieutenant Charles E. Drew was appointed agent to the Mimbres, a brave, good-hearted man with a fondness for hard liquor. He was to prove one of the best, if short-lived, agent-advocates for the Apache.

CHAPTER V: A FRAGILE PEACE

1. The conference took place on October 10, 1869, on the outskirts of the mostly Mexican community of Canada Alamosa, near present-day Monticello, which was the northern edge of the territory the Chihenne hoped to be granted as a reservation.

2. Lieutenant Drew's efforts to crack down on the black market trade in whiskey among the Mimbres apparently led to his confrontation with traders Thomas Jeffords and Elias Brevoort, with Brevoort playing the leading role in the dispute. Brevoort and Jeffords, in March 1870, sent a letter claiming Loco had demanded whiskey from them, saying Drew had already given him some. Drew denied the allegations and asked the government to revoke the traders' licenses. This triggered a series of charges and counter-charges that exonerated Drew and resulted in the revocation of Jeffords's and Brevoort's licenses.

3. The conflict between Agent Argalus Garey Hennisee and Justice of the Peace Jose Trujillo and Constable Juan Montoya indicates the political complexity of the system the Chihenne had to placate and predict. Trujillo and Montoya were among the chief traders on the still unofficially declared reservation. They induced warriors to steal one hundred bushels of corn from the farm of Hennisee's translator. Hennisee attempted to curtail the illegal whiskey trade on the reservation by sending a detachment to search Montoya's house, where the soldiers found twenty-eight gallons of whiskey that had been paid for with a stolen army mule. Montoya could expect to sell the whiskey to the Chihenne for about ten mules, which provided a major incentive for continued raids by the warriors. Hennisee arrested Montoya and Trujillo, who summoned a forty-man posse that chased the agent and his three soldiers out of town. The army sought a writ against the constable and the magistrate in Socorro while Montoya arrested the translator at Canada Alamosa and filed an assault charge against Hennisee. The agent was convicted by a Mexican jury in Canada Alamosa and sentenced to three months in jail. In his appeal, he concluded that the entire Mexican population of the region was engaged in trading for stolen property with the Indians, and that the local authorities made it almost impossible to recover stolen livestock. Hennisee didn't serve the time, but the dispute indicated the confusion that prevailed in this division between the army and the local authorities.

4. In September 1870.

5. The remarks of Cochise and Victorio at this 1870 conference were reported by Special Indian Agent William Arny, who toured the region with Hennisee. His November 21, 1870, report no. 8 recommended establishing a reservation at one of six sites. He estimated that the Chiricahua Mimbres Mogollon and Gila Apache totaled 910 warriors, 1,502 women, and 1,226 children, for a total of about 3,638. One of the reservation sites he recommended included Ojo Caliente. Establishing the reservation would cost eleven thousand dollars to buy out fifty-two white and Mexican families, who were essentially squatting on government land anyway. Other alternatives included

moving the Apache to near Fort Stanton adjoining the Mescalero Reservation or establishing a reservation on the Tularosa River, eighty miles west of Socorro.

6. The Camp Grant massacre was led by several white Tucson residents whose force
consisted mostly of Pima Indians and Mexicans. They attacked the Apache camp at
dawn and killed approximately 150, almost all of them women and children. The commander at Camp Grant, Royal Whitman, convinced the warriors not to retaliate and
pushed for the trial of the murderers. But a Tucson jury quickly acquitted the perpe-
trators and extended the thanks of the citizens of Tucson. Whitman, a high-minded,
abolitionist New Englander, remained a staunch advocate for the Apache. He underwent
repeated court-martials on apparently trumped-up charges of drunkenness and ultimately resigned his commission—an honorable, idealistic, but bitterly disillusioned man.
However, news of the Camp Grant massacre spurred outrage in the East, especially
among former abolitionist groups who had taken up the cause of Indian rights. It helped
inspire the peace policy of incoming president Ulysses S. Grant.

7. Orlanda F. Piper replaced Hennisee on November 30, 1870, when the government
shifted control of the Indians from the War Department to the Interior Department,
another in the repeated shifts of authority that contributed to the chaotic, confusing,
and often corrupt administration of Indian affairs. This shift was part of President
Grant's peace policy, which featured the appointment of reform-minded civilian agents,
many selected from the ranks of religious organizations.

CHAPTER VI: THE MIRAGE OF PEACE

1. Local officials and settlers blamed the one thousand Apache gathered at Canada
Alamosa awaiting a decision on a reservation for every murder and theft in the territory.
Small groups of warriors who slipped away from the reservation undoubtedly stole livestock and perhaps killed herders and settlers, but the bulk of the thefts and murders
were probably committed by bandits, outlaws, bands from Mexico, or other bands that
had refused to settle on the reservation. Nonetheless, local officials and Governor William Pile continually stoked the fears and anger of the settlers and directed it against
the Apache bands clustered around Canada Alamosa. Governor Pile repeatedly predicted an attack by the locals that would put the Camp Grant massacre in the shade.

2. Colyer was a devout, high-minded man convinced the Indians had been wronged
and determined to use extraordinary powers granted to him by President Grant to finally
settle the Indian troubles in the Southwest. He was reviled by the settlers as a corrupt,
idiotic, doddering Indian lover and generally criticized by the military commanders as a
foolish, addled easterner who didn't understand that Apache warriors would never settle
peacefully on a reservation until they'd been decisively beaten militarily. Colyer established the White Mountain Apache Reservation, which formed the basis for the long-
term peace with the White Mountain bands who later provided the core of army scouts
who helped defeat the Chihenne and Chiricahua. However, Colyer considered it "pre-
posterous" to buy out some three hundred settlers near Canada Alamosa when the
reservation could be established on vacant land at Tularosa. He never adequately con-

sidered the deep-felt objections of the Apache to settling permanently at Tularosa, with its harsh, high-altitude winters. However, the government accepted his recommendation and General Phil Sheridan on November 20, 1870, designated the valley of the Tularosa as a thirty-mile-long, ten-mile-wide reservation for the Southern Apache. The attempt to force the Chihenne and Chiricahua to settle at Tularosa ultimately proved disastrous, ensuring a generation of warfare on the frontier.

3. President Grant sent Assistant Inspector General of the Army Colonel Nelson Henry Davis, who described Cochise as "dignified, commanding, able and shrewd" to help resolve the apparent impasse (Thrapp, *Victorio and the Mimbres Apaches,* 142). Davis noted the Tularosa Reservation probably contained mineral deposits, which might cause trouble later if settlers wanted the land. Colonel Davis recommended letting the Apache remain at Canada Alamosa, which Interior Secretary Columbus Delano agreed to do as a temporary measure.

4. The council was held on September 11 and 12, 1872, at Fort Tularosa. The following dialogue between Victorio and Howard and the other leaders is taken from Edwin Sweeney, ed., *Making Peace with Cochise, The 1872 Journal of Captain Joseph Alton Sladen,* 115.

5. Howard's promise later proved controversial. Victorio and the other leaders believed he had promised they could live at Canada Alamosa. However, Howard said he told the leaders the government could only afford to establish a reservation at Canada Alamosa if Cochise and his Chiricahua agreed to live there. Ultimately, Cochise refused to move his band to New Mexico and Howard established the Chiricahua Reservation in Arizona.

6. One of Howard's guides, Ponce, was from a band of about forty people led by Sancho, who was not living on the reservation. In order to secure Ponce's services, Howard gave Sancho's band permission to remain off the reservation until he returned. Other officials already opposed to Howard's mission complained that warriors from Sancho's bands continued to raid in the area, which caused a furor in Howard's absence.

7. Dudley was appointed in February 1873 to replace Nathaniel Pope as superintendent of Indian affairs for New Mexico. The constant turnover of agents and officers together with the tensions between the Indian Bureau and the military complicated management of the reservation.

8. The incident took place in January 1873, and an investigation later concluded the incident might not have taken place if the post commander hadn't been drunk.

9. I am here making an assumption as to the advice Lozen offered. Almost all of the accounts of this period rely on official dispatches and reports by the agents, who mostly quoted Victorio and Loco to represent the Apache point of view. The agents and the army never fully appreciated Lozen's influence over her brother. Apache sources indicate Victorio regularly consulted with Lozen, even in matters of military strategy. Apache decisions emerged as a result of this nonconfrontational search for consensus and so it

seems reasonable to suppose Lozen urged restraint and patience, since this is the course Victorio followed despite his occasional outbursts of anger and impatience.

10. Dudley ultimately concluded the government would save money by moving the reservation to Canada Alamosa and advised the move, but Indian Commissioner Edward P. Smith insisted Dudley obtain Cochise's consent to leave the Chiricahua reservation and move his people to Canada Alamosa. As Historian Dan Thrapp concluded in *Victorio and the Mimbres Apaches,* the refusal of the officials to establish a reservation for the Chihenne near Ojo Caliente seems almost irrational. "Why? Search the records from end to end, the thousands upon thousands of documents, and you discover no valid reason. There was no reason. It was simply that, since they desired to remain, they must be moved" (p. 99).

11. Cochise died on June 8, 1874.

12. In the summer of 1874 Dudley concluded that the effort to force the Chihenne to remain at Tularosa had been a failure and ordered Mimbres Agent Thomas to move the agency to Canada Alamosa. John Shaw took over as agent there on November 15.

13. John Shaw was named agent and assumed control in November 1874. He soon reported 1,317 Indians drawing rations, probably an inflated number. He drew increasingly ample rations, all the while complaining he had so many Indians on his hands he had to shift to half-rations. Throughout this period, most agents treated their commission as a license to fleece the government, and the Apache were keenly aware of the tendency of the whites to steal their supplies.

14. Throughout this account, I am using the names most familiar to whites for the Apache, as their own Apache names would be harder for most readers. Most prominent Apache had nicknames they used with the whites, in part to deny the whites the power of knowing a person's true name. It is unclear how Victorio's son got the nickname "Washington," and his Apache name has not survived in the historical record. It might have been because his Apache name sounded vaguely like "Washington."

15. This description of the composition of the families of Loco, Washington, Victorio, and Nana comes from the census produced by Shaw in 1874 showing a total of 916 Indians on the reservation. Shaw resigned in June, probably because of irregularities in his books, and produced the census in an effort to justify the rations he was issuing. At one point, he claimed to have issued 200 days' rations in 130 days, yet the Apache reported they were starving.

16. These statements by Victorio and the other leaders were reported by Colonel Edward Hatch of the Ninth Cavalry who met with them in the summer of 1874. Hatch's report that the Indian Bureau had not been issuing rations prompted the army to issue rations to forestall the outbreak of war.

17. San Carlos Agent John Clum was directed to move the Chiricahua to the San Carlos Reservation on May 3, 1876, after several incidents involving Poinsenay's band, even

though Taza and the majority of the Chiricahua even fought a pitched battle with the renegades on behalf of the soldiers. The government never offered a clear justification for breaking General Howard's promise. The proximity of the reservation to the Mexican border had caused ongoing problems, since Agent Thomas Jeffords proved unable to prevent Chiricahua warriors from raiding in Mexico and returning to the reservation. Jeffords came in for considerable criticism for his outspoken support of the Chiricahua and was also accused of diverting or selling supplies. The accusations are hard to evaluate at this distance, but it seems more likely Jeffords bent the rules to maintain the peace and the confidence of Cochise—perhaps even augmenting the rations with beef from his own ranch. The truth remains that Jeffords and Cochise virtually eliminated raiding in the United States and the government acted on flimsy pretext. The decision to concentrate all the bands at San Carlos spawned a decade of needless warfare. Clum removed 325 Chiricahua to San Carlos, but perhaps as many as 500 others slipped away, including Geronimo and Juh.

18. On September 4, 1874, a company of soldiers led by Navajo scouts attacked the reservation at Canada Alamosa.

19. In March 1875, First Lieutenant Austin Henely of the Sixth Cavalry reported seeing Geronimo at the Warm Springs agency, noting Geronimo was indignant that he could not draw rations for the time he had been out raiding.

20. I am here speculating as to Lozen's train of thought, based on her later actions.

21. Clum's account of the April 20, 1877, capture of Geronimo is a matter of some dispute. Clum left a vivid, detailed account with himself as the clever hero. Apache accounts maintain most of Clum's details are exaggerated or fabricated. In any case, Geronimo and the other leading Chiricahua were disarmed and taken to San Carlos in chains. For a detailed description see either *Apache Agent* by Clum's son, or *Geronimo* by Debo, or *The Fox and the Whirlwind* by myself.

22. The number of Indians at the Ojo Caliente reservation before it was closed remains unclear, as are most reservation counts in this period. Thrapp reports that Ojo Caliente Agent Dr. Walter Whitney advised the army there were 175 men, 200 women and 250 children on the reservation, and the military reported that 434 made the trip to San Carlos, about 323 of them Mimbres. The remaining 200 either slipped away or were off raiding. The estimate of about 600 on the reservation might also have been inflated so the agent could draw extra rations for sale on the black market, a relatively common practice.

CHAPTER VII: SAN CARLOS—ESCAPING THE TRAP

1. Clum did push for the concentration policy and did push for a pay raise when he assumed supervision of many different tribes. In three years he had concentrated three agencies into one, increasing the Indians under his supervision from eight hundred to five thousand and saving the government twenty-five thousand dollars annually for each of the reservations closed.

2. James Kaywaykla told historian Eve Ball that "as agents went, John Clum was one of the best. The Apaches conceded that; but they knew also that he was responsible [for the concentration policy]. . . . And they knew, too, that his motive for attempting to bring all Apaches under his rule was an increase in salary . . . but they respected the arrogant young man in spite of that, for he was both courageous and honest. They liked his using Indian police and Indian judges . . . [for] it was commendable to have a man who realized that our standards differed from theirs and felt that a man should be judged by the mores of his own people." Ball, *In the Days of Victorio*, 114.

3. They left the San Carlos Reservation on September 2, 1876.

4. Army reports list half a dozen fights with the fleeing Apache, but it's unclear which fights involved Victorio's band and which involved Poinsenay's. No detailed account of the flight survives from among Victorio's band, so it's hard to reconstruct the sequence. In the end, Victorio headed for Fort Wingate near the Mescalero Reservation in New Mexico and Poinsenay headed into Mexico.

5. The following exchange comes from Ball, *In the Days of Victorio*, 35. James Kaywaykla, who was a boy in Victorio's band, recounts the dialogue. Therefore, the conversation represents an Apache oral tradition rendered as dialogue years after the event.

6. This description of the conference and the dialogue comes again from Ball, *In the Days of Victorio*, 21. Kaywaykla observed, "Much has been written of the low regard in which Indian women were held. Among my people, that was not true. Instead they were respected, protected and cherished. I knew of no other woman bidden to the council, but that was because no other had the skills as a warrior that Lozen did. She could ride, shoot and fight like a man; and I think she had more ability in planning and military strategy than did Victorio. At the time I speak of, she had not married, she went on the warpath with the men, which no women other than the wives of the warriors were permitted to do; and she was held in the greatest respect by them, much as though she were a holy person. But Lozen did not let the esteem in which she was held prevent her doing the tasks that of necessity fell to the women. Women did much hard work, but how else could the tribe have existed?"

7. I am here speculating that Lozen would have thought about Grey Ghost in such a manner all these years later. It is also possible that the whole, somewhat implausible story of Grey Ghost is simply an element in the legend that has grown up around Lozen, since it relies on the recollections of a single source and has almost supernatural overtones.

8. Lozen often served as an intermediary with the soldiers as there was less chance the soldiers would kill or imprison a woman. The records on this occasion don't specifically state Lozen was the first point of contact, but the assumption seems reasonable.

9. Military and civilian leaders were embroiled in a debate about where to put the Mimbres as they seemed unaccountably determined not to let the Mimbres remain in the one place they longed to be. They feared that moving the turbulent Chihenne to

the Mescalero Reservation would stir up trouble there, but they also realized it would be impossible to keep the Mimbres on the San Carlos Reservation. The army and the Indian Bureau finally agreed to let the Mimbres gather there with the ultimate goal of moving them to Oklahoma to the Indian Territory. General Philip Sheridan ultimately concluded it would cost too much to move them to the Indian Territory and recommended reestablishing the Ojo Caliente Reservation. However, the Indian Bureau concluded it would be "inconvenient" to change its policy since it had already decided to sell the property and buildings at the Ojo Caliente Reservation. Meanwhile, the army and the Indian Bureau continued to argue bitterly about which agency should pay for feeding the hundreds of people gathered at Ojo Caliente.

10. Captain Charles Steelhammer, the commander at Ojo Caliente, reported, "when I look back upon the condition of these Indians a year and a half ago and contrast it with their present, it seems almost incredible that such a long step in their civilization could have been taken in so short a time. Everything connected with the Indians at Ojo Caliente is done well and with that regularity, precision and temperance which breed obedience and contentment. . . . The Indians wished me to say that they are happier than they ever have been were it not for that they feared removal and that if the government would permit them to remain where they now are they would gladly accept only one-half of their present ration." Thrapp, *Victorio of the Mimbres Apaches*, 208.

11. On September 18, 1879, Colonel Hatch issued orders to remove 266 Mimbres Apache from Ojo Caliente to San Carlos in response to apparent Apache raids in Mexico and the insistence of the Indian Bureau on the closure of Ojo Caliente and the sale of the assets there.

12. This account comes from Kaywaykla's recollections in Ball, *In the Days of Victorio*, 182.

13. This group returned to San Carlos on November 26, 1878.

14. Lieutenant Merritt considerably exceeded his authority when he opened negotiations with Victorio on February 7, 1879. When he reported the discussions he was initially reproached, but when he explained that he could not corner Victorio but could through negotiations induce his surrender, General Hatch changed his mind and supported the negotiations. Hatch then convinced the Indian Bureau to accept the transfer of the Chihenne to the Mescalero Reservation.

15. This was evidently a mistranslation, or a misunderstanding on Victorio's part. Actually, Lieutenant Merritt had said the government would let the Chihenne settle on the Mescalero Reservation.

16. They set out in June 1879.

17. The dialogue between Victorio and Blazer comes from Ball, *In the Days of Victorio*, 63.

18. Victorio's final outbreak was evidently a tragic mistake. Indictments for murder and horse theft had been lodged against Victorio in Grant County, where Billy the Kid was also earning his reputation. However, the army apparently had no intention of turning Victorio over to civilian authorities. A judge and a prosecutor did enter the reservation, but they were on a hunting party, not seeking the arrest of Victorio. Tragically, at the time of the outbreak the Indian Bureau had finally decided to relent and reestablish the Ojo Caliente Reservation. The army concluded there was sufficient land at Ojo Caliente to sustain one thousand people with two hundred thousand sheep and twenty-five thousand cattle. Such a decision at any time in the previous four years could have saved hundreds of lives and millions of dollars and averted one of the most tragic injustices in the long, bitter history of the Indian conflicts.

CHAPTER VIII: WAR

1. The precise number who left with Victorio is unclear, particularly since his force continually grew and shrank as others joined him or left and filtered back onto the reservation. Apache sources indicate Victorio's force never numbered more than about seventy-five Chihenne warriors and that Mescalero and Chiricahua warriors added another thirty or forty to his strength. He generally had two or three times more women and children with him than warriors.

2. The following account of the river crossing comes directly from Kaywaykla's recollections set down in Ball, *In the Days of Victorio*. I have altered the words slightly to take it out of Kaywaykla's first-person narration.

3. This represents speculation as to what thoughts must have gone through Lozen's mind as she approached the Sacred Mountain. She left no firsthand account of her life or her thoughts.

4. About forty warriors stole almost the entire horse herd from Captain Ambrose Hooker's Ninth Cavalry posted at Ojo Caliente.

5. Major Morrow, the Fort Bayard commander, clashed with an estimated one hundred warriors at the McEver's ranch south of Hillsboro and reported ten troopers dead, several wounded, and the loss of most of the stock. Estimates of Victorio's strength varied sharply from one clash to the next. This stemmed from the difficulties of making estimates in a battle with warriors trained to never expose themselves to fire and the way Victorio constantly divided his forces, detaching groups of warriors to scout, capture supplies, and confuse the pursuit.

6. Lieutenant Matthias Day disobeyed direct orders to withdraw and leave his wounded, advancing alone under fire to rescue a wounded man. His enraged commanding officer wanted to have him court-martialed, but instead he was awarded a gold medal. The fight was a decisive defeat for the soldiers.

7. I am assuming specific uses of Lozen's Power, relying on Apache statements that her Power was critical in this period in evading their pursuers and that Victorio consulted

her often on matters of strategy. Unfortunately, the few surviving Apache accounts of this campaign make only scattered and anecdotal references to the actions of individuals.

8. Gatewood left a vivid account of his service with the scouts. Thrapp quotes Gatewood's account of the advance of the scouts against Victorio's forces: "I didn't believe there was a sane man in the country except the corporal, who coolly informed me after a while that I was sitting on the wrong side of a rock to be safe from a cross fire. Up to that time, it seemed to me, we would all be killed for every man had lost his head and was yelling with all his might and shooting in the air. But once anchored on the right side of the rock, I was astonished to see how cool they were, and how steady was their aim, some even laughing and joking." *Victorio and the Mimbres Apaches,* 243.

9. Historians have debated whether Victorio and Geronimo joined forces at this point. Juh and Geronimo remained on the San Carlos Reservation when the Chihenne left San Carlos, but they too left the reservation sometime later. They may have sought to take advantage of the chaos caused by the Chihenne breakout in August 1879 by raiding independently. Historian Dan Thrapp, Victorio's biographer, said that reports of a sharp increase in Victorio's strength at this time suggests the two groups did join forces. I am accepting Thrapp's supposition from *Victorio and the Mimbres Apaches,* 250.

10. I am assuming here Lozen played a role in predicting the arrival of the second detachment of Mexicans, since Victorio relied on her to determine the whereabouts and intentions of the enemy. Neither Mexican nor American accounts of the fight in the Candelaria Mountains at a place called Victorio's Tanks indicates the people of Carrizal intended to lure Victorio to a treacherous fiesta. But here I have accepted James Kaywaykla's account to Eve Ball (Thrapp, *Victorio and the Mimbres Apaches,* 254). Kaywaykla's account also suggests the trap was sprung after the Mexicans stopped to water their horses in a stream. An account by George Baylor who came upon the scene of the battle a few days later said the Mexicans were fired on as they reached the crest of a ridge, which drove them across the canyon into a place of seeming cover which was actually a trap. (Thrapp, *Victorio and the Mimbres Apaches,* 254).

11. Louis Scott, American Counsel at Chihuahua in northern Mexico, reported that Juh and Geronimo with about forty-five warriors had joined with Victorio and that raiding parties killed about 150 people in a six-week period in the summer of 1879. He urged coordination between the American and Mexican armies to attempt to trap Victorio's force between them.

12. I am assuming that the linkup between Victorio and Juh and Geronimo did take place, although it's debatable. I am also speculating here as to Lozen and Victorio's attitude toward their abandonment by the Chiricahua in light of the later combination of forces when Nana and Lozen finally took refuge with Juh in the Sierra Madre. Interestingly, Victorio had a very different reaction when a large contingent of Mescalero warriors attempted to abandon the group.

13. They neared Ojo Caliente on January 16, 1880.

14. Basso, *Wisdom Sits in Places,* 53. This is a place-name story told by the White Mountain Apache. I am taking the liberty here of attributing it to the Chihenne, on the assumption Lozen would have heard similar stories. Each member of the band learned hundreds of such place-name stories.

15. I am here assuming that Lozen carried Victorio's offer to surrender to Agent Andy Kelly at Ojo Caliente. Lozen often served as an intermediary because the whites were unlikely to take a woman prisoner.

16. The new band of soldiers they fought was the Ninth Cavalry.

CHAPTER IX: POWER TURNS

1. On May 23, 1880, Chief of Scouts Henry K. Parker struck a heavy blow against Victorio at the headwaters of the Palomas River with a force of sixty to seventy-five Apache scouts operating independently of the soldiers, whose horses had been worn out in the long pursuit.

2. I am here speculating Lozen would have been disturbed by this rare instance in which Victorio was taken completely by surprise. Opler, in *An Apache Lifeway,* provides several detailed explanations about the relationship between a person and her Power and the sorts of offenses that might disrupt the relationship with Power, which was viewed as personal and often difficult, 207, 209–210, 212, 243, 255, 270.

3. Several sources report that the women in this fight shouted out that they would eat Victorio's body rather than let it fall into the hands of the scouts and one of Ball's informants attributed the remark to Lozen.

4. Parker did send word back to Morrow's command, but the messenger was unaccountably assigned to Morrow's pack train and no reinforcements were sent. Out of ammunition and suffering greatly from thirst, Parker had little choice but to withdraw the scouts. Morrow later complained that the scouts should have pursued the Chihenne instead of breaking off the fight. Hatch, Morrow's commander, reported that the soldiers had won a great victory over Victorio with slight assistance from the scouts. In fact, Apache scouts had administered the only major defeat suffered by Victorio in the United States.

5. The following exchange between Victorio and Nana comes from Ball, *In the Days of Victorio,* 142.

6. They entered Texas in August 1880. The estimates of his force vary from 125 to 150, according to Thrapp, 288.

CHAPTER X: ALONE AMONG THE ENEMY

1. This account of Lozen's journey with the woman and her baby to the Mescalero Reservation is based on the account of Kaywaykla as told to Eve Ball and reproduced in *In the Days of Victorio*, 116. Kaywaykla heard the story from Lozen.

CHAPTER XI: DEATH AND REVENGE

1. This dialogue comes from Ball, *In the Days of Victorio*, 88.

2. Joaquin Terrazas was frustrated by the Mexican Army's inability to deal with Victorio. So the tall, energetic, vain, chain-smoking former scalp hunter, successful rancher and insightful organizer and campaigner, assembled a force of up to five hundred. It is unclear why Victorio abandoned the mountains in which he had for so long eluded his enemies to strike out across an open plain for Tres Castillos, which was outside his normal range of operations. He might have been trying to stay out of the way of both Terrazas and a force of Texas Rangers that had moved into Mexico searching for Victorio. Following fresh tracks, Terrazas did encounter the Americans and ordered them out of Mexico. Later, he came across the tracks of Victorio's main force, surmised they might head for the reliable water of Tres Castillos, and arrived there ahead of them. On October 15, 1880, Terrazas climbed one of the three small hills overlooking the ephemeral lake and the permanent spring and saw the dust of the approaching Apache, whereupon he sent runners to hurry his main force to Tres Castillos. Accounts of the battle differ. The Apache version, recounted by James Kaywaykla, is presented in the text here, in keeping with my practice of accepting the Apache version when possible. Terrazas's report of the battle indicates his 260 soldiers spotted the main body of Apache when they were one thousand yards distant and that thirty warriors charged the Mexicans, presumably to give the women and children time to escape. The Apache took refuge on the southernmost peak, where they were surrounded and trapped.

3. Kaywaykla reports Victorio killed himself with his own knife. The Mexicans generally gave Juan Mata Ortiz, captain of the Indian auxiliaries, credit, and he was reportedly rewarded with Victorio's saddle. Other accounts said Victorio was killed while atop a white horse or while directing the defense or that he was the last man left alive on the peak. One other Apache account holds Victorio was captured alive and boiled to death in a vat of oil. First Lieutenant Henry Beck, of the Tenth Cavalry, reported that Terrazas lined up ten warriors and asked them, one at a time, to show him Victorio's body. He executed each man who refused until he reached the tenth man, who led the soldiers to the spot where Victorio lay mortally wounded—tended to by several women. Terrazas then ordered Victorio executed. However, as Thrapp observed, the terrain at Tres Castillos makes this story unlikely. Other accounts suggest Victorio and the last group of warriors surrendered when they ran out of ammunition, whereupon they were executed. I have here accepted Kaywaykla's account, which is based on Kaytennae's examination of the bodies after the battle.

4. Kaywaykla reported this execution of the boys, which he learned about later from Huera, who was taken prisoner but escaped. The Mexican accounts of the battle make no mention of these executions.

5. Kaywaykla related this speech of Nana's in Ball, *In the Days of Victorio*, 100.

6. I am here speculating on Lozen's reaction to the death of her brother, based on the Apache worldview which emphasizes a certain stoic fatalism and the idea that the world is dominated by forces that can be only faintly understood or controlled.

7. Ball, *In the Days of Victorio*, 102. Kaywaykla remembers this advice from Nana after the death of Victorio in connection with telling the cycle of stories about Child of Water.

8. Thrapp, in *Victorio and the Mimbres Apaches*, 310, cited local newspaper articles describing the killing of the nine soldiers. A contemporary account by the captain of a band of Texas Rangers who had trailed Victorio's band to Tres Castillos reported that Nana's warriors killed at least two hundred Mexicans after Tres Castillos in retaliation.

9. The estimates of Nana's force in the epic 1880 raid through the Southwest vary considerably. I am here accepting the estimates reported by Donald Worcester in *The Apaches, Eagles of the Southwest*.

10. This took place around June 1881. Long known as Nana's raid, the war party covered a total of three-thousand miles in two months, averaging fifty miles a day. They won seven pitched battles with the pursuing cavalry, attacked a dozen towns and ranches, killed at least thirty-five people, and captured two hundred horses and mules, all without losing any warriors.

CHAPTER XII: DEATH OF A PROPHET

1. We don't actually have a description of Lozen's reaction to the Ghost Dances. However, Juh's son in Eve Ball's *Indeh* described Juh's and Nana's reactions to the movement and I have made the assumption that Lozen's reaction would have been consistent with Nana's, 53.

2. The Green One was Lieutenant Thomas Cruse, who left a compelling account of the Battle of Cibecue in his fascinating *Apache Days and After*. Cruse had qualms about taking his detachment of White Mountain Apache scouts to arrest the Prophet, but Colonel Eugene Carr in command of the Sixth Cavalry detachment stationed at Fort Apache decided to go ahead before a replacement detachment arrived from San Carlos. On August 29, 1881, Carr arrived at Cibecue with 117 men, including 23 scouts.

3. Army reports suggest the Indians started shooting first and the scouts joined in the attack on the detachment. Several scouts were later tried and executed for mutiny, although the trial testimony was conflicting and ambiguous.

4. The timing of the departure of Nana and Lozen from the reservation is unclear from available sources. Juh's son, Ace Daklugie, told historian Eve Ball in *Indeh*, 54, that Lozen was at the Battle of Cibecue and that she made off with a mule loaded with

ammunition. But no sources describe precisely when Lozen left the San Carlos Reservation. By contrast, the departure of Juh and Geronimo and their Chiricahua warriors on September 30, 1881, a month after the battle, has been amply documented—partly because they left such a bloody trail back into the Sierra Madre. James Kaywaykla, in *In the Days of Victorio,* provided the next solid accounting of Lozen's actions when he recounted the reunification of the Chihenne and the Chiricahua in the Sierra Madre as described above, 210.

5. This dialogue and incident comes from Ball, *In the Days of Victorio,* 112.

6. Kaywaykla's description of the feast and Nana's words come from Ball, *In the Days of Victorio,* 128.

CHAPTER XIII: THE GREAT GAMBLE

1. James Kaywaykla does not specifically include Lozen on the list of leaders at the council in Ball, *In the Days of Victorio,* but elsewhere he notes she was asked to attend the councils, and so it is reasonable to assume she attended this meeting as well.

2. All the direct dialogue in this council comes from Ball, *In the Days of Victorio,* 139. It is based on Kaywaykla's recollection in adulthood of events that took place when he was a boy. It is also colored by the later deep divisions between the war leaders who fought to the end like Lozen and Geronimo and those who became scouts, like Chato. Other accounts depict Chato in a much more sympathetic light, but I have adopted Kaywaykla's view as being closest to the probable view held by Lozen.

3. Most accounts of the April 1882 raid suggest Geronimo was the primary leader, although Juh's role remains open to debate. Geronimo may have served as a chief of his own Bedonkohe band at one time, but the Bedonkohe suffered so many deaths they ceased to exist as a group. He then fought as subordinate to Juh with the Nednhi. At some point, Geronimo shifted to a Chiricahua band led by Naiche, the son of Cochise. Although Naiche was the leader, Geronimo took the lead on raids as he had Power in warfare. Kaywaykla, who left a secondhand account of the raid, does not mention Juh at all. Nor does John Rope, a White Mountain scout who left another secondhand account. More tellingly, Jason Betzinez, a cousin of Geronimo's and one of the kidnapped band, also makes no mention of Juh in *I Fought with Geronimo.* Historians disagree about Juh's participation. Angie Debo, who wrote a biography of Geronimo, concluded Juh was not present. However, Dan Thrapp, one of the leading historians of the period, believes Juh was present and played a leading role in planning the expedition. I am here accepting Geronimo's leadership role in deference to Betzinez's firsthand account.

4. Debo indicates the incident at the sheep camp came on the approach to the reservation. David Roberts, in his excellent *Once They Moved Like the Wind,* suggests the incident took place as they fled the reservation. I have accepted Debo's version, both here and in my biography of Crook and Geronimo, *The Fox and the Whirlwind.*

5. Several firsthand Apache accounts cited by Debo and others note that the party paused for a day in their flight to hold the Sunrise Ceremony for a girl who had begun to menstruate. I am here making the assumption Lozen would have advocated pausing long enough to have an abbreviated ceremony.

6. Several Apache sources cited by Debo and others claim Geronimo delayed the dawn by two or three hours, one of several remarkable demonstrations of supernatural power attributed to him by his admirers. I have accepted that claim here in keeping with my effort to present an essentially Apache view of these events.

7. I am speculating here as to Lozen's reaction to this battle, fought on April 27, 1882, eight days after the breakout from San Carlos, which took place on April 19.

8. Jason Betzinez, in his *I Fought with Geronimo,* says that in fleeing he saw the advance guard including Naiche, Chato, and Kaytennae smoking under a tree and making no attempt to return to the fight. Scout Al Seiber found tracks consistent with Betzinez's account shortly after the battle. This behavior seems completely out of character for these warriors, whose courage and fighting abilities were demonstrated repeatedly. It's possible they had some sort of argument with Geronimo and had effectively left the group. However, both Naiche and Chato remained allies of Geronimo and leading fighters in the months to come. Moreover, it seems strange Kaytennae would remain apart from the battle, since most of the people being killed were his own Warm Springs or Chihenne people.

9. All of the dialogue in the description of this battle and the account of Lozen's role in fending off the charge comes from James Kaywaykla's secondhand account in Ball, *In the Days of Victorio,* 135. Geronimo's behavior in this fight is controversial. Geronimo gave a different account in his autobiography, which included the incident in which he shot the Mexican officer. Kaywaykla's account is based on a version of the battle relayed to him by Talbert Gooday, a Chihenne warrior bitterly critical of Geronimo for stirring up the trouble that cost the Chihenne their reservation and for driving Loco's Chihenne band off the San Carlos Reservation. Therefore, Gooday's account is suspect. However, Geronimo did repeatedly escape from battles in which even his wives and children were killed, which demonstrates the high value he placed on self-preservation. Moreover, most of the women and children in the ditch were Chihenne, not his own Chiricahua. Therefore, I have accepted Kaywaykla's version, as I have in most cases when the evidence warrants, in part because he's the best single source for describing Lozen's activities and viewpoints.

10. Fun was actually Geronimo's cousin, but in Apache the terms for brother and cousin are the same.

11. This detail comes from Betzinez's secondhand account in *I Fought with Geronimo.* However, Betzinez wasn't in the arroyo, having already fled to the mountain with his mother.

12. I am here speculating as to what Lozen felt as she waited for the last charge.

13. Kaywaykla quotes Loco as saying they would have suffered more deaths at San Carlos, although the dismaying reservation death rate never rose to 33 percent in a year. Moreover, Loco later proved willing enough to return to the reservation.

14. Lieutenant Colonel George Forsyth had made the decision to take his force of about four hundred, including about fifty Apache scouts, into Mexico after the fleeing Apache without consulting his superiors. However, in his official reports he said the Sierra Embudo fight took place in New Mexico instead of Mexico. Colonel Lorenzo Garcia, in command of the 250-man Mexican force, ordered the Americans out of the country. However, cooperation between the Mexicans and the Americans was eventually to break the Apache will to fight.

CHAPTER XIV: THE LAST FREE PEOPLE

1. Estimates of the numbers of people gathered varies. About half of the total came with Loco's band from the reservation. The rest were the Chiricahua and Nednhi bands living in the area before Geronimo's raid on the reservation.

2. The attack on Galeana was made in November 1882.

3. The raid took place in March 1883. It came shortly after General George Crook, the nation's most successful Indian fighter, had returned from fighting the Sioux to pacify the Apache. The raid spurred an almost hysterical public reaction throughout the Southwest, especially after the raiders killed Judge H. C. McComas and his wife and kidnapped their young son, Charlie. The territorial press screamed for action against the Chiricahua in Mexico.

4. I have made the assumption Lozen would have performed her ceremony on this occasion, as Apache reports indicate Nana and Geronimo continued to rely on her ceremony.

5. Debo, *Geronimo,* 170. Kaywaykla's account of the battle differs sharply from the official Mexican report of the engagement by Colonel Lorenzo Garcia, who was also the commander of the Mexican force that had ambushed Loco's band previously. Garcia commanded eighty-six federal troops and fifty auxiliaries, many of them Indians from tribes who had long been enemies of the Apache. Garcia reported he made a frontal assault and drove off the Indians, killing eleven. However, descriptions of the battle scene later by Americans supports the Apache version of the battle offered here in the text.

6. This was in May 1883.

CHAPTER XV: TRAPPED BY THE GREY FOX

1. General Crook arrested Tsoe shortly after his arrival on the reservation, relying on a well-developed system of informants to let him know when any of the renegades showed up on the reservation. Tsoe then readily agreed to lead the expedition into the Sierra Madre, saying he had been forced to live with the Chiricahua who had not treated

him well. Tsoe noted that several of the key leaders wanted to return to the reservation. Crook assembled 193 scouts and 50 soldiers, together with a pack train of 266 mules with 76 packers. Captain John Bourke's *An Apache Campaign in the Sierra Madre* offers a compelling description of the expedition, which was a bold gamble on Crook's part. Crook sent the scouts under the command of Captain Emmett Crawford and Lieutenant Charles Gatewood ahead of the slow-moving soldiers and pack train, and they located and attacked Chato's camp on May 15, 1883.

2. Jason Betzinez, in *I Fought with Geronimo*, 113, recounted this incident.

3. It is possible Crook merely blundered in going hunting, which was an obsession with him. Captain John Bourke, Crook's aide, doesn't mention the incident in his excellent *An Apache Campaign in the Sierra Madre,* perhaps because of the later controversy that arose when Crook's critics suggested he'd offered the Apache favorable surrender terms because they had captured his whole command. The incident only came to light years later with the publication of an account of the expedition by John Rope, a White Mountain scout. For a full account of the incident and Crook's complex relationship with Geronimo, see my own *The Fox and the Whirlwind*. The public initially gave Crook and his command up for dead, but when they appeared with most of the women and children but only half the warriors and no Geronimo, criticism began to build. Many newspapers suggested the army should immediately hang all the men, sell the women, and offer the children for adoption.

4. Lozen's movements in this period aren't clear, partly because the army never understood her importance and influence and so never bothered to make mention of her whereabouts. Debo in *Geronimo,* 189, and Worcester in *The Apaches, Eagles of the Southwest,* 275, report that Nana, Lozen, and Kaytennae returned to San Carlos with Crook while Geronimo, Chato, Chihuahua, and others remained behind. Debo's account is based on army reports on the movements of Kaytennae, who was recognized as an important war leader, and Nana, who was thought to be an old man with little remaining influence. However, Kaywaykla, Kaytennae's adopted son who usually traveled with Nana and Lozen, described coming in with Geronimo some months later with a herd of cattle Geronimo had gathered up (Ball, *In the Days of Victorio,* 148). He says Lozen acted as the intermediary for Geronimo when he finally did cross the border seven months later. Kaywaykla's account is confusing on several points. He makes no mention of Crook's expedition into the Sierra Madre and said Nana and Geronimo decided to return to the reservation when they "heard" Crook was in charge. I am here accepting Kaywaykla's account as to Lozen's movements, although it seems to conflict with army records.

5. They set out in February 1884.

6. Davis only told Geronimo half the story. One of the men was a customs official who wanted to seize the herd. The other was a marshal with a warrant for Geronimo's arrest on murder charges. The marshal deputized Davis and ordered him to help arrest Geronimo. This put Davis in an impossible position, as Crook had ordered him to bring

Geronimo safely to the reservation. Davis knew that any attempt to arrest Geronimo would provoke a bloody fight that would deter any other bands still in Mexico from surrendering and might provoke the breakout of the warriors already settled uneasily on the reservation. Fortunately, another officer arrived that afternoon and Davis came up with a bold plan. He got the two civilians drunk so Geronimo could slip away with the herd and then placed the rest of his detachment under the command of the other officer. Davis remained at the empty camp until morning in obedience to the deputization. The ruse worked and Davis suffered no more serious consequence than the curses of the two civilians.

7. Geronimo wrote in his autobiography that he had been promised land along Eagle Creek, but Crook maintains he made no such promise. It seems unlikely Crook would have promised a camp on Eagle Creek as that area had already been occupied by settlers. However, I am here accepting the Apache view of disputed events in order to remain faithful to Lozen's perspective. For a full discussion of this issue see *The Fox and the Whirlwind*.

8. This incident and all of the direct dialogue comes from Ball, *Indeh*, 67, and was recounted to Eve Ball by Ace Daklugie, the son of Juh.

9. The views of the Lozen and Geronimo faction are reflected by the accounts of Kaywaykla and Juh's son, Daklugie, gathered by Eve Ball in *Indeh* and *In the Days of Victorio*. They maintain that Chato, Tsoe, and Mickey Free stirred up trouble and lied to Davis about the others. Davis, in his excellent account *The Truth about Geronimo*, lays the blame mostly on Geronimo and Kaytennae and indicates Chato was an honorable and faithful advocate for peace. I am here accepting the view Lozen probably held, which would be consistent with Kaywaykla's and Dakulgie's accounts.

10. Kaywaykla related this incident in Ball, *In the Days of Victorio*, 160, evidently after Nana concluded that the picture of a devil on a can of deviled ham indicated the can contained human meat. Kaywaykla told historian Eve Ball that the incident confirmed suspicions the whites ate human flesh and that he believed this to be true as a boy. It's unclear whether Nana really believed the whites were canning human flesh or simply seized on this incident to spread fear and suspicion of whites.

11. This dialogue comes directly from Kaywaykla's secondhand recollection (Ball, *In the Days of Victorio*, 162). I have accepted his version of the character and motivations of Chato largely because it would have reflected Lozen's view. However, the account is undoubtedly biased because Kaytennae was Kaywaykla's adored stepfather. In fact, it is possible Geronimo was manipulating people's reactions and putting Chato in the worst possible light.

12. The accounts of Davis on one side and Kaywaykla and Daklugie on the other side differ significantly. Davis believed Kaytennae was fomenting unrest, based on information from Chato and others. Kaywaykla and Daklugie insist Chato fabricated the inci-

dents. I have here accepted Kaywaykla's version as the best reflection of Lozen's likely viewpoint.

13. Kaytennae was convicted of inciting unrest in a brief trial at which he was apparently not present and sentenced to imprisonment on Alcatraz. He remained in prison there for a month, where he learned some English and the rudiments of reading and writing. Crook then ordered that Kaytennae be given the run of San Francisco, on the shrewd and ultimately correct calculation that Kaytennae would be so overwhelmed by the power and numbers of the whites he would become a strong advocate for accommodation and surrender.

14. Crawford was relieved by Crook at his own request and sent to rejoin his regiment in Texas. Crawford had administered the reservation honestly and fairly, but he had come under bitter criticism from certain factions in the Indian Bureau and among traders with licenses to sell goods on the reservation. He was caught in the conflict between the army and the Interior Department for control of the reservations and the potential for patronage and graft it offered. The reservations shifted constantly back and forth from military to civilian control and the evidence suggests graft increased dramatically under most civilian administrations. Efforts by Crawford and Davis to crack down on graft provoked a political counterattack—including allegations of corruption leveled against Crawford. An independent investigation cleared him, but he was so disgusted by the politics of the job he requested a return to field service. His transfer proved fateful, as the loss of Crawford's cool judgment and experience in dealing with Indians contributed significantly to the outbreak of the Chiricahua.

15. Davis's telegram seeking instructions from Crook never reached the general. Davis, going through channels, had sent the message for Crook to his immediate superior, Captain Francis Pierce, who had replaced Crawford. The inexperienced Pierce showed the telegram to veteran scout Al Sieber, who was sleeping off a binge, and told Pierce not to worry about it. Pierce simply put the telegram aside, leaving Davis as much in the dark as Geronimo. It seems likely that if Crook had actually received the telegram he could have averted the outbreak.

16. This incident remains controversial. Geronimo makes no mention of it in his autobiography. In addition, Geronimo's later close cooperation with Naiche, Mangas, and Chihuahua casts some doubts on the alleged rift between them. The claim Geronimo tricked Naiche, Mangas, and Chihuahua into leaving the reservation comes from Sam Kenoi, a Chihenne Apache who blamed Geronimo for many of the losses suffered by his people. However, the splitting of the bands shortly after they left the reservation and the attempts by both Chihuahua and Naiche to return to the reservation lend credibility to this incident. It is unclear what role Nana and Lozen might have played in this dispute, but they appear to have remained with Geronimo. None of the Apache leaders themselves mentioned this incident in subsequent accounts.

17. I am here speculating as to Lozen's reaction to the breakout, as we have no firsthand account of her thinking. However, this seems consistent with her life and with her repeated returns to the warpath after relatively brief stays on the reservation.

CHAPTER XVI: INDEH

1. The scouts on August 7, 1885, initially reported killing Nana and three others, including the son of Geronimo. They claimed to have wounded Geronimo and Mangas. However, subsequent events demonstrated that Geronimo, Chapo, and Mangas all emerged from the battle unscathed. However, the scouts' attacks killed or captured one-third of the women and children who left the reservation.

2. This raid happened in November 1885. It is known as Ulzana's raid.

3. They made the trip to the Canyon, which was about eighty-four miles south of Fort Bowie in Apache Pass, in March 1886. The negotiations represented a calculated gamble for General Crook, who had faced a firestorm of criticism as a result of Geronimo's outbreak and the inability of his soldiers and scouts to recapture them. Many newspapers vociferously criticized Crook's reliance on Apache scouts to do most of the fighting, although in the long history of the war with the Apache the scouts were almost the only units to win battles with the renegades.

4. These quotes come from transcripts of the negotiations made by Crook and are taken from Debo, *Geronimo,* 263.

5. Geronimo, Naiche, and Lozen bolted on March 28, 1886. Their departure set in motion a fateful chain of events. Crook was already in political difficulties with his commander, General Philip Sheridan, who had on orders of President Grover Cleveland already rejected the terms on which Crook had accepted the surrender of the Chiricahua. Crook had promised they would be imprisoned with their families for not more than two years and then returned to the San Carlos Reservation. He was acting in accordance with previous orders giving him discretion in establishing surrender terms. But the public had grown almost hysterical as a result of continued raids like Ulzana's, so Sheridan and Cleveland now felt the unconditional surrender of the Chiricahua was a political necessity. This placed Crook in an ethically impossible position, which he resolved by simply not telling Chihuahua, Nana, and the others that he could not keep his promise. The news that Geronimo, Naiche, and the others had fled proved a political bombshell, as Geronimo was the best known of the renegades. General Sheridan suggested the scouts must have helped Geronimo escape and ordered Crook to simply defend the frontier. Offended by the implications and the criticism, Crook resigned his command. General Sheridan replaced him with General Nelson Miles, a longtime rival of Crook's with fewer scruples about the use of deceit as a negotiating ploy. Crook later assumed command of most of the interior western United States and spent the closing years of his life stamping out the last few Indian disturbances and struggling to force

the release from imprisonment of the Apache scouts who had helped him battle Geronimo and the other renegades.

CHAPTER XVII: THE FINAL SURRENDER

1. This description of their state of mind comes from Geronimo's autobiography. He said, "We were reckless of our lives, because we felt that every man's hand was against us. If we returned to the reservation we would be put in prison and killed; if we stayed in Mexico they would continue to send soldiers to fight us; so we gave no quarter to anyone and asked no favors."

2. General Miles had discharged most of the scout units, partly in response to the widespread criticism of Crook's reliance on the scouts and allegations the scouts had let Geronimo escape. Miles established a handpicked unit that pursued Geronimo for four months, covering fourteen hundred miles. In addition, Miles requested and received reinforcements so he eventually had five thousand men trying to find Geronimo and his group—about one-quarter of the United States Army. Despite this mobilization, Miles could neither stop Geronimo's band nor force them to turn and fight. Miles eventually sought out Lieutenant Charles Gatewood, one of Crook's most effective officers in command of Apache scouts, and asked him to find Geronimo and talk him into surrendering. Gatewood enlisted the help of two warriors with relatives in Geronimo's band and set out for Mexico with a small party in July 1886.

3. Opler, *A Chiricahua Apache's Account*, 375. This dialogue comes from an account by an Apache warrior named Sam Kenoi, who was a critic of Geronimo but who knew personally many of the warriors involved in this incident.

4. The direct dialogue here comes from Gatewood's account in Sonnichen, *Geronimo and the End of the Apache Wars*, 63.

5. Sonnichen, *Geronimo and the End of the Apache Wars*, 64.

6. Miles had been frantically telegraphing and dispatching messengers, trying to determine whether to undertake the considerable political risks of a face-to-face meeting with Geronimo. He had earlier sent a ten-man Apache delegation headed by Loco and Chato to Washington, DC, to negotiate the removal of the Chiricahua from Arizona to the Indian Territory or some other place where they could no longer provide supplies for the bands who continued to raid. Chato and Loco both spoke eloquently against removal, but Miles had the train bringing them home diverted to Leavenworth, Kansas, where he imprisoned these strong peace leaders and scouts. Miles called for the Chiricahua to come in for counting and then disarmed them and shipped them to Florida. Gatewood's message that Geronimo was willing to surrender after a face-to-face meeting threw Miles into a quandary. Geronimo was by then already famous. Miles knew Geronimo's on-again, off-again surrender had proved a political disaster for Crook, but he also hoped to reap enormous career benefits from being the man to capture Geronimo. Miles knew his superiors, including the President, had balked at Crook's terms promising a return to Arizona after a two-year term in Florida. Miles's message suggested

Lawton disarm the prisoners by any means possible, but ultimately left matters to Lawton's judgment. Lawton responded he could attack the band and kill several warriors, but he could not capture them. Therefore, Miles vacillated in an effort to avoid the blame if Geronimo once again bolted.

7. The precise nature of Miles's terms became a matter of controversy. Miles did not put the terms in writing, realizing he could face serious political difficulty as a result of any promise to return the Chiricahua to Arizona after two years in Florida. His superiors had not approved anything more lenient than unconditional surrender and President Grover Cleveland had expressed preference for terms that would allow him to hang Geronimo. Miles's description of the surrender terms proved so vague and conflicting that General Sherman ordered the train carrying Naiche's band stopped and the prisoners questioned about the terms. Each prisoner reported the promise of a quick reunion with their families, livestock, and tools on a reserve in Florida and a return to Arizona after two years. I am here accepting their version of the surrender terms.

8. I am speculating here as to Lozen's thinking at the time of surrender.

9. Debo, *Geronimo*, 228, quoted from Geronimo's autobiography.

10. This is the explanation Kaywaykla offers and would account for the complete absence of military records concerning Lozen's disposition as a prisoner. Apache accounts indicate she was with Geronimo's band through the final surrender, and the only known photograph of Lozen shows her with Geronimo and Naiche and the others in front of the boxcar waiting to take them to Florida. However, her name does not appear on the roster of those prisoners. On the other hand, few of the women were listed by name. Most were simply put down as a named warrior's wife. She may have therefore been listed as one of the warriors' wives as a way to protect her from possible retaliation by the soldiers if they learned her full role, as Geronimo and some of the others expected execution despite Miles's promises.

BIBLIOGRAPHY

▼▼▼

Adams, Alexander B. *Geronimo: A Biography*. New York: De Capo Press, 1971.

Aleshire, Peter. *Reaping the Whirlwind: The Apache Wars*. New York: Facts on File, 1998.

———. *The Fox and the Whirlwind: General George Crook and Geronimo: A Paired Biography*. New York: John Wiley & Sons, 2000.

Altshuler, Constance Wynn. *Starting with Defiance, Nineteenth Century Arizona Military Posts*. Tucson: Arizona Historical Society, 1983.

Ambrose, Stephen. *Crazy Horse and Custer: The Parallel Lives of Two American Warriors*. New York: Meridian, 1975.

Ball, Eve. *In the Days of Victorio: Recollections of a Warm Springs Apache*. Tucson: University of Arizona Press, 1970.

———. *Indeh. An Apache Odyssey*. Provo, Utah: Brigham Young University Press, 1980.

Barnes, Will C. *Apaches and Longhorns: The Reminiscences of Will C. Barnes*. Tucson: University of Arizona Press, 1941.

Barrett, S. M. *Geronimo's Story of His Life*. New York: Duffield and Company, 1906.

Basso, Keith H. *The Cibecue Apache*. Prospect Heights, Ill.: Waveland Press, 1973.

———. *Wisdom Sits in Places: Landscape and Language Among the Western Apache*. Albuquerque: University of New Mexico Press, 1996.

———. ed. *Western Apache Raiding and Warfare: From the Notes of Grenville Goodwin*. Tucson: University of Arizona Press, 1971.

Betzinez, Jason. *I Fought with Geronimo*. Edited and annotated by Wilbur Sturtevant Nye. Harrisburg, Pa.: Stackpole, 1959.

Bigelow, John. *On the Bloody Trail of Geronimo*. Edited by Arthur Woodward. Tucson: Westernlore Press, 1986.

Bourke, John G. *An Apache Campaign in the Sierra Madre*. New York: Charles Scribner's Sons, 1958.

———. *Apache Medicine-Men*. 1892. Reprint, New York: Dover Publications, 1993.

———. *On the Border with Crook*. New York: Charles Scribner's Sons, 1891.

———. *A Scout with the Buffalo Soldiers*. Palmer Lake, Colo.: Filter Press. Reprint, 1973. Originally published in *Century Magazine*, April, March, 1891.

————. *With General Crook in the Indian Wars*. Palo Alto: Lewis Osborne, 1968.

Browning, Sinclair. *Enju: The Life and Struggle of an Apache Chief from the Little Running Water*. Flagstaff: Northland Press, 1982.

Carr, Camillo Casatti Cadmus. *A Cavalryman in Indian Country*. Library of Congress catalog card no. 73-91060.

Clum, Woodworth. *Apache Agent: The Story of John P. Clum*. Boston: Houghton Mifflin, 1936.

Colyer, Vincent. *Peace with the Apaches of New Mexico and Arizona*. Washington, D.C.: U.S. Government Printing Office, 1872.

Corle, Edwin. *The Gila, River of the Southwest*. Lincoln: University of Nebraska Press, 1951.

Cortes, Jose. Edited by Elizabeth John. *Views from the Apache Frontier, Report on the Northern Provinces of New Spain*. Norman: University of Oklahoma Press, 1994.

Cremony, John Carey. *Life Among the Apaches*. 1868 reprint. Glorieta, N. Mex.: Rio Grande Press, 1969.

Crook, George. *General George Crook: His Autobiography*. Edited by Martin F. Schmitt. Norman: University of Oklahoma Press, 1960.

Cruse, Thomas. *Apache Days and After*. 1941. Reprint, 1987, 10th Edition.

Davis, Britton. *The Truth about Geronimo*. 1929. Reprint, Lincoln: University of Nebraska Press, 1976.

Debo, Angie. *Geronimo. The Man, His Time, His Place*. Norman: University of Oklahoma Press, 1976.

Faulk, Odie B. *The Geronimo Campaign*. New York: Oxford University Press, 1969.

Forbes, Jack D. *Apache, Navaho, and Spaniard*. Norman: University of Oklahoma Press, 1960.

Goodwin, Grenville. *The Myths and Tales of the White Mountain Apache*. Tucson: University of Arizona Press, 1996.

Haley, James L. *Apaches: A History and Culture Portrait*. New York: Doubleday, 1981.

Hand, George. *The Civil War in Apacheland*. Edited by Neil B. Carmony. Silver City, N. Mex.: High-Lonesome, 1996.

Howard, O. O. *Famous Indian Chiefs I Have Known*. New York: The Century Company, 1907.

————. *My life and Experiences among our Hostile Indians*. Hartford, Conn.: A. D. Worthington & Company, 1907.

Leermakers, J. A. *Great Western Indian Fights*. Lincoln: University of Nebraska Press, 1960.

Lockwood, Frank. *The Apache Indians*. Lincoln: University of Nebraska Press, 1938.

Lummis, Charles. *General Crook and the Apache Wars*. Flagstaff: Northland Press, 1985.

Mails, Thomas. *The People Called Apache*. New York: BDD Illustrated Books, 1993.

Miles, Nelson A. *Personal Recollections*. Chicago and New York: The Werner Company, 1897.

————. *Serving the Republic*. Freeport, N.Y.: Books for Libraries Press, 1971.

Olge, Ralph Hedrick. *Federal Control of the Western Apaches, 1848–1886*. Albuquerque: University of New Mexico Press, 1992.

Opler, Morris Edward. *An Apache Lifeway*. Chicago: University of Chicago Press. 1941 original. 1996 Bison Book reprint, 10th edition.

———. "A Chiricahua Apache's Account of the Geronimo Campaign of 1886." *New Mexico Historical Review* 13, no. 4 (1938).

———. *Myths and Tales of the Chiricahua Apache Indians*. Lincoln: University of Nebraska Press, 1942.

———. *Myths and Tales of the Jicarilla Apache Indians*. New York: Dover Publications, 1994.

Perry, Richard. *Western Apache Heritage, People of the Mountain Corridor*. Austin: University of Texas Press, 1991.

Redstorm, Lisle. *Apache Wars: An Illustrated Battle History*. New York: Barnes and Nobel Books, 1990.

Rickey, Don. *Forty Miles a Day on Beans and Hay: The Enlisted Soldier Fighting the Indian Wars*. Norman: University of Oklahoma Press, 1963.

Roberts, David. *Once They Moved Like the Wind: Cochise, Geronimo and the Apache Wars*. New York: Simon and Schuster, 1993.

Santee, Ross. *Apache Land*. New York: Charles Scribner's Sons, 1947.

Schellie, Don. *Vast Domain of Blood: The Story of the Camp Grant Massacre*. Los Angeles: Westernlore Press, 1968.

Simmons, Marc. *Witchcraft in the Southwest*. Lincoln: University of Nebraska Press, 1994.

Sladen, Joseph Alton. *Making Peace with Cochise*. Norman: University of Oklahoma Press, 1997.

Smith, Cornelius C. *Fort Huachuca, The Story of a Frontier Post*. Washington, D.C.: U.S. Government Printing Office, 1981.

Smith, Sherry. *The View from Officer Row: Army Perceptions of Western Indians*. Tucson: University of Arizona Press, 1990.

Sonnichen, C. L. *Geronimo and the End of the Apache Wars*. Lincoln: University of Nebraska Press, 1986.

———. *The Mescalero Apaches*. Norman: University of Oklahoma Press, 1958.

Stockel, Henrietta. *Women of the Apache Nation: Voices of Truth*. Reno: University of Nevada Press, 1991.

Sutherland, Edwin Van Valkenburg. "The Diaries of John Gregory Bourke: Their Anthropological and Folklore Content." Graduate School of Arts and Sciences, University of Pennsylvania, Philadelphia, 1964.

Thrapp, Dan L. *Al Sieber, Chief of Scouts*. Norman: University of Oklahoma Press, 1964.

———. *The Conquest of Apacheria*. Norman: University of Oklahoma Press, 1967.

———. *General Crook and the Sierra Madre Adventure*. Norman: University of Oklahoma Press, 1972.

———. *Juh: An Incredible Indian*. Southwest Studies, monograph no. 39. El Paso: Texas Western Press, 1973.

————. *Victorio and the Mimbres Apaches*. Norman: University of Oklahoma Press, 1974.

Tiller, Veronica E. Velarde. *The Jicarilla Apache Tribe, A History*. Lincoln: University of Nebraska Press, 1992.

Utley, Robert. *A Clash of Cultures: Fort Bowie and the Chiricahua Apaches*. Washington, D.C.: Division of Publications, National Park Service, 1977.

————. *Frontiersmen in Blue: The United States Army and the Indian, 1848–1865*. Lincoln: University of Nebraska Press, 1967.

Weems, John Edward. *Death Song: The Last of the Indian Wars*. New York: Indian Head Books, 1994.

Wellman, Paul I. *The Indian Wars of the West*. Garden City, N.Y.: Doubleday & Company, 1947.

Worcester, Donald. *The Apaches, Eagles of the Southwest*. Norman: University of Oklahoma Press, 1979.